112
120
221-2

Other titles in the series

Labour:
The Unions and
the Party

A Study of the Trade Unions and the British Labour Movement

by Bill Simpson

London. George Allen & Unwin Ltd
Ruskin House   Museum Street

First published in 1973

ISBN 0 04 331057 5 hardback
     0 04 331058 3 paperback

Printed in Great Britain
in 10 *point Times Roman type* by
Clarke, Doble & Brendon Ltd
Plymouth

The true life is the common life of all,
not the life of one.
All must labour for the life of others.

Leo Tolstoy, 1828–1910

Preface

Writing a book on the Trade Unions and the Labour Party is like trying to empty Loch Lomond with a teaspoon! At the same time many have already attempted to chart the depths – some perhaps in search of monsters.

This book is different in that it sets out to study the political relationship between the Labour Party and the trade unions in Britain. The ultimate aim of the book is to determine what factors have created trade union political attitudes, and to pass some judgement on which attitude holds most relevance for our present day society. It is impossible to do this without looking at the strands of socialist thought that led to trade union political activity, and eventually to the formation of the Labour Party.

The book is therefore initially historical, tracing briefly early British socialist thinking, but the historical narrative is selective in that it concentrates on the events and periods in our history which have had a bearing on trade union political thought at that time. In studying each historical phase, comment is made and questions are posed (and answered) and, where appropriate, lessons are drawn for future consolidation. So the history is laced with dashes of modern analogy. The book gives ample historical coverage to the events around 1900 to 1910, which concerned the creation of the Labour Party. Some of the arguments of that period are still with us today!

It also deals in some detail with the Syndicalist period from 1910 to 1914, when the direct actionists were rampant, and takes a close look at the 1926 General Strike and the events which preceded it. All these periods were watersheds in socialist political thinking within the unions and influenced the Labour Party then and now.

Less time is devoted to the 1930s and 1940s because none of the events which occurred in this period is comparable in a political sense with those already mentioned, but some attention is

focused on the emergence of political theories which challenged
the basic tenets of Marxism.

The historical examination then looks at the 1945–51 Labour
Government and the 1950s under the Tories, and the section
finishes with a review of the lessons to be drawn from this period
and from the recent experience of the 1964–70 Labour Government.

The second half of this book is the analytical and policy section,
where the various political theories are studied against the modern
political and industrial background. Here we examine the
contending streams of political thought within the trade unions
and look in depth at the Marxist case, widely expressed at present
by many active trade union members.

The conclusions formed in this section lead us on to examine
some policy areas which intimately affect the trade union movement, namely: ownership and control of the economy; industrial
relations; and prices, incomes and inflation. All three are 'crunch'
political issues at present. Policy proposals are made on each of
these issues.

The final section deals with how the Labour Party and the trade
unions should organise for power.

The directions and structure of this book have been developed
as a contribution to the continuing debate on policies and the
future political direction of the Labour movement. If you like
the sound of it – read on.

Contents

Chapter 1

Introduction

The rule which I dare to enact and declare,
Is that all shall be equal and equally share.
All wealth and enjoyments no longer endure
That one should be rich and one should be poor,
That one should have acres far stretching and wide,
And another not even enough to provide
Himself with a grave; that this at his call
Should have hundreds of servants, and that none at all.
All this I intend to correct and amend:
Now all of all blessings shall freely partake,
One life and one system for all men I make.

Aristophanes, 440–380 BC

An examination of the future relationship between the trade unions in Britain and the Labour Party must commence with some analysis of what the trade unions expect from a political party and how far the unions themselves have what could be called a coherent political philosophy.

It is ninety years since the trade unions first actively moved towards united political action, and the divergence of views which was present then is still with the unions today. The argument within the unions has, in fact, been sharpened by the experiences with the Labour Government from 1964 to 1970. The defeat of the Labour Government in 1970 inevitably resurrected, in private if not in public, talk about the need for firmer trade union control of the Labour Party, and some have expressed the view that the Labour Party has had its day and that there is a place for a new party to represent organised workers in Britain.

With these factors in mind, under a Conservative Government

which has shown ample evidence of its attitude to the unions and with the experience of a recent Labour Government behind us, this is perhaps a good time to examine the political role of the unions and to question how far the arguments and conditions which led to the formation of the Labour Party seventy years ago are still valid today.

This is no idle historical exercise because not only is it necessary from time to time to look afresh at the reasons why the trade unions in this country decided on a different political link up with a Labour Party from the unions in Germany or the Scandinavian countries (where the unions are not affiliated to a political party), but also because it will help us assess whether the Labour Party has an assured future in its present form or what changes in policy, structure and organisation are necessary for its survival.

According to some political writers the future of the British Labour Party, along with other Labour Parties in the world, is far from assured. Mr D. W. Rawson, writing on 'The Life Span of Labour Parties' in the September 1969 issue of *Political Studies*, examines the growth and decline of membership of all Labour Parties and concludes that 'sponsored [Labour] parties not only have a limited life span but are actually self-destructive in the sense that their success removes the special factor which produces them, namely the lack of balance between the political weakness and the relative industrial strength of their members'.

Rawson argues that the decline of the trade union affiliated Labour Parties is inevitable because of the changing occupational patterns in industrial countries and the growth of trade unionism among non-manual workers in those countries, including Great Britain. Rawson ends by saying that Labour Parties 'are unlikely to survive in their present form into the next century'.

Whether Mr Rawson is right or not is open to argument, but as his conclusions are based on the fact that changes in industry and in the status of trade unions in their respective countries will cause unions to think seriously about what form of political approach is right for them at the present time, they do warrant some analysis. These views, plus the criticism of any trade union leaders about the political direction of the Labour Party, make some assessment of past attitudes an essential part of any study of the trade unions in Britain and the Labour Party.

THE POLITICAL ROLE OF THE UNIONS?

It is impossible to embark on such a study without referring to the wide ideological chasm which has always existed within British trade unions over what their political purpose should be.

FOR NON-ALIGNMENT

Many unions are resolutely opposed to political alignment with any party. Unions favouring non-alignment are mainly in the professions and cater for what are loosely called non-manual, staff or white collar workers. They are not in the main affiliated to the Labour Party but have some significance in this study because they are a part of the Labour movement and have an increasing influence on the policy of the TUC. They also hold views on non-alignment which might well be attractive to other unions who are at present aligned but disillusioned and inclined to question which political road to tread in the future in the interest of their members.

There is a grain of truth in the argument that trade unions probably are maligned more by Conservatives and the mass media simply because of their link with the Labour Party, but on present evidence there does not seem to be any discernible shift towards a politically non-aligned trade union movement in Britain. The arguments against non-alignment are developed in a later chapter.

The divergence of views on the political purpose of trade unions is not confined to the unions not affiliated to the Labour Party. The history of the Labour Party is littered with the whitened bones of arguments over the years between the political extremists in the trade unions and those holding 'moderate' views. Although Britain is probably unique in the Western world in having trade unions whose rule books embrace political objectives, these definitions have remained unaltered in most cases for a hundred years or more and are no help in fashioning a picture of what politically motivates unions today.

All unions are united in their criticism and distaste of a *purely* capitalist, unbridled, free enterprise society, and a large measure of agreement is possible about what is most objectionable in such a society. There is also agreement about the basic require-ments for a more just and fair society, but on the ultimate desirable system of government and on the path towards it, the arguments today are as diverse as they ever were.

THE MARXIST ROLE FOR THE UNIONS

The Marxist view shown in the text books is that the industrial organisation of the workers is an instinctive expression of the class struggle and that members are to be regarded as class-conscious proletarians holding basically socialist views and seeking to use the trade unions to overthrow capitalism.

To those holding such views, agreements with employers are merely temporary truces and the struggle ends only with the victory of the working class and the creation of a socialist society.

Of course present day Marxists have sophisticated and distilled these views, but they still essentially regard the trade unions as an instrument of political change. Though few in number, they exercise considerable influence over trade union affairs at present.

LIMITED POLITICAL ROLE

Between the Marxists and the non-affiliated trade unionists there are many shades of opinion among those active in trade union politics but with no hard, coherent philosophy, and in fact the majority of trade unionists do realise the need for some kind of political action by the unions, but part company with the Marxists on how this should be done and how far the unions should be involved.

This majority includes left-wing socialists (other than Marxists), middle- and right-wing socialists who disagree not only about the ultimate shape of their ideal society but also about the way to achieve it.

The political ravine in the views of the unions is inevitably reflected in the arguments about policy in the Labour Party and also in the industrial attitudes of the unions. Small wonder then that to those looking on, the Labour Party seems incessantly riven with arguments and dispute. The wonder is that with all these strains the party has held together at all.

All these factors lead us to question whether the reasons for a Labour Party created by the unions seventy years ago are still viable today, and this needs some historical assessment.

Chapter 2

A Trade Union Historical Perspective

Without the labourer the land is nothing worth. Therefore the labouring people whether in sickness or in health, are to have the first maintenance out of the land.

William Cobbett, 1762–1835

THE UNIONS' POLITICAL AWAKENING

The present trade union link with the Labour Party dates officially from 1900, but the unions had political associations and were involved in political action much earlier than that.

The middle classes in Britain secured the first fruits of political agitation in 1832 with the introduction of the Reform Act which gave them the vote, but the working class had to wait until the enfranchisement reforms in 1868 and 1884 before they got the vote in the towns and counties.

Following this the unions hitched their political star to the Liberal Party and some unions were so firmly hitched that their association with the Liberal Party continued long after the Labour Party was formed in 1901. The Miners' Federation (the forerunner of the present National Union of Mineworkers) did not break with the Liberals until 1909!

The move towards a new political party created by trade union finance and support had its roots in the two sets of reformers who campaigned intelligently and effectively in the early part of the nineteenth century. Both of these were opposed to the existing system of society, but one set influenced by the theories of Ricardo were opposed to socialism as an alternative and wanted a return to a society composed of small independent producers governed

B

by the laws of exchange and without any government interference. The other group – the Owenite Socialists led by Robert Owen – wanted a co-operative socialist society.

These movements will be discussed later; we will examine first the seeds of trade unionism and political action which were already being fertilized by small, isolated groups.

THE EMERGENCE OF TRADE SOCIETIES AND CLUBS

The early societies and clubs, which grew into what have come to be known as trade unions, derived their impetus from the immediate needs of the working man rather than the ideas of political thinkers. The early groups, composed as they were of working men, relied on their immediate surroundings to influence their thoughts. Most of the members were barely literate, and even if they were, had at the beginning of the nineteenth century little or no access to books and journals. News and original ideas spread slowly both in a geographical and social sense.

EARLY UNIONS

It is not surprising to find that these early associations were locally based and often derived more from masonic or quasi-religious ideas than from political movements. Even today journalists and printers refer to their local groups as 'chapels' and not branches.

The earliest forms of trades unions were associations of journeymen who found themselves as qualified as their masters but had insufficient capital to set up in business on their own. Journeymen, as their name implies, journeyed round the country looking for employment in the trade of their choosing.

FROM TUDOR INCOMES POLICY TO THE COMBINATION LAWS

Until the seventeenth century with the fast growth of commerce and industry, the old State of Artificers 1563 had worked successfully. It had given local magistrates the power to fix the wages of artisans and labourers, and for many years these orders were effective. But the quickening pace of industrial development in the second half of the seventeenth century made it almost impossible to restrict wages by law in the face of a rising demand for labour.

By the late eighteenth century public unrest in Europe was widespread. The 'combination' of groups of working men was quickly seen as a 'Jacobin conspiracy' following in the wake of the French Revolution, a reaction which was to repeat itself 150 years later when general strikers in 1926 were labelled 'Bolshevik agents' allegedly bent on spreading the Russian Revolution.

The rebellion in Ireland in 1798 and the support given there by French Republican forces added weight to this interpretation. In this highly charged atmosphere it was almost inevitable that Parliament should pass in 1799 and 1800 the infamous Combination Laws which prohibited combinations of both employers and employees. As time went by these Acts were more and more used against combinations of employees rather than against their masters.

So with the Industrial Revolution barely out of infancy, Parliament was already using the Law as a means of combating embryonic trade unions. An aspect which will not be lost on trade unionists of the present day is the way in which this, the first anti-union Bill of the industrial age, was (like the Industrial Relations Act of 1971) allegedly impartial in discriminating between restrictive practices by working men or their bosses. In fact, the Combination Laws were used as the 1971 Act is at present being used, almost solely against the worker.

THE VIOLENT YEARS

With industrialisation in full swing and the Napoleonic Wars depressing living standards, it was almost inevitable that violence should be seen as the only means to which workers could resort to defend their interests.

The movement of machine breakers (which came to be known as the 'Luddite' movement) was perhaps, with the Peterloo Massacres of 1819, the best-known example of the violent era in which the early industrial labour movement grew.

The Luddites got their names from the *nom de plume* 'Ned Ludd' which appeared as signatory to letters declaring their intention to destroy new machinery in the lace industry in the years 1812–14. The name was also taken by some other groups of workmen engaged on the same activity in other industries.

A misconception which has gained currency over the years is that the Luddite movement was indiscriminate in its opposition to machines. In fact, as Professor E. J. Hobsbawm points out in *Labouring Men*, 'He [the Luddite] was concerned not with technical progress in the abstract, but with the practical twin problems of preventing unemployment and maintaining the customary standard of life which included non-monetary factors such as freedom and dignity as well as wages. It was thus not to the machine as such that he objected.'

Instances of machine breaking were not uncommon towards the end of the eighteenth century, but increased at the turn of the century. Whether this increase was related to the Combination Laws is unclear, but it is clear that the Combination Laws forced trade unions underground and in so doing pushed them closer to violent acts such as machine breaking, and generally closer to clandestine activities.

THE FIRST MARTYRS

Despite the ending of the Napoleonic Wars in 1815 the Government was still uneasy about political agitation, and this unease was disastrously displayed in 1819 when eleven members of a peaceful political protest in Manchester were killed by a charge of yeoman soldiers, at what was called the 'Peterloo Massacre'. With this last tragic flourish, the early age of violence subsided as the infant Labour Movement aimed its sights more and more at legal reform.

In 1824, as a result of a recommendation by a Committee of Inquiry of the House of Commons, the Combination Laws were repealed, thanks largely to the effort of Francis Place. The Committee report said of these Laws: '. . . the laws have not only been efficient to prevent Combinations either of masters or workmen, but on the contrary have in the opinion of many of both parties had a tendency to produce mutual irritation and distrust, and to give a violent character to the Combination, and to render them highly dangerous to the peace of the Community.'

It is interesting that besides Place many working men active in societies and clubs gave evidence before this Committee in favour of repealing the Combination Acts. It was one of the first occasions on which organised labour had worked through the parliamentary process to meet their grievances. Appropriately, they met with success.

THE FIRST UNSTEADY STEPS

Although the Repeal of the Combination Laws in 1824 was not in itself the cause of trade union growth, it did, by giving trade unions a new-found legality, create a more favourable climate in which they could develop more easily.

For the first twenty-four years of the nineteenth century the only legal grouping in which working men could band together for the purposes of mutual welfare had been through friendly societies. These societies or clubs aimed mainly at providing for members when they were sick, unemployed or retired, and on death for their funeral expenses. The more direct trade union activities were confined to secret meetings and illicit organisations. Often the only outward effect of these illegal gatherings was to intimidate workmen who 'overworked'.

After 1824 the industrial purpose of the various clubs and societies came to the fore, although membership tended to be confined to particular areas and particular crafts. Communications in the 1820s were insufficiently developed to support the growth of large national unions.

THE GENERAL UNIONS

There had been an unsuccessful attempt to start a general union as early as 1818. In that year the Manchester Spinners tried to co-ordinate the activities of several trades in Manchester to support joint industrial action against the new powerful mill owners.

The Philanthropic Society, as this group was called, lived a short, dramatic life, for on 29 August 1818 five members of the Spinners' Executive were arrested for conspiracy and the Treasurer absconded with the funds. Under this dual blow the union and the strike collapsed, but the experience influenced a young spinner, John Doherty, to revive the idea some years later in 1830, when he set up the National Association for the Protection of Labour (NAPL).

This 'union of all trades' quickly spread across the industrial north-west and Midlands, but relied mainly on the Spinners' Union for support. Its structure was democratic and its aim was to prevent cuts in wages.

The NAPL did not have long to wait for its first confrontation, for in the winter of 1830 Manchester clothiers attempted to cut the spinners' wages. Despite scattered support from some spinning union members outside the area, the NAPL showed itself to be largely ineffective in bringing members out on strike.

By March 1831 the strike had collapsed, and with it the effectiveness of the NAPL. The spinners themselves continued to put up a spirited fight, going as far as murdering the son of one of the leading mill owners in Ashton, with the result that over a thousand troops had to be called in.

POLITICAL REFORM

The demands for political reform eventually succeeded with the passing of the first Reform Act in 1832, and this had a major effect on the trade union movement.

The general growth of political awareness in working-class organisations owed much to the influence of two men mentioned earlier, David Ricardo and Robert Owen, and we now examine the philosophies of these men briefly.

THE RICARDIANS

Although the Ricardians were anti-socialist in outlook they have a place in this examination of trade union thinking in the 1800s because they, even more than the Owenites, laid bare in incisive terms the basic antagonisms between capital and labour and breathed dignity into those who laboured for a living. The Ricardians are also important because of the work of one young naval officer, Thomas Hodgskin (1783–1869), whom these new ideas transformed into a social critic of a new stamp.

Hodgskin was one of the principal founders of the London Mechanics' Institution (1823) which was a centre for discussion and action of some of the most active working-class minds at that time. At that centre Hodgskin explained the theories of Ricardo and Locke to the British working class in terms they could understand. Thomas Hodgskin's role in the development of working-class awareness to the problems and solutions of society at that time is seriously underrated by many historians. A sample of the core of his thinking is contained in the following extract from his *Labour Defended*:

I am certain however that till the triumph of labour be com-
pleted; till productive industry alone be opulent, and till idleness
alone be poor, till the admirable maxim that 'he who sows shall
reap' be solidly established; till the right of property shall be
founded on principles of justice and not on those of slavery, till
MAN shall be held more in honour than the clod he treads on,
or the machine he guides – there cannot and there ought not to be
either peace on earth or goodwill amongst men'.

Elie Halévy's biography *Thomas Hodgskin* (1903) is extremely
revealing, and his disappearance from the social scene in 1833 is
one of the mysteries of Britain's political history. His link with the
Ricardians and the working class, his active years from 1820 to
1830, were a powerful influence at the start of one of the most
revolutionary periods in our history, and with great significance in the development of trade union political thought and
action.

The Ricardian group with Hodgskin were responsible in 1821
for the publication of what was probably the first anti-capitalist
case set out in understandable terms. An anonymous writer from
the group published a pamphlet entitled *A Letter to Lord John
Russell*. Lord John Russell was a Whig who later introduced the
Reform Bill in 1830. The letter was a devastating attack on the
capitalist system and is set out admirably by Max Beer in the first
volume of his *History of British Socialism*.

This letter was rather ponderously called 'The Source and
Remedy of the National Difficulties', but there is nothing ponder-
ous about the logic which revealed the paradox that the people of
Britain were suffering while the nation's revenue was rising.
'Political Economists,' the letter went on, 'say that the nations are
richest where the greatest revenue can be raised, as if the power of
compelling or inducing men to labour twice as much at the "mills
of Gaza" for the enjoyment of the Philistines were a proof of
anything but a tyranny or an ignorance twice as powerful.'

Having stated the 'arsis' the letter then developed the thesis of
this Ricardian group and proceeded to give their own 'theory of
surplus value'. This they described by showing that labour which
produced beyond the requirements of the individual and his family
could be termed as surplus labour, and that such surplus could
be regarded as capital. 'As this surplus labour is not owned by
those who produced it, but instead by those who provided the

necessaries while he was producing it, the surplus labour could be regarded as capital taken away from the producer'.

The pamphlet went on to deal with the accumulation of capital and gave an analogy of a simple society following through in logical steps the injustices inflicted on the workers by the operation of the capitalist system. The employer is described here as 'an idle consumer' – 'maintained on the surplus value of others'.

'Wealth is Liberty, Liberty for recreation, liberty to enjoy life, liberty to improve the mind. Wealth is disposable time and nothing more,' this masterly exposition thundered on. 'The less useful the idle consumer becomes,' said the letter 'the stronger is his lust for accumulating the surplus labour of others – the more he wastes the more he extracts from the producers'.

Strong meat this glistening slice of Ricardian critique for those able at that time to understand and with a conscience to appreciate it, and more remarkable still as a political document because it was written in 1821, twenty-seven years before the publication of the Communist Manifesto in 1848. Marx himself, in fact, acknowledges the thinking of this group in his *Critique of Political Economy* published in 1859, and also in the English edition of *Capital* in 1888.

A Letter to Lord John Russell may not have put forward a socialist answer to the problem of British society in the 1820s, but it undoubtedly set many social reformers off on the road which was eventually to end in an exposition of the socialist alternative.

THE 'OWENITES' – ROBERT OWEN (1771–1858)

From this principle of individual interest have arisen all the divisions of mankind, the endless errors and mischiefs of class, sect, party and of national antipathies, creating the anger and malevolent passions and all the crimes and miseries with which the human race have hitherto been afflicted.

In short, if there be one closet doctrine more contrary to truth than another, it is the notion that individual interest as that term is now understood is a more advantageous principle on which to found the social system for the benefit of all, or of any, than the principle of union and mutual co-operation.

Robert Owen: Report to the County of Lanark

In these terms the Owenites drew liberally from the anti-capitalist deductions of the Ricardians and expounded their doctrine of co-operative socialism spanning the political bridge from *laissez-faire* liberalism to socialism and then towards an independent workers' political party. They had even stronger links with the trade unions than the Ricardians, and because of Owen's work within the unions, a more powerful influence on trade union political direction.

Robert Owen himself was wrongly labelled a crackpot and a dreamer, but he did have a conscience about the way the Industrial Revolution was developing in Britain and its effect on the working peoples. Although the owner of the largest cotton-spinning mill in Britain at the age of twenty-nine, he devoted his life to industrial experiments and social reforms.

His labour laws for factories, his views on free education, his teacher training colleges and his model villages and communities are all with us today in some form. The model factory village at New Lanark, which he purchased from David Dale in 1799, was a paternalistic experiment in which tickets were issued instead of wages, cashable only at the village store. Drunks were reported by caretakers and fined – all this in the name of Owen's moral code. Owen regarded the village at New Lanark as a success and as a blueprint for all society.

Robert Owen founded the first really political union in 1834, the Grand National Consolidated Trades Union, which was unashamedly dedicated to achieving socialism. Although the union only survived for ten years it was a noble exercise and showed that the dreamer had practical tendencies.

Owen was a leading figure in the universal protest against the deportation of the Tolpuddle Martyrs in 1834, the same year in which he formed the 'Grand National'. As a radical he commands a place in any work which links together those who work and politically aspire. Dreamer he may have been; paternalist he was; but his workers in New Lanark were happy, contented and fed, which was not the lot of many at that time. His failures at Orbiston in Scotland, Queenwood, Hampshire and New Harmony, Indiana (USA) were the forerunner of ideas that others carried on and his work to dignify labour is a sufficient monument to a man who laboured to prove that working people, however ignorant or unenlightened, would respond to improved conditions and a new environment.

Owen had not sufficiently studied the economic system in Britain and his conception of socialism was Utopian. He therefore was wide open to attack as being an unpractical socialist. He placed too much emphasis on changing society by changing the hearts of those in it. The spirit of competition proved too strong for Owen's spirit of co-operation, and his 'New Moral World' never looked feasible at any time, even when he was relatively successful in a small way. Still, his faith in the essential goodness of working men, which he backed by cash and dedication, shines brightly in the annals of British Socialism. The battle for trade unionism was laid down by Owen, but was plucked up by the more cautious 'Aristocrats of Labour'.

THE ARISTOCRATS OF LABOUR

The trade depression of 1837–42 had the effect of weakening unionism while strengthening political struggles and these conditions saw the rise of the Chartist movement. Although this movement met with limited success, its lessons were not lost on trade unionists of the 1840s. Its overt political challenges had been ineffective. Many felt that what was needed after the setbacks of the 1830s was a cautious policy based on financial and industrial strength.

Unions which began to make headway were those that adopted this course, being reluctant to strike, having high dues and restricting membership to a particular skilled trade. These tactics were effective at a time when the Victorian economy was truly reaching its peak. In the 1860s Britain was supplying over half the total of world coal production, 83 million tons in 1860 and 111 million in 1870. Coal was the major source of energy for industrialization, and those who owned it benefited as the owners of oil wells in Texas and the Middle East do today.

The skilled artisans were as vital to the new industrial economy as the coal which powered the machines of the new capitalism. In 1867 a skilled man could command an average weekly wage of 50s per week, whilst both the agricultural worker and the unskilled labourer were receiving 24s 10d per week, a differential in excess of 100 per cent, which meant a vital difference in bargaining power and in the power to organise.

REFORM NOT REVOLUTION

With the collapse of the more ambitious general unions, especially the GNCTU, tradesmen tended to look upon their own trade as being the only effective base to work from. While copying the general unions in aiming at a national rather than a regional basis of organisation the new unions were exclusive to skilled craftsmen, and relied not on voluntary organisers but full-time officials with offices in one of the large industrial centres. To run such an organisation meant a high level of subscriptions, which in itself barred the lower paid labouring class from supporting such unions.

The union, regarded as a model of the times, representing the new generation of strong, cautious and highly skilled unions, was the Amalgamated Society of Engineers, Machinists, Smiths, Millwrights and Patternmakers (ASE). This union was created, as its name implies, out of a merger of several craft unions in 1851. From the beginning the ASE had a high rate of subscriptions and a full-time General Secretary in the form of the conservative William Allen. Its sickness, retirement and funeral benefits were generous, and aimed essentially to provide for the needs of its highly skilled artisan members. One of the important achievements of the ASE was in effectively running a national union with a London-based leadership. Travel and communication were still major obstacles to running such an organisation, despite the rapid construction of the railways networks in the 1840s, and during the twenty years between 1854 and 1874 there were only two delegate conferences of the ASE. Between these conferences the union was run by an Executive elected from amongst London branches, in co-operation with the General Secretary.

'THE DOCUMENT'

Although the ASE was blessed with early success, it suffered a prompt challenge to its existence. In January 1852 employers in London and Lancashire acted in concert when ASE members refused to allow an increase in the number of unskilled men working in their shops. The ASE members were locked out, and despite some £1,200 being raised by other ASE members, the strike failed and members were forced to sign the infamous 'document', allowing the opening up of the shops.

Although the ASE suffered a setback as a result of this defeat, it was not disastrous. Despite the exhortation of one member of the ASE Executive to work for a co-operative society as a solution to their ills, Allen won over the union to support his policy of gradual consolidation.

A NEW SOLIDARITY

As union funds grew employers gradually gave recognition to this somewhat cautious union and the membership figures picked up after the defeat of 1852. By 1859 the ASE was in a healthy position with strong reserves and widely recognized at the bargaining table.

Some writers have wrongly assumed that these 'New Model Unions', as Beatrice Webb described them, shunned political activity, or indeed failed to recognize the common interest they shared with their less skilled brothers. On the contrary, instances abound where not just the ASE but other new craft unions indulged in overt political actions. They were tempered in these activities by the experience of the past, of course, and the general tendency was to avoid conflict wherever possible, unless it either threatened existing wage rates or the existence of unionism itself.

A tangible example of this was the strike in the London building industry, 1859–60. Although the dispute was originally over negotiations for a nine-hour day, it soon snowballed into an anti-union offensive when other London master builders locked out their employees until they had not only dropped the nine-hour day request, but signed the 'document'. This strike was supported by skilled and unskilled building workers alike, and it was to support this defence of trade unionists' rights amongst all workers that the ASE rallied by giving £3,000 to the strike fund. After six months the employers withdrew the demand to sign the 'document' and the workers their demand for a nine-hour day. Besides the deterrent effect which this strike had on anti-union employers, it also had a beneficial effect on union organization. The London Trades Council had been set up in May 1860 to Co-ordinate trade union support for the building workers. This Council was the genesis of the first TUC and continued to co-ordinate union activities long after the building workers' strike ended until the first TUC in 1868.

At the same time, impressed by the strength of the ASE in helping fellow unionists, the woodworking unions joined together to form the Amalgamated Society of Carpenters and Joiners, with Robert Applegarth as their General Secretary, creating the second major national craft union of the 'new model' type.

PUBLIC OPINION

With the growth of unionism in numbers and in financial strength, society and the law inevitably began again to take notice. The Molestation of Workmen Act, 1855, had given trades unionists the right to peaceful picketing, but soon public opinion was angered with the reappearance of violence in industrial disputes.

In 1866 the Sheffield Grinders blew up the house of a non-unionist, and in the following year four miners were killed and twenty-six injured when troops opened fire on a demonstration in North Wales as the Government of the day swung once more into an attack on the unions. The courts, as ever, were not slow to take up the cudgels, and in 1867 the Hornby v. Close decision laid down that trade unions were still illegal, although not criminal, as they tended to act in 'restraint of trade'.

TRADES UNIONS AS A PRESSURE GROUP

The 'restraint of trade' decision led to the first Royal Commission on Trades Unions, which opened its inquiries at Westminster on Monday, 8 March 1867.

The unions, in an effort to present their case coherently, formed a 'Conference of Amalgamated Trades'. This 'Conference', later labelled the 'Junta' by Sidney and Beatrice Webb, comprised W. Allen (ASE), R. Applegarth (Carpenters), D. Guile (Iron Foundries), E. Coulson (Shoemakers). The representations made by this group were both eloquent and well received. Their representations, and the report of the Royal Commission, showed just what could be done by the unions acting in concert.

The Royal Commission Report in 1869 helped to satisfy the public mind that much of the work done by trade unions was, in fact, entirely beneficial.

THE BIRTH OF THE TUC

The trade union movement, in the meantime, had been cementing the links which had been forged during the building workers' strike. In June 1868 the first Trades Union Congress met in Manchester. The Congress was attended by thirty-four delegates, representing seventeen trade unions and six trades councils. They were invited in the following words:

> The Manchester and Salford Trades Council having recently taken into their serious consideration the present aspect of trade unions, and the profound ignorance which prevails in the public mind with reference to their operations and principles, together with the probability of an attempt being made by the legislature during the present Session of Parliament to introduce a measure which might prove detrimental to the interests of such societies unless some prompt and decisive action be taken by the working classes themselves, beg most respectfully to intimate that it has been decided to hold in Manchester, as the main centre of industry in the provinces, a Congress of the representatives of Trades Councils, federations of trades, and trade societies in general.

The first TUC was called primarily to discuss how to influence the Royal Commission which was still sitting. The Congress concluded by calling for further annual congresses to bring 'the trades into closer alliance and to take action in all parliamentary matters pertaining to the general interests of the working classes'.

This was a particularly apt point to make, with the 1867 Reform Act extending the franchise to many members of the working class. From then on trade unionists did not have the right just to lobby Parliament, but actually to have a say in who sat there. And as their representations at the Royal Commission had shown, labour was perfectly capable of providing its own representatives.

A NEW POLITICAL ATMOSPHERE

The period of the 1870s and 1880s found the British Labour movement entering an intellectual renaissance. The booming trade conditions of the mid-Victorian economy had provided full employment, while the harshness of the capitalist ethic ensured that the rewards were shared unevenly. Not surprisingly, a large number of political groups had sprung up channelling the wide divergence of socialist, Christian and radical views which were currently held by working men and women.

POLITICAL TRENDS

Although not influential during his lifetime, the writings of the German philosopher Karl Marx have undoubtedly received the widest attention of all. His ideas on the inevitability of class war were never widely accepted by the British Labour movement, largely because they minimised the value of Parliament, an institution that was becoming increasingly the focus of trade unionists' attention during this period.

As early as 1864 Marx had sat alongside two Junta members, George Odger of the London Trades Council, and Robert Applegarth, at the formation of the International Working Men's Association in London. This body aimed at forging links between the labour unions of all countries, and this was perfectly acceptable to the cautious men of the Junta.

Although Marxist ideas had a great influence on the direction of socialist thought, not until Hyndman founded the Social Democratic Federation in 1881 was there a separate Marxist Party. The theories of Marx in relation to the Labour movement are examined in a later analytical chapter.

In addition to this 'scientific' stream of political thought, there were the Christian Socialists, the Owenites, the Fabians, various monetary reform associations, the Land Nationalization Society, the National Secular Society, the Vegetarian Society, and a host of smaller groups, all contributing to the ferment of ideas in the Labour movement.

Adjacent to these groups were a large number of publications of both regional and national standing, often produced by local Trades Councils or associations of working men. The most influential of these papers at the time was *The Beehive*, whose editor, George Potter, was a member of the Building Workers' Union and an unrelenting critic of the Junta. *The Beehive* ran from 1861 to 1877, and it was for the most part used to support strikes and actions of work people when and where they took place. The President of the ASE condemned Potter's criticism of the Junta and said he 'had become the aider and abettor of strikes. He thought of nothing else; in short, he was a strike-jobber, and *The Beehive* newspaper was his instrument.'

THE PARLIAMENTARY COMMITTEE

The TUC was at first reticent to use the electoral strength it had been given by the second Reform Act, and it was not until its second Congress in August 1869 that a Parliamentary Committee was set up to lobby Parliament on matters concerning labour.

For some years the Parliamentary Committee was over-shadowed by the Junta which, with its London-based leaders and established parliamentary contacts, was in a better position to exert influence. In 1875 the Parliamentary Committee appointed Henry Broadhurst as Secretary, and he served for fourteen years. Broadhurst was a fervent Liberal, and from 1880 served as a Liberal MP. Not surprisingly, under his influence the Parliamentary Committee saw its role more as a lobbying force than as a separate power group.

PRESSURE FROM BELOW

The Broadhurst line was consistently being threatened by the success of 'Labour' candidates in municipal and constituency elections. In 1873 a 'Labour' candidate stood against the two major party nominations in the Greenwich by-elections. The result was that the Conservatives gained a Liberal seat, and Professor Beesly, writing in *The Beehive*, said: 'The result of the Greenwich election is highly satisfactory. . . . The workman has at last come to the conclusion that the difference between the Liberal and Tory is pretty much that between upper and nether millstone.'

The increasing antipathy of working people to the Liberal Party was due to the growing indifference to their problems which that party displayed during Gladstone's administration. William Morris, in a private letter dated 11 February 1878, wrote later:

I am full of shame and anger at the cowardice of the so-called Liberal Party. A very few righteous men refuse to sit down at the bidding of these yelling scoundrels and pretend to agree with what they hate: these few are determined with the help of our workmen allies to get up a demonstration in London as soon as may be.

In 1871 the Criminal Law Amendment Act was passed, which, while not making strikes as such illegal, made preparations and other supporting activities for strikes criminal offences. As a result, in the same year seven women from South Wales were im-prisoned for saying 'Bah' to a blackleg, while in December of the following year gas stokers were imprisoned for a year merely for preparing to strike.

The 1874 elections saw a number of unions supporting independent candidates. In all, thirteen 'Labour' candidates stood in 1874, with the result that two officials of the National Union of Mineworkers, Alexander Macdonald and Thomas Burt, were elected for Stafford and Morpeth respectively. More important, Gladstone's Government was routed and the Tories, pledged to review the Criminal Law Amendment Act, were elected.

FROM LABOUR LOBBY TO LABOUR PARTY

The working man was not just increasing his influence in the Palace of Westminister during the 1870s, but was also increasing his influence through wider trade union organisation, especially amongst the ranks of the unskilled.

In 1872 a formidable figure, Joseph Arch, a Methodist lay preacher, laid the foundation of the National Agricultural Labourers' Union. By 1873 the union, having amalgamated with numerous local societies, had over 100,000 members. Despite opposition from the Established Church the union grew rapidly in a field of labour which still employed a sizable proportion of the working population.

Other unions of the unskilled grew up. In 1871 the wealthy brewer and philanthropist, M. T. Bass, financed the organisation of the Amalgamated Society of Railway Servants as a result of his concern for the condition of his constituents in Derby, where he was Liberal MP.

The unskilled workers suffered from the post-1875 recession in trade, later called the Great Depression. The uncontrolled savagery of the trade cycle caused widespread misery amongst the ranks of the new industrial workers. Demonstrations of the unemployed met with harsh treatment, and a demonstration held in London on 11 November 1887 resulted in such repressive police action that the demonstration was referred to thereafter as 'Bloody Sunday'.

THE MATCH GIRLS STRIKE A LIGHT

The first significant industrial action by the unskilled was especially notable because it involved women. The 672 women employees

C

in the East End Match Factory of Bryant and May came out on strike in 1887 against the conditions under which they had to work. Annie Besant, an ardent Fabian, assisted the girls by publicising their plight.

As a result of this publicity £400 was subscribed which enabled the two-week strike to reach a successful conclusion with improved pay and conditions. As a direct result the TUC in the following year passed a resolution supporting equal pay for women for equal work. A similar resolution was passed by the TUC eighty years later, and in 1969 Parliament at last passed the Equal Pay Act.

The match girls' strike was a signal for further strikes by the unskilled, and in the following August 20,000 gas workers in the East Ham Gas Works successfully struck under the leadership of Will Thorne, a radical socialist and himself a gas worker.

THE 1889 DOCK STRIKE

The next and more momentous act was that of the dockworkers, who were paid fourpence an hour and had irregular work. On 12 August 1889, a small dispute at the South-West India Dock quickly snowballed into a general demand for sixpence an hour, or the 'dockers' tanner', as it was later described. Tom Mann, John Burns and Ben Tillett, all leading socialists, took a part in the dispute. After two weeks, with the strike at breaking point, financial help arrived from Australian dockers, who eventually contributed some £30,000 which together with other contributions saved the strike.

As Tom Mann later wrote: The London Dock Strike of 1889 involved a much wider issue than that of a large number of port workers fighting for better conditions. There had been no more than a dogged acquiescence in the conditions insisted upon by the employers, more particularly on the part of those classed as unskilled labourers.

After five weeks and many meetings and marches through London, the dockers got their 'tanner' and general unionism, after sixty years, experienced a rebirth as the growing strength of Labour began to assert itself.

THE INDEPENDENT LABOUR PARTY

Increasingly the floor of the Trades Union Congress had shown impatience with the prevailing party system. Demands for stronger ties on candidates seeking votes of trade unionists were heard increasingly. (Shades of *Tribune* 1972!) Both Liberals and Conservatives had courted the newly enfranchised electors, but had done little to deserve the support of their voters.

A Scottish miner named Keir Hardie, after many hours studying the activities of the Liberals and Conservatives from the public gallery in the House of Commons, decided that the only way for Labour to ensure loyal representation was to start its own party.

In 1893 Hardie was instrumental in founding the Independent Labour Party, of which he wrote in the same year:

High over the Tent of Labour a gallant standard is floating proudly in the breeze, and on it are emblazoned in letters of gold the words 'INDEPENDENT LABOUR PARTY', and under that flag will be found those who love Humanity more than material greatness.

The year previously three supporters of this party had been elected to Parliament, John Burns, Havelock Wilson and Keir Hardie himself.

The ILP was indirectly the result of a resolution passed on the floor of the TUC in 1892 calling the Parliamentary Committee to draw up a scheme for a labour representation fund. In 1893 Congress urged trade unions to support only candidates pledged to 'the collective ownership and control of the means of production, distribution and exchange'.

The Parliamentary Committee were loath to follow such instructions, and it was not until the Courts unleashed a further attack on the trade union movement in 1900 that the Committee finally stirred itself to meet with the ILP and others and form the Labour Representation Committee.

The seeds planted and tended by the early clubs at the start of the nineteenth century were about to flower into political action.

Chapter 3

The Birth of the Labour Party

Capitalism is the creed of the dying present;
Socialism throbs with the life of the days that are to be.
J. Keir Hardie, 1856–1915

In 1887 Keir Hardie, writing in *The Miner* about the importance of having Labour representation independently of the Liberals, asked this question: 'Have we a grievance as a class, and if we have, do we have sufficient intelligence to state what the grievances are and what would constitute a remedy?'

The remedy was, according to Hardie, a new society – an economic and social system based on socialist principles.

Keir Hardie knew that the socialist remedy could not be applied without political organisation and his efforts in establishing the Scottish Labour Party in 1888 which led to the formation of the ILP, and his leading part in the formation of the Labour Representation Committee in 1900, showed him as the major figure in the attempt to form a new party for labour in Britain.

THE 'FORMATION' RESOLUTION

Many trade union leaders (aligned with the ILP) believed with Hardie that independent political organisation was necessary if socialist remedies were to have a chance. They believed the new party should be 'fathered' by the trade unions.

From 1895 onwards ILP union leaders had resolutions on successive TUC agendas asking for some action to be taken by the TUC Parliamentary Committee to set up a new independent political organisation. In 1899 they were at last successful when

James Holmes of the Railwaymen moved, and James Sexton of the Dockers seconded, the following resolution at the TUC:

That this Congress, having regard to its decisions in former years, and with a view to securing a better representation of the interests of Labour in the House of Commons, hereby instructs the Parliamentary Committee to invite the co-operation of all the Co-operative, Socialistic, Trade Union and other working-class organisations to jointly co-operate on lines mutually agreed upon in convening a special congress of representatives from such of the above-named organisations as may be willing to take part to devise ways and means for securing the return of an increased number of Labour Members to the next Parliament.

This was the resolution which led to the Parliamentary Committee of the TUC convening the Special Conference on Labour Representation in the Memorial Hall, London on 27 and 28 February 1900.

THE 'AGENDA' COMMITTEE

The Agenda for the conference was drawn up by representatives from the Parliamentary Committee, the ILP, the SDF and the Fabian Society. The leading trade union and political figures of the day were all on the 'Agenda' Committee – Sam Woods, W. C. Steadman, MP, Will Thorne, C. W. Bowerman, and Richard Bell were the five from the TUC Parliamentary Committee. Keir Hardie and Ramsay MacDonald represented the ILP with R. H. Taylor and H. Quelch from the SDF and E. R. Pease and George Bernard Shaw representing the Fabian Society.

What an interesting committee this must have been; what was said we will never know because no notes or accounts of the discussions are recorded. We can only guess at the sparks which flew from the clash of these strong-minded men of their time.

Keir Hardie, MacDonald, G. B. Shaw and Will Thorne we all know, but Sam Woods, along with John Burns, was one of the Whips of the trade union group of MPs in Parliament and was a Liberal MP at the time. This group was itself split between pro-Labour and pro-Liberal views. We have all heard that 'committee' is a noun of multitude signifying many but not signifying much, yet this could certainly not be said of the Agenda Committee who set out clearly the issues upon which decisions had to be made.

The socialists were, however, very much in the majority and although some compromise was made with the older trade unionists on the 'Agenda' Committee, the proposals which came from them were very much the aims which Hardie and other ILP supporters had in their political sights.

LABOUR REPRESENTATION CONFERENCE: 27 FEBRUARY 1900

When the 129 delegates assembled in the Memorial Hall, London, on that morning, feelings were divided. Although most of the delegates from seventy organisations, representing 568,177 members, were undoubtedly favourably inclined towards the Committee's proposals, there was also a sizable faction who were not.

Ramsay MacDonald said later of the conference, 'Some delegates met to bury the attempt in good-humoured tolerance, a few to make sure that burial would be its fate, but the majority were determined to give it a chance.'

The stage was now set and the lines of division at the conference separated out three distinct groups. Firstly there were the older trade union leaders who remained faithful to the liberal principles which had propelled them in their earlier days. This group, although anxious for the representation of the workers in Parliament, did not necessarily want to be at loggerheads with the two older political parties. The second group was composed of the socialist delegates from the ILP and the Fabian Society, and the SDF supported this group with some reservations. The trade unionists who represented what they called 'new unionism' also stood with this group. This group wanted to have the Labour representation in Parliament carried on by only avowed socialists who were prepared to form a separate party. They felt that all those who were in Parliament should recognise the class war and should stand for the socialisation of the means of production, distribution and exchange.

The third defined group at conference were those simply prepared to have representation in Parliament by those who belonged to the working class.

When the conference opened, the first resolution submitted read as follows: 'That this Conference is in favour of the working classes being represented in the House of Commons by members of the working classes, as being the most likely to be sympathetic with the aims and demands of the Labour Movement.' This resolution was far from an ambitious one and very much represented the view of the third group at conference. It was, however, a serious attempt to get some unity in the conference, particularly in the early stages.

This resolution was amended by the ASE who proposed to add to the end of the resolution the following qualifying clause: 'whose candidatures are promoted by one or another of the organised movements represented by the constitution which this conference is due to frame'. There was little discussion on this amendment which was carried by 102 votes to 3.

THE PROPOSALS BEFORE CONFERENCE

The conference then proceeded to deal with the other proposals drawn up by the Agenda Committee, which were as follows:

Labour Members in the House of Commons
A resolution in favour of establishing a distinct Labour Group in Parliament which should have its own Whips and agree on a policy which must embrace a willingness to co-operate with any party which for the time being may be engaged in promoting legislation in the direct interest of labour, and be equally ready to associate itself with any party in opposing measures having an opposite tendency.

Constitution of Committee
The Committee shall consist of twelve representatives from trade unions, ten for Co-operative Societies provided they are represented as a body at the conference, two from the Fabian Society, two from the ILP and two from the SDF.

Duty of Committee
This Committee should keep in touch with trade unions and other organisations which are running Labour candidates.

Financial Responsibility
The Committee shall administer the funds which may be received on behalf of the organisation and each body shall be required to pay 10s 0d per annum for every thousand members

or fraction thereof, also that each shall be responsible for the expenses of its own candidates.

Reporting to Congress
It should also report annually to the Trades Union Congress and the annual meetings of the National Societies represented on the Committee and take any steps deemed advisable to elicit information from the members of the organisations to whom the Committee is ultimately responsible.

Basis of Representation
Societies by whatever name they may be known shall be entitled to one delegate for every two thousand members or fraction thereof, and they must pay 10s 0d for each delegate attending the conference.

Voting
The method of voting shall be by card to be issued to the delegates of trade societies according to their membership and paid for on the principle of one card for every thousand members.

The convening of the conference and the clear proposals which formed the agenda ensured that the issues could not now be shelved.

With this conference and these proposals the history of the Labour Party began and the pioneering period of the socialist movement in Britain ended. The first steps had been taken. It now remained for the conference to respond to the challenge laid down by the eight proposals.

The second resolution given above was the most important, and it immediately drew fire from both the extreme wings of the conference. The right-wing view was expressed by the ship-wrights who proposed that the Labour Group should simply have a programme embracing four or five main principles upon which the vast majority of workers could be united, but that outside the main principles the members of the Parliamentary Group should be left entirely free on what they called 'purely political questions'.

The SDF, representing the left-wing point of view, moved a resolution which was in favour of a Parliamentary Group being entirely separate from what it called 'the Capitalist parties', and having for its ultimate object the socialisation of the means of production, distribution and exchange. The resolution from the SDF would also have given the Parliamentary Group the power to formulate its own policy for legislative measures which it felt to be in the interests of the workers. This resolution, although it did propose a measure of co-operation with other parties either in support of or in opposition to issues before Parliament, neverthe-less bound the Group to recognise the existence and the full implications of the class war. The Marxists had brought the argument out into the open.

KEIR HARDIE'S AMENDMENT

As the discussion at the conference proceeded it became fairly obvious that neither the original resolution nor the resolutions from the SDF or the shipwrights could secure the near unani-mous approval of the conference which was thought to be advisable. It was at this point that Keir Hardie, who was representing the ILP, put forward the following amendment to the original resolution: 'and further, members of the Labour Group shall not oppose any candidates whose candidature is being promoted in terms of Resolution (1)'. Although there was some debate, the amended resolution was.eventually carried unanim-mously and the establishment of the first Parliamentary Labour Party was under way.

Looking back today, and especially in view of Clause 4 of the Labour Party Constitution at the present time, it seems peculiar that the SDF resolution should raise the anger which it did at this conference, but in 1900 the political conditions in the Labour Movement were such that there was no chance at all of a resolu-tion such as that proposed by the SDF securing a majority at the conference.

Having dealt with the first two proposals the conference then went on to discuss the third, and the first Executive Committee of the Labour Party was elected. Seven members were chosen to represent the trade unions, these being: Frederick Rogers (Vellum Book Binders); Thomas Greenall (Lancashire Miners); Richard Bell (Amalgamated Society of Railway Servants); Peter Curran (Gas Workers and General Labourers); Allan Gee (Yorkshire Textile Workers); Alec Wilkie (Shipwrights); and John Hodge (British Steel Smelters).

Keir Hardie and James Parker were elected to represent the ILP, and James McDonald and Harry Quelch were elected from the SDF. The Secretary of the Fabian Society, Edward R. Pease, was also elected and Ramsay MacDonald, ILP, was eventually unanimously elected as Secretary. Frederick Rogers was the first Chairman and the newly elected Executive was called the Labour Representation Committee.

The conference then went on to approve the other five proposals. One other resolution proposed by the Railwaymen that Trades Councils should be invited to send delegates to the next conference was later amended to include Co-operative Societies, and ultimately was carried by 218,000 votes to 191,000.

Although a political party had been established it is strange that at this conference there were no proposals to set up any electoral machinery which was necessary if the sponsored candidates were to be elected. There were no proposals, for example, for the establishment of Labour Parties in the constituencies, and this was probably the reason which motivated the resolution by the Railwaymen, as the Trades Councils were the only local unit of organisation which could be used for electioneering purposes.

The election of Ramsay MacDonald as Secretary of the Committee was done in a rather haphazard manner as though once the conference had got rid of the important business there was a light-hearted attitude to some of the rest.

Initially, John Ward, who represented the Navvies, asked whether Sam Woods, who was then Secretary of the Parliamentary Committee of the Trades Union Congress, would agree to be Secretary. This was found to be impossible, firstly because Sam Woods's trade union had not sent any representative to the conference, and secondly because, as the conference suddenly realised, Sam Woods was a Liberal Member of Parliament. The conference obviously had to think again.

Mr Brocklehurst, representing the ILP, suggested that perhaps it would be better if two Secretaries were appointed, but this met with no support. Then John Hodge of the Steel Smelters moved that Mr Brocklehurst himself should act temporarily as the Secretary but Brocklehurst declined and himself nominated J. Ramsay MacDonald, who was unanimously elected to the office.

This most casual selection of Ramsay MacDonald as Secretary of the party proved later to be one of the most important decisions

taken by any conference. Regardless of the reputation which
he now holds in the movement, and however much his actions in
1931 were to be condemned, there is little doubt that no other man
could have brought such power and drive to the secretaryship of
the LRC as MacDonald did in those early years. It is obvious from
reading reports of the conference that the delegates inside the
conference did not appreciate the importance of the decision they
had taken when Ramsay MacDonald was elected Secretary,
whilst people outside the conference appreciated this even less.

The manner of MacDonald's election is rather reminiscent of
the atmosphere which still exists at some Labour Party conferences
In my experience the conference is very prone to become screwed
up tight over a particular issue on the agenda, leaving some in-
portant events both before and after this issue to go through on
the nod. So in a sense, the casualness of this MacDonald election
in 1900 may be said to have preceded a tradition which is still
carried on to some extent in our conferences today.

George Shepherd's NCLC pamphlet *Labour's Early Days* gives
an interesting account of some of the personalities who attended
the first conference, and relates that of the 129 delegates who were
present twenty-six were afterwards to become MPs, some of them
attaining high office in the Labour Party. Ramsay MacDonald
became Labour's first Prime Minister; Philip Snowden Labour's
first Chancellor of the Exchequer; G, N. Barnes was a member of
the War Cabinet from 1914 to 1918; F. W. Jowett was Minister
of Works; J. R. Clynes was Home Secretary; and John Hodge of
the steel smelters was the first Minister of Labour.

In addition to these, there were others present at the conference
who were later to make their mark in the trade union movement.
They included C. W. Bowerman (later Secretary of the TUC),
Ben Tillett and James Sexton of the dockers, Will Thorne and
Pete Curran of the Gas Workers, and Alex Wilkie, who later
united a plethora of local Shipwrights' societies and welded them
into a powerful trade union.

Chapter 4

The Shaping of Union Political Action

'What we want is to get away as far as possible from mere trade representation.
  We want Labour representation in the proper sense of the term.'

Arthur Henderson: 1904 Conference, LRC

THE CESSATION OF THE SDF

To obtain a 'rounded knowledge' of the 1900 LRC conference it is necessary here to extend our historical perspective by another five years, because three further major events occurred during that time which shaped trade union political thinking and spurred on political action by the unions.

In 1901 the ILP and the SDF, at the first annual LRC conference held in Manchester, again tried to persuade the unions to adopt a more socialist programme, and the ILP had a long resolution called 'Collectivism' which was moved by Bruce Glasier.

The resolution said:

This Congress of representatives of organised labour, recognising that the inevitable tendency of privately owned capital is towards combination in monopolies known as trusts, is of the opinion that the ownership and control of such vast aggregations of capital by private individuals are disastrous to the welfare of the consuming public, inimical to the social and political freedom of the people, and especially injurious to the industrial liberty and economic condition of the worker, that our policy must be to transfer all such private monopolies to public control as steps towards the creation of an Industrial Commonwealth founded upon the common ownership and control of land and capital and the substitution of co-operative production for use in place of the present method of competitive production for profit.

The ILP hardly believed in short resolutions or short sentences in those days, and the same genre of resolutions, long and involved, without punctuation, still appear frequently today on trade union and Labour Party agendas.

The SDF moved an amendment to the ILP resolution to add the following:

And this conference further declares that no candidate for Parliament should receive the support of the Labour Representation Committee who is not pledged to the above principles and to the recognition of the class war as the basis of working class political action.

The SDF were not going to be satisfied even with the acceptance of the wide programme of social ownership put forward by the ILP. They wanted individual candidates completely committed or else they would be disowned by the LRC. In the event the conference did not support any of the resolutions and the previous year's statement was again moved and carried.

The attitudes of the ILP and the SDF to their defeat at this conference are extremely important historically. The SDF peremptorily cut its connection with the LRC and disaffiliated soon after the conference, whereas the ILP, which had always shown more patience than the SDF, decided that there would be another day – another chance, and they stayed in. The SDF star declined from that time, and the ILP went on to make an important socialist contribution to the thinking of the Labour Party in later years.

TAFF VALE CASE: 1900–1902

When Richard Bell (Amalgamated Society of Railway Servants) read a telegram to the 1900 TUC announcing the judgement against his union in an action brought by the Taff Vale Railway Company, not many of the delegates realised then how far-reaching the decision was going to be.

The ASRS had engaged in a dispute with the Railway Company during which the Company obtained an injunction against the union for picketing and molestation, and another injunction which stopped the union from using union funds to defend the union officers concerned. Action was also started by the Taff Vale Company against the workers involved for breach of contract, but this was later shelved.

The Railway Company carried through the legal action against the union for £23,000 in respect of damages and costs in the dispute and eventually, after much argument and campaigning by the union, the House of Lords decided in 1902 in favour of the Company.

The Union bill for the action, including their own defence and the £23,000 awarded to the Company came to £42,000.

This decision struck the unions like a thunderbolt, and at the 1902 LRC Conference the Executive Committee described the position of the unions as being 'menaced on every hand, in workshop, court of law, and Press'. 'Trade Unionism,' the Executive report said, 'has no refuge except the ballot box and Labour representation.'

This judgement more than any other single event in history made the unions politically conscious. The 1901 TUC had already declared in favour of an alteration of the law to restore the legal position of the unions, and there was a flood of workers into the LRC. The figures speak for themselves. In 1901 there were 41 unions affiliated to the LRC. In 1904 it increased to 165. In a single year the affiliated membership, which was 455,450 in 1901, had gone up to 847,315 and in 1904 was up to almost a million.

In the campaign to reverse 'Taff Vale' three important trade unionists were elected in by-elections – David Shackleton of the Darwen Weavers was elected unopposed in Clitheroe, Will Crookes won at Woolwich in 1903, and Arthur Henderson, President of my own union, the Foundry Workers, was also elected for Barnard Castle.

The fight was engaged and David Shackleton, though generally little mentioned now, became a force in the House of Commons and was a leader in the struggle to have the trade union laws amended.

Although the argument raged over Tariff Reform (and this was an issue at the three by-elections mentioned), to trade unionists there was only one issue – Taff Vale – and this was the real battering-ram of the movement. With this point as their inspiration the unions eventually forced Balfour, the Tory Prime Minister, to set up a Royal Commission, but the TUC boycotted this and eventually the General Election of 1906 saw the Liberal Party win with 377 seats against the Tories' 167. LRC had 29.

The Labour Party, as it had now become (the change is described in detail later) set its hand once more to the task of reversing the Taff Vale decision. Asquith, a leading Liberal and a lawyer, was against writing into the law anything that would give trade union members a privilege not given to other citizens, and the Liberal Government Bill, influenced by his thinking, was therefore unacceptable to the Labour MPs who had drafted the following crucial clause:

Any action against the Trade Unions, whether of workmen or masters, or against members or officials thereof, on behalf of themselves and all other members of Trade Unions, in respect of any tortious act alleged to have been committed by or on behalf of the Trade Union, shall not be entertained by any Court.

During the debate on the second reading of the Government's Bill, the Liberal Prime Minister, Sir Henry Campbell-Bannerman, dropped a bombshell when he told the House that the Bill drafted by the Labour MPs was the better of the two and the above clause was included in the 1906 Trade Union Act.

It is tempting at this stage to go into detail about the parallel of the Taff Vale campaign by the unions to establish a legal status and protection for their funds in disputes, and the campaign which is still raging around the Industrial Relations Act, but as a later chapter deals specifically with an industrial relations policy for the unions, I have decided reluctantly not to pursue the analogy further at this point.

LRC CONFERENCE: 1905

The LRC refused to abandon their pragmatic, federated type of policy and organisation, despite attempts at the conference between 1901 and 1905 by the left wing to obtain a declaration of ultimate aims and to stimulate political discussion on programmatic lines which the LRC so far had set their face against. This silence on political objectives ended with the conference of 1905.

The 1905 conference is particularly important because one of the resolutions carried with slight amendments later became the famous Clause 4 of the Labour Party Constitution.

The resolution stated:

The Annual Conference of the LRC hereby declares that its ultimate object shall be the obtaining for the workers the full results of their labour by the overthrow of the present competitive system of capitalism and the institution of a system of public ownership of all the means of production, distribution and exchange.

This historic resolution went through without discussion – a surprising fact because it was virtually the same resolution which the SDF representatives had moved at the 1900 Conference and which had led to their secession at the Manchester Conference in 1901.

Although the SDF were not represented as a group at the 1905 conference it is generally accepted that their persistence and lobbying were responsible for the resolution being on the agenda again and ultimately passed. It may seem strange too that an organisation outside the Labour Party should be responsible for that part of its constitution which has proved to be an inspiration to many and a source of annoyance to others.

As we have said, during the years 1900 to 1905 the annual conferences of the LRC had resolutely refused to put a programme before the public, whilst left-wing influences in the party argued strongly for the adoption of ultimate aims and the declaration of a programme. The moderate elements meanwhile argued that this was unnecessary because each year the TUC passed resolutions and all that was really needed was to weigh up the issues at any given time, pick out the appropriate TUC resolutions, and with a bit of intelligent linking you had a programme.

Even in 1905 when the party had adopted the 'Clause 4' type resolution, it still refused to declare a political programme. Action was, however, taken on some of the burning issues at that time, and even before the 1905 Conference the NEC of the LRC had already held conferences in January to deal with unemployment. The resolutions carried at these conferences are the first public policy statement by the LRC and deserve examination.

THE UNEMPLOYMENT RESOLUTION OF 1905

(a) That unemployment is not caused by scarcity of land, of capital, of national wealth, or by incapacity to consume.

(b) That unemployment prevails in Protectorates and Free Trade countries alike.

(c) That the presence of aliens in Britain is not a cause of unemployment amongst British workers.

(d) That unemployment, on the contrary, is due to the existence of monopoly and the burdens which the non-producing sections impose on the industrious classes, together with the lack of such an organisation of industry as will prevent alternate periods of overwork and unemployment,

It will be seen that apart from (b), which deals with issues which have long since disappeared, the remainder of the points covered in the resolution are still valid today.

In the second resolution dealing with this subject, the Members of Parliament were urged to introduce legislation so that local authorities could acquire and use land and reorganise local administrative machinery in order to provide alleviation for poverty and unemployment. They were also urged to bring pressure on the Government to put the recommendations of the Afforestation Committee into effect to the same end. The resolution also stated that the Board of Trade should undertake a programme of reclamation of foreshores and also create a Labour Ministry in order to create further job opportunities.

David Shackleton, who has been mentioned in the events surrounding the Taff Vale judgement, later moved a third resolution which stated that local authorities should have a programme of public work to bring forward at times when the labour market is depressed and should in consequence schedule improvements, housing schemes, etc., with a view to putting these programmes in hand immediately, and should also wherever possible employ direct labour paying standard trade union rates under standard conditions.

These resolutions and the detailed proposals are remarkable for the clarity with which they stated the LRC's political position, and the methods by which they were to be achieved were indeed practical, foreshadowing the action which was taken by future Labour Governments.

Keir Hardie had a burning hatred of the effects of unemployment which had reached 5 per cent in 1904, and he was the first to lead Labour's fight against unemployment. To him was due the honour for that first Act – the Unemployed Workmen's Act

D

of 1905 – and although it looks puny seen from the 1970s, its enactment was a triumph for Hardie who stirred the public conscience of the country by his unsparing efforts in defence of those who were 'on the scrap-heap of industry'.

The six years from 1900 to 1906 were formative years in the political thinking of the unions. The resolution regarding objectives carried at the 1905 Conference was later to be embodied in the constitution and, as we have mentioned, led to the Clause 4 argument in 1959–61. The Taff Vale decision united the unions on a single political issue, and for the first time in their history caused them to pursue political action through their own party. Finally, the LRC changed to the Labour Party and similarly changed its attitude towards setting out a separate political programme for the party, beginning to organise itself in Parliament as an independent political party.

With these events in mind, the following chapter examines the basic attitudes of the unions in this period, and draws conclusions for today and the future.

Chapter 5

The Unions and Political Alignment in the 1970s

'Suddenly politicians of all parties realised that a new factor in politics had appeared. Organised labour as a political force is already a mence to the easy-going gentlemen of the old school who have slumbered for so long on the green benches at St Stephen's.'

L.R.C. Executive Committee, 1906

With the 1905 Conference issues fresh in our minds and the wry reflection that the spectre of unemployment still stalks our present society, we can see clearly that there are also many other problems which were endemic in the 1900s that are still awaiting a lasting solution. For example, one other special issue which had a major place in the 1905 Agenda was 'The Feeding of School Children', which is certainly still capable of causing a political and social storm as the controversy about school milk not so long ago reminds us.

I quote these two easily recognised examples because I wish to show that not only have we failed to clarify our political philosophical outlook since then, but there are also some elementary problems which the unions and their political organisation regarded as social evils seventy years ago yet which are still far from resolved, although the degree of the problem may have changed.

One of the tasks set out for this book is to question whether the reasons why the unions created the Labour Party are still valid today. Now that we have looked at the events and the thinking which shaped the Labour Party at its formation, we are

better equipped to approach the two questions which are asked as
frequently today as they were in the early 1900s.

These questions concern the trade unions' participation in
policies in Great Britain, and whether it is in their interests to be
aligned with the Labour Party.

SHOULD UNIONS BE IN POLITICS?

Of course a Conservative would have a vested interest in arguing
that trade unions should not be involved in politics – after all,
their exclusion would remove a powerful mass workers' organisation from the political arena. But many trade unionists also have
the notion that it is possible for unions to confine their activities
to industrial questions only, and that 'politics' as they see it, is
something private, to be decided only by ballot at election times.

I realise that this argument may be regarded by many as being
too naive to answer, but these are views which were expressed in
opposition to the creation of a trade union political party a
hundred years ago, and at least some trade union members and
some of the public today hold these views strongly enough to
write to newspapers, or indeed to voice them at union meetings.

Although the majority of members of the unions organising
manual workers agree with the need for unions to carry out some
kind of political action, even in those unions only about two-
thirds are politically affiliated. This is an important fact, especially
when it is realised that a member must make a conscious, physical
action to contract out of the political levy.

The four million fewer members affiliated to the Labour Party
than are within the TUC are also an overall indication of how large
a number of trade unions are non-political when these manual
non-politicals are joined by those of the white collar unions. Of
course, these four million trade unionists do not all believe that
the unions should stay out of politics altogether. Some do want
and need political action, but they do not agree with being tied
financially or even policy-wise to the Labour Party.

Yet the arguments for being involved in politics are stronger
today than they were for the unions a hundred years ago. Ignoring
for the moment the obvious higher political reasons concerned
with eradicating social evils and the building of a better society,
there are still practical, industrial reasons why trade unions must
be involved in political action.

The TUC in the 1880s was administered by the Parliamentary Committee even before there was a combination of unions to form a political party. A look at the political items which flowed from the industrial interests of the unions at that time is revealing. In 1889 the Parliamentary Committee discussed Old Age Pensions, 'Half Tanners' Bill, Amendment to the Compensation Act, Miners' Eight-hour Day Bill, Workmen's Cheap Trains Bill, Bakehouses' Hours Bill, Merchandise Marks Amendment Bill, Bills dealing with anchors, chains, cables, watermen, steam engine, boilers, as well as the more general questions of electoral reform, banking of trade union funds, and so on.

These matters which concerned the day-to-day work of the unions at that time were being advanced in some way by pressure in the lobbies of the House of Commons. Political action was necessary then even in a primitive form to enable the unions to fulfil their industrial role.

POLITICS AND INDUSTRY

This relationship is even more necessary today. In recent years politics in the form of Acts and Statutes have increasingly been entering the works gate. The Contracts of Employment Act, the Redundancy Payments Act, Earnings Related Benefits – are all very recent political actions which have left their mark on industry. Factory Acts, special regulations for dangerous industries, or special conditions of work for women and young persons, all needed political action to put them on the statute book and need continuing political pressure to have them amended as industrial aspirations rise.

The whole range of industrial benefits that are interwoven with the social insurance scheme concerning disablement benefits, pneumoconiosis and other industrial diseases all require constant political vigilance if the injured or sick trade union member's interests are to be fully protected. So even on the primary level of serving its members' immediate interests, a trade union would be doing only half a job if it were completely non-political.

In the more general sense, unions cannot truly improve the real wages and standard of living of their members unless they concern themselves with the economic direction of our resources and the distribution of wealth in our society. If trade unions are to be concerned with their unemployed members, how can they be effective without having some analysis about the cause of unemployment and the means to put it right? How can the unions be concerned with what gross wages will be for their members and remain unconcerned with what the member takes home after tax and insurance? How can a union be concerned with a member when he is well and working and yet stay inactive on his or her behalf when he is sick and not working?

Trade unions, to do their job intelligently and efficiently, must be ever seeking to establish the kind of economic and social framework within which they can best carry out their responsibilities on behalf of their members. Looking after the whole man or woman is the only sensible way the unions can fulfil their duties to their members. This means being politically active about ante-natal grants for women as well as concessionary fares for members who have retired and so on across the spectrum. Workers expect a universal service from the union. They get it, but the service would be seriously limited if political action were excluded.

The trade unionists of the 1880s and 1900s came slowly to see the inevitability of political action if the unions' job was to be done. Today the fact that Governments are trying to regulate the conditions under which the unions will operate and the precise way in which workers shall behave is an even more compelling reason why unions must continue to be in politics!

ALIGNED OR NON-ALIGNED

Aside from the 'non-political' trade union arguments there is still the case to be examined of those who, while agreeing the unions must indulge in political action, are emphatically opposed to their being part and parcel of the Labour Party.

It is understandable that this cry is heard loudest after the election of each Conservative Government and, of course, as already mentioned, the growth of membership in white collar unions, many of whose members identify with management, swells the ranks of those who want a break between the unions and the Labour Party.

It is also beyond doubt that many trade unionists vote Conservative and they, along with the militant Tories who have 'contracted out' of paying the political levy, are quick to exploit occasions when they think the unions are exceeding what they regard as their traditional functions.

These groups, with a little help from the Conservative Party, are vociferous within the unions at local level. Not many of them are interested in attending the national conferences of their union where they doubtless do not relish being in a minority, but they do wield influence in union branches and on the shop floor, and their campaign to push 'contracting out' starts annually about November.

In their letters to local newspapers, who usually oblige each year by publishing 'contracting out' letters, they point to the USA and the European countries where, they say, trade unions and workers do all right and are courted by all the political parties. They also hint that the trade unionists are attacked more strongly in Britain because they are aligned with the Labour Party!

How much truth is there in these assertions?

EXPERIENCE IN OTHER COUNTRIES

It is true that in the USA and in many European countries there is no formal link with the Labour or Social Democratic Parties and the unions, but there is an extremely powerful chain of interest which binds the unions in these countries to the respective Labour Parties.

In the Scandinavian countries most of the finance of the Social Democratic Parties comes from the unions, either nationally or locally. In West Germany too the links are strong, and in policy matters every bit as effective, if not more so, than they are in Britain in keeping the Social Democratic Party in tune with the unions.

In France and Italy a divided trade union movement and splintered workers' political representation make comparisons with Great Britain difficult, but even there splinter groups receive financial support nationally and locally from the unions which support their views.

In the USA elections the unions usually support the Democrats, although it must be said that they are not always uncritical of the party. Of all the examples mentioned the American trade unionist is probably the most disposed towards the non-aligned political position of the unions.

There is, however, in the USA a powerful lobbying system by

which the unions on occasions can use their weight on legislation affecting their interest, and this method of political pressure leads to more horse-trading and chicanery than almost anywhere in the Western world. The lobby system is bound to be a political approach made up of unrelated bits and pieces. It is certainly no substitute for a political programme of trade union action. As a democratic form of action the lobby system is more open to criticism than the formal link which we have in Britain between the unions and the Labour Party. MPs' motives are often questioned with good reason when a powerful lobby is in action at their backs.

Many trade union leaders in Europe admire the structure of the British Labour Party and its union base, and there is little doubt that this union base has been responsible for the comparative stability of the Labour Party here, compared with the Continental Social Democratic parties. In conversation these leaders have often admitted that if they could start afresh on the construction of an organisation for promoting trade union political objectives, they would build on the lines of the British model.

I conclude from the experience in the USA and in the European countries that the unions there would certainly be no worse off if they had formal financial links with their traditional political parties.

The argument that the link with the Labour Party automatically makes the unions the Conservative's whipping-boy is so thin as to be almost transparent. Trade unions are unpopular with Tories not because they are linked with the Labour Party, but because of their functions in industry. Looking after our members automatically means that we are in perpetual conflict with those who run industry. Getting the best deal for our members means having more power and rights in decision-making in industry, and this in turn means that the unions are continually involved in 'rolling back the frontiers of management'. The unions have won the right to have a say today in spheres that would have been unthinkable even twenty-five years ago.

The elaborate dismissals procedures which involve a number of verbal and written warnings and have appeals stages for the worker concerned are a graphic example of how even the much quoted right of management to 'hire and fire' has been modified by modern industrial development and trade union organisation.

The right to be consulted effectively over a wide range of matters has been won from, not given benevolently by, managements in this country, and the unions' power in delaying or facilitating the introduction of new working practices has also meant that private enterprise as a group has always regarded the unions as its *bête noire* in attempting to run business in the time-honoured, free enterprise fashion.

Like many trade unionists, the Tories recognise that governments may come and go in this country, and frequently do, but the unions are always industrially in power to some extent.

BUSINESS BEFORE POLITICS

It is for these reasons that the unions can never expect fair treatment from a Conservative Government. Conservatives are tolerant of trade unions because the alternative is industrial chaos, which would be bad for business and would impose strains on the unity of the Conservative Party itself. The private industry pay increases in 1971 and 1972, which were diametrically opposed to the Conservative incomes philosophy, are recent proof that what is right for business takes precedence even over political loyalty to the party which stands for 'free enterprise'.

The agreements now widely signed in which private employers have agreed not to use the provisions of the Industrial Relations Act are also an indication that 'private enterprisers' who are in sections of industry which are well organised by unions had no intention of being the 'Flodden fields' on which the Tories could reap a harvest of political plaudits.

The Conservative dilemma is that the constituency Tory supporters demand from their party an anti-trade union policy which in practice is damaging to the interests of private enterprise.

The trade unions are disliked by Conservatives because they have power in industry, not because of their formal links with the Labour Party. In protecting the interests of their members, the unions restrict the right of management to manage as they used to. This process is dynamic because industry itself is dynamic and because the aspirations of workers are changing. They require more qualitatively and quantitively from their jobs. This means that the rights of management will be perpetually cut back because the balance of forces and interests on the shop floor demands that this must be done. It is the law of the situation in industrial Britain and only a complete collapse of trade union organisation can halt the process.

Once again, it is for these reasons concerned with industrial power that the Tories try to defeat the unions, not because they are politically connected and aligned with the Labour Party.

My conclusion is that in the interests of their members the trade unions must continue to be political and to be aligned with the Labour Party. But let us finish this chapter by hearing Robert Blatchford's case for the trade union link with the Labour Party. In his book *Britain for the British* (1902), Blatchford puts the case for alignment with the Labour Party like this: 'My chief object in writing this book,' he tells the British trade unionist, 'has been to persuade you that you need the Labour Party.' He then takes up the analogy between the trade union and the Labour Party:

What is a trade union? It is a combination of workers to defend their own interests from the encroachments of the employers. Well, the Labour Party is a combination of workers to defend their own interests from the encroachment of the employers or their representatives in Parliament and on municipal bodies. Do you elect your employers as officials of your trade unions? Do you send employers as delegates to your Trade Union Congress? You would laugh at the suggestion. You know that the employer could not attend to your interests in the trade union which is formed as a defence against him. Do you think the employer is likely to be more useful or more disinterested in Parliament or the County Council than in the trade union? Whether he be in Parliament or in his own office, he is an employer and he puts his own interest first and the interests of labour behind, yet these men whom as trade unionists you mistrust, you annually send as politicians to make laws for you. A Labour Party is a kind of political trade union, and to defend trade unionism is to defend Labour representation. If an employer's interests are opposed to your interests in business what reason have you for supposing that his interests and yours are not opposed in politics? To be a trade unionist and fight for your class during a strike, and to be a Tory or Liberal and fight against your class at an election is folly. During a strike there are no Tories or Liberals among the strikers, they are all workers. At election times there are no workers, only Liberals and Tories.

Blatchford had of course, written this before the Labour Party was politically organised and therefore at that time the choice was between Liberals and Tories. Although written almost seventy years ago, the basic logic contained within this statement is as valid today as it was then.

We leave the last word with Blatchford on the necessity for trade union formal alignment with the Labour Party. We take up our historical narrative in the next chapter by looking at the events in the years 1906–13, which made political life difficult for the unions and which shaped the framework of the law within which the unions have worked until the present time.

The unions, having just survived the Taff Vale decision and seeing the Trade Union Act of 1906 as the first fruits of their political action, were to find that not all our society at that time were pleased with the way in which the unions had flexed their political muscles and put Taff Vale behind them.

Chapter 6

Osborne. The Remedy – Then and Now

'At one stroke the financial resources of the Labour Party
or of the political activities of the unions appear to have
been cut off.'

Max Beer: *History of British Socialism*, Vol. 2

The General Election of 1906 saw twenty-nine Labour members
elected out of fifty candidates approved by the Labour Representation Committee. These members, with Keir Hardie as their
leader, started work as a Parliamentary group and established a
system of standing committees which have been a feature of every
Parliamentary Labour Party since that time.

At the Annual Conference of the LRC in 1906 after the election,
the first Parliamentary Report was presented which established the
procedure giving the Parliamentary Party direct representation at
the Annual Conference. This was, in fact, the constitutional
basis for the much-disputed independence of the Parliamentary
Party. It acted then as a constitution group within the party but
was not subject to the direction of the National Executive Committee. It still operates in this way today, but the roots of the
present status of the PLP were first put down in the 1906
Conference.

What's in a Name?
The 1906 Conference is also noted for the change in the name of
the LRC to Labour Party. The argument over the change of name
was typical of the many 'cautious-moderate versus left-wing'
rows which have been a feature of the party since its birth.

The left wing wanted the party to be called the Socialist Party, but the moderates (dominated by the trade unions) felt that the name of the party should convey a sense of belonging for all working men and women and should appeal to the majority who were only marginally interested in politics.

In a strange way they wanted a name for the party which transcended politics. The name Labour, they felt, conveyed that the party was a party for the working man. It is still a good name and a name which brings working people together. To work is to labour, and certainly in those days when the party organisation was being built, to labour was to belong to and vote for the Labour Party.

OSBORNE JUDGEMENT

The years between the 1906 Conference and the start of the Great War in 1914 were important years in the formation of trade union political attitudes. The Osborne case in 1908, in which Mr W. V. Osborne, the Walthamstow Branch Secretary of the Amalgamated Society of Railway Servants, objected to changes in the constitution of the union which added the securing of parliamentary representation to the objects in the union rule book, was a milestone in any study of British trade unions and their political development.

Osborne contended that spending money on parliamentary representation was not included in the objects on which money could be spent in Section 16 of the Trade Union Act of 1876. Section 16 read as follows:

The term 'Trade Union' means any combination whether temporary or permanent, for regulating the relations between workmen and workmen or between masters and masters, or for imposing restrictive conditions on the conduct of any trade or business whether such combination would or would not, if the principal Act had not been passed, have been deemed to have been an unlawful combination by reason of some one or more of its purposes being in restraint of trade.

The principal Act referred to in Section 16 was the Act of 1871, but the whole argument put forward by Osborne was that the clause did provide an exhaustive definition of what a trade union could have in its objects.

Osborne's case was first dismissed with costs against him, but on appeal later judgement was given against the Union, and Lord Justice Cozens-Hardy (Master of the Rolls) in his judgement said that the definition of a trade union and its purposes as defined in the 1871 and 1876 legislation was purposely limited and restricted, and that it was not competent for a union to add to its objects 'something so wholly distinct from the objects contemplated by the Trade Union Acts (of 1871 and 1876) as a provision to secure Parliamentary Representation'.

LABOUR – A PLEDGE-BOUND PARTY

The union took the case to the House of Lords, but there it had to face not only the reasons for the judgement given by Cozens-Hardy but also the opinion offered by another member of the Court of Appeal, Lord Justice Fletcher Moulton, who said that it was *ultra vires* for trade unions to collect money for securing or maintaining parliamentary representation by the means of compulsory contributions from the members.

He also said that other amendments to the unions stated objects prescribed that those who were supported by the union for parliamentary representation were thereby bound to vote a certain way (i.e. with the Labour Party) and, further, that a pledge-bound party like the Labour Party was an anomaly and contrary to public policy.

JUDGEMENT WIDENED

The case was therefore widened by this statement. It now dealt not only with Osborne's original point, but also struck at the constitution of the Labour Party itself as decided by the 1900 Conference.

The House of Lords delivered their judgement on 21 December 1909 and found against the union.

Lord Halsbury, one of the leading Tory lawyers of the day, said in judgement that the political contribution collected by the union was to his mind manifestly beyond the powers possessed by a trade union. Almost all the other law lords took substantially the same view, although a few, including Lord James of Hereford, said that it would not be illegal for trade unions to have a separate fund to pay the expenses of Members of Parliament.

THE IMPORTANCE OF 'OSBORNE'

The Osborne Judgement was therefore important because of two things. Firstly, it persuaded nearly all active trade unionists that they could not expect anything other than obstruction and hindrance from the law as made by British judges. Secondly, it was the start of a virile political campaign to have the law altered to legalise trade union political participation, including the financing of MPs.

THE TRADE UNION ACT OF 1913

The campaign was successful and the Liberal Government of 1910 eventually introduced the Trade Union Act of 1913, which although not giving the unions all they wanted in that they could not spend the general funds on political purposes, gave them the avenue by which they could be politically active once again.

The Trade Union Act of 1913 is still with us today and governs how political levies will be collected and spent. This was the Act which introduced 'contracting out', and although some think that even today this is too favourable a method for the trade union collection of political contributions, it must be understood that from 1874 up to the date of the Osborne Judgement trade unions had used their *general* funds without impediment for political purposes, including the precise point which was at issue in the Osborne case.

The Trade Union Act of 1913 therefore was a compromise born broadly of the views expressed by Lord James of Hereford in his musings on the Osborne case.

FINANCING POLITICS FROM GENERAL FUNDS

As politics flow more and more into our industrial life it is almost impossible to define at certain points what is political expenditure and what is legitimately general fund expenditure.

The dichotomy between the two is becoming more artificial as one Act of Parliament succeeds another. Shareholders who buy shares in private companies are not asked whether they agree or not to the company using their money for political activity. The directors are empowered to act in all matters, including political interests of the company. Private companies have no restrictive clause in their company rules governing their political spending, or a special registrar to watch over them.

Although there are disadvantages, the time is ripe for a fresh look at the restrictions placed on trade union financing of political activities which are legally allowed in their rules and without which the unions could not carry out the legal objects of their organisation. The present procedure with separate funds will always encourage, as it did in 1927, 'backwoodsmen' 'to do a modern Osborne'. As long as political financing is not an integral part of trade union general activity and is not met from the general funds of unions, there will always be those who will try to castrate the unions politically. This would be bad not only for democracy in this country but for stability and industrial peace.

An alteration to the law to permit political expenditure from general funds could well be one of the trade union reforms which a future Labour Government could introduce. In doing so it would be recognising the narrowing border separating the political from the industrial, and it would also be helping to balance the scales of power by at least giving the Labour Party a source of revenue approaching the amounts spent each election-tide by the Conservatives. Modern 1970-style elections cannot be fought on finances governed by Acts of Parliament forged about sixty years ago. The Trade Union Act of 1913 was a move forward, a historic step forward in the development of political democracy in this country. It should now give way to the changing times and the changing needs of funding modern political parties.

LABOUR STANDS FOR ALL WHO WORK

PLATE I

YESTERDAY-THE TRENCHES

PUBLISHED BY THE LABOUR PARTY 33 Eccleston Square London S.W. & PRINTED BY VINCENT BROOKS DAY & SON LTD 48 Parker St. Kingsway London W.C.

PLATE II

Chapter 7

The Fermenting Years

'Force is the midwife of every social system pregnant with
a new one.'

Karl Marx

The reforms introduced by the 1910 Liberal Government, including the Trade Union Act of 1913, were auguring well for the
unions. Although SDF denounced the reforms as worthless, the
enactment of the National Insurance Act of 1911, the provisions
for Workmen's Compensation, Old Age Pensions, the eight-hour
day and a minimum wage for miners, and the payment of MPs,
did bring the Labour Party closer to the Liberals during the life
of this Parliament.

But things were not as 'cosy' in the workshops as they were in
the House of Commons. Wages were falling behind prices and
many trade unionists were beginning to look again at the political
organisation which the trade unions had fashioned. Some had
been critical all along of the belief of the older trade unionists in
peaceful political evolution which they regarded as being either
illusory or so far distant as to be irrelevant. They began to look
more and more to the power of the trade unions to settle the basic
economic problems of the workers rather than to seek a constitutional political answer.

They soon found philosophical roots for their views in the
doctrine of Industrial Unionism or Syndicalism, which had
originated in Europe from the ideas of a Frenchman, Georges
Sorel, who expounded a programme of direct action by the
workers, through their unions (French *syndicats*).

The Syndicalists' propaganda was based on the class war theme
that there could be no real peace between the employers and

E

employed because of the nature of the struggle between the classes. The message blazed far and wide by the Syndicalist propagandists was that the workers were only respected when they were feared. It followed therefore that to make progress the workers had to use their power effectively and ruthlessly if necessary.

The Syndicalists, who included the 'Wobblies', IWW (Industrial Workers of the World), followed the teachings of the American industrial unionist Daniel De Leon, and the British Tom Mann. Mann's message to British workers was that political reforms were a delusion, a device to keep in being the capitalist system and to deflect real working class power.

In industry the Syndicalists believed that craft unions should be garnered into great industrial unions until eventually only four or five unions would represent all of the workers in Britain. The next step, the revolutionary change of society, would come by a carefully timed General Strike, by civil disorder, and by the unions appropriating the industries which they represented to run them in the interest of the community.

THE BRITISH SYNDICALISTS

This doctrine of revolution based on the unions fell on fertile ground, not only in the minds of many younger trade union leaders at the time but in certain industries, notably mining, where Arthur Cook and Noah Ablett published *The Miners' Next Step* advocating in a series of pamphlets and leaflets the use of the unions in a take-over of industry.

Sorel pulled all 'real Marxists' into action in support of the Syndicalist view by insisting in his book *Reflections on Violence* that 'real Marxists' were in fact direct actionists.

Tom Mann in the 1911 March issue of the *British Syndicalist* translated Sorel's theories into practical strike propaganda:

We most certainly favour strikes, and we shall do our best to make strikes successful to prepare the way as rapidly as possible for the General Strike of national proportions. This will be the actual Social and Industrial revolution and the workers will refuse to any longer manipulate the machinery of power in the interests of the capitalist class and there will be no power on earth to compel them to work if they refuse. When the capitalists get tired of running industry the workers will cheerfully invite them to abdicate and through their unions will run the industries themselves in the interests of the whole community.

Tom Mann, like other British Syndicalists, believed that only in the workshops of Britain was there the sense of solidarity which was capable of surmounting all the smaller difficulties which would inevitably beset a political party on lines established by the Labour Party. The trade union, according to Mann, was immune from the corrupting and debilitating influences of middle-class leaders and could be inspired with a revolutionary *élan* engendered by a militant minority.

There was at that time, in addition to the unrest caused by wages lagging behind prices, a growing discontent with the results of the first decade of the Labour Party. The Syndicalists were able to plant their ideas in the soil of dissatisfaction with the results of the orthodox political action so far taken by the unions.

INDUSTRIAL UNREST

The years that followed between 1910 and the outbreak of the First World War in 1914 were times of frenzied political and industrial activity. Strikes involving transport workers, carters, dockers and railwaymen all hoisted danger signals for the Asquith Government which did a King Canute with forms of conciliation machinery, including industrial arbitration.

The *Daily Herald* appeared for the first time in 1912 as an Independent Labour daily paper, later with George Lansbury as editor. It was hostile to the Labour leaders and the Syndicalists became regular contributors with Will Dyson providing the biting social comment in cartoons that for many months had the unions in ferment.

The one lasting industrial achievement of this period was the amalgamation of three railway unions to form the NUR (the present National Union of Railwaymen) in 1913. By a stroke of fate or irony, the General Secretary of this new model industrial union, on which so many Syndicalists' hopes were pinned, was J. H. Thomas.

The other industry to receive the attention of the 'industrial unionists' was the building industry. The officials of the unions here were opposed to the amalgamations and used legal difficulties to frustrate the 'unionists' within their ranks. Eventually after the unions were defeated in a national lock-out in 1914, the building trade Syndicalists cut adrift and set up their own union, The Building Workers' Industrial Union. The new union started just as war broke out, and sank without trace.

THE WAR AND THE POLITICAL FREEZE

The outbreak of war halted more than the BWIU. It almost immediately froze industrial militancy and political activity. The voice of the Syndicalists was silenced as the *Daily Herald* ceased publication and a milder, more orthodox *Weekly Herald* took its place. The Triple Industrial Alliance formed in the Spring of 1914 between the Miners, the NUR and the Transport Workers' Federation also went into cold storage for the duration.

BEVAN AND DIRECT ACTION

This period of history was an exciting time for those at the time who were politically interested. Nye Bevan in his book *In Place of Fear* describes the electric effect which Noah Ablett had on him and others. Bevan depicts the burning yet simple intellect of Ablett, who argued that Parliament was a roundabout way to change society. 'Why cross the river to fill the pail?' Ablett said, and the South Wales intellectuals lapped up the message.

The reason for the magnetic attraction which the direct action philosophy had for those interested in social change at the time, was that it was absolutely relevant at that moment to the way they were living and working. It had substance and a vitality which made an immediate impact.

Bevan, who was in the centre of the direct action exponents in the Welsh coalfields, said later, 'The relevance of what we were reading to our own industrial and political experience had all the impact of a divine revelation. Everything fell into place.' The lessons of the doctrine stuck with Bevan who had as the centre of his dogma that 'politics was about power' and the revolutionary Syndicalists showed him how his goal could be achieved using the power of the unions. There were many like Bevan, young, impatient, and deeply committed to social change who must have felt in 1914 that the revolution lay just beyond the next wages or hours claim.

WOULD BRITAIN HAVE BOILED OVER?

What would have happened if the war had not started is difficult
to forecast. This much can be said: if there was a time when
revolutionary change was near in Britain it was surely then. The
war took the movement off the boil and it has never really got
to the same point again – so far at any rate.

Although Syndicalist ideas never gripped the movement as
much after the war, they have influenced many trade union
leaders, and there are signs that today there are neo-Syndicalist
groups operating in many unions. Some older trade union
socialists still inhale the fragrance of the strong, heady four years
from 1910 to 1914, and like those on St Crispin's Day in another
battle, stand a-tiptoe when they tell of it.

As Syndicalism is still a force today in the trade union movement and we shall be visiting its theories again in a later chapter
when we examine the groups within the present day Labour Party.

Chapter 8

Failure of the Triple Alliance and the Birth of the Communist Party

'The outbreak of war stilled everything. Like the Gorgon's head it seemed to have frozen the combatants into immobility.'

> Raymond Postgate: *Pocket History of the British Working Class*

Before leaving this action-packed period in political industrial development, let us look briefly at the phenomenon of the 'Triple Alliance' of Miners, Railwaymen and Transport Workers which, as already mentioned, was formed in the spring of 1914 and was frozen by the outbreak of war.

This initial link between three powerful unions was obviously important politically, because there was some Syndicalist prompting in the birth of the idea. Some Syndicalists certainly saw the forging together of major unions on the industrial front as a prerequisite of the powerful concerted action by the unions on the political front, so although the declared purpose of the Alliance was industrial, it did have important potential.

The initiative to form the Alliance was taken by the Miners' Executive who had been so instructed by their Annual Conference in 1913. The mandate from this conference was for the Miners to approach the executives of other large trade unions 'with a view to co-operative action and the support of each other's demands'.

After the discussions with the Railwaymen and the Transport Workers the programme of the Triple Industrial Alliance was for the three unions simultaneously to formulate a policy of progress in the appropriate trades covered by each union, and then all three were to put in their claims at the same time. Each claim was also to contain a notice terminating existing agreements with their respective employers. Plans were also made for a cessation of work to take place simultaneously in each of the three trades if the employers did not concede a satisfactory agreement to the three unions.

The outbreak of war occurred before the plan of the small conference of the three unions had been approved by each of the unions. This ratification was overtaken by the events of the first few months of the war when the unions became pre-occupied with the 'War Emergency Measures' and the arguments which ensued in the Labour Party about what the movement's attitude should be towards the war. During the war years the 'Alliance' lay fallow. No form of organisation had been set up even to tend the idea, and when the war finished the Miners' attempt to use the Triple Alliance failed primarily because the purpose for which the 'Miners' sought to use the Alliance was not that which was agreed in 1914.

1921 MINERS' CLAIM

When in 1921 the coal owners said there would be no more national negotiations with the union, the Miners sought support from the NUR (Railwaymen) and the National Transport Workers' Federation for a claim submitted to the coal owners to set up a national pool out of the surpluses of the profitable mines, and from this to increase miners' wages. The NUR and the NTWF both felt that they could not recommend a stoppage of work in their own particular industries to support the Miners' claim.

Doubtless the call for united action would have had much more support had all three unions been involved in claims of their own. The Miners' action placed too great a strain on an idea of solid-darity and identity of interest which would certainly have had more appeal if each union had acted as provided for in the original plan devised in 1914. The miners' conditions at the time in the summer and autumn of 1920 undoubtedly contributed to their 'jumping the gun'. But their call for sympathetic action from the other two unions was doomed to failure because the purpose for which the alliance was originally created would not be realised in a dispute in the coalfields which only affected one of the partners of the 'Alliance'.

THREE REASONS FOR NON-SUPPORT

It was also apparent from the obstacles raised by the Railwaymen and the Transport Workers against supporting the Miners that many administrative and constitutional matters had been overlooked. It was found that there were considerable differences in rules to be surmounted before the three unions could have acted together simultaneously, and uppermost of these, no doubt, in the minds of the Railwaymen and Transport Workers, was the industrial fact that the Miners' dispute was likely to be a long one.

This was evident for three reasons. Firstly, it takes some time before the effects of a coal strike are felt, either in the industry (depending on coal stocks) or in the economy in general, and secondly, the coal owners had already made no secret of their determination not to concede the kind of increases which the union was demanding.

BLACK FRIDAY, 22 APRIL 1921

The third reason why the NUR and NTWF did not support the Miners exposed the weakness of the Alliance. This chain of events started off with a statement by Frank Hodges, the Miners' General Secretary, on Friday, 22 April 1921, when at an inter-party meeting of MPs in the House of Commons he said that the Miners would consider a compromise offer which would leave aside the demand for a national pool, as long as it ensured that wages would not fall below the cost of living.

This answer may sound an innocuous and even sensible reply to a loaded question by an MP, but it proved calamitous for the Miners' Federation. On the basis of this answer by Hodges, Lloyd George invited the representatives of the Miners' Federation to discuss a compromise settlement. The Miners' Executive refused to meet Lloyd George on these terms, repudiated Frank Hodge's statement, and reaffirmed that a settlement was only possible on the principles already laid down in the claim.

The split in the Triple Alliance was thus accomplished, because the Railwaymen and the Transport Workers thought that Hodge's attitude did warrant serious consideration, and so became at loggerheads with the Miners' Executive.

Soon the argument was also adduced by both these unions that if they were being asked to support the Miners' claim, they should have some say in the eventual settlement. The Miners' Executive adhered to their attitude that no compromise offer which did not give them a National wages board and national wages pool could be considered. The NUR and the NTWF in turn stated that it was not their idea of a triple *alliance* that decisions which affected the members of all three unions should be left to be decided by only one of the executives, and when this line of reasoning was not accepted by the Miners, the break was complete.

The Railwaymen (NUR) and the Transport Workers (NTWF) then cancelled such strike notices as had been tendered and the Alliance was ended.

The events concerning Hodge's speech in the Commons and all the consequences that flowed, including the official ending of the Triple Alliance, occupied only one day in our industrial history. It was called 'Black Friday' by those inside the movement, who saw the dramatic collapse as a major setback for the working-class movement.

The high hopes that the Syndicalists had built into this concept of a trade union united front challenging a government also lay buried in a venture which failed primarily because it was founded on theory and not rooted in the realities of industrial life. With the decision of the Railwaymen and the Transport Workers not to give support, the morale of the Miners was shaken, and although the threatened strike which had been decided on by ballot vote in the coalfields did eventually take place in April 1921, it lasted for only about seven weeks before the union reached agreement with the employers. Charges of betrayal were laid against the other two unions by Miners' members and also by 'militants' in other unions, but when history is examined on this point it will be seen that the venture was ill thought out and ill prepared.

The collapse of the Triple Alliance in 1921 was undoubtedly a crucial point in the political history of Great Britain because of the strong philosophical influence of direct action which lay at the heart of the idea. The disintegration of the Alliance was used by trade union and political leaders at that time to show that the political aims of ordinary men and women could not be achieved by such futile, isolated actions as that envisaged by those who fathered the 'Alliance'. The argument that political change would be more surely achieved by working through the Labour Party by constitutional means fell on receptive ears in 1921, and also in 1922, when the Engineers also bit the industrial dust in a strike which failed.

The failure of the Triple Alliance also holds lessons for us today. As the leaderhip of major unions change and some affinities are established, there are muted voices who talk even now of a new union alliance. Whether we will have open advocacy of a new 'Dual Alliance' remains to be seen, but an alliance which has not recognisable and attainable industrial objectives, and is not effectively organised and administered, is not likely to be successful. No amount of political affinity can provide the cement in industrial disputes to bind the workers in unity. In working-class eyes an identity of interest is the only enduring link which holds workers together. Without it the sacrifices of each section are inevitably weighed, with a selfish eye on the balance, and the likely gains are estimated with a view to querying the equity of the possible successful outcome. Forging an alliance which equates all these gains, between separate industrial organizations operating in differing industries, is not impossible, but it is difficult.

Those unconcerned with the day-to-day running of the unions can afford to sit above these considerations and muse on higher things, but those of us who see the trade union task in a more practical way, have to ensure that the trade union movement does not embark on industrial pacts which are ill fitted to stand the stresses of modern industrial action. A modern trade union alliance which collapsed would set our movement back industrially and politically now, just as much as it did in 1921 and 1922.

Those who do advocate this kind of political action in the future should be asked, not only for their credentials, but also for their detailed organisational and administrative plans for action.

The threat of major confrontation by powerfully organised unions linked to a common purpose was not lost on the Government of the day. The proposed use of the Triple Alliance in 1920 was later to be exploited by the Government in 1926 when this supposed threat was cited to secure the Emergency Powers legislation which was used during the General Strike, and which is the subject of our next chapter.

THE COMMUNIST PARTY IS BORN

Before moving on to examine the events leading up to the General Strike, there must be some mention at this period of the formation of the Communist Party of Great Britain in 1920–1, which absorbed the British Socialist Party and some other minor political groupings.

The formation was inspired in part by the upsurge of working-class aspirations as the soldiers returned in 1918. The membership of the unions swelled to six million, a record figure, and there was a feeling of unrest permeating the country in 1919 and 1920 which was akin to the 1906–14 period. General Councils were formed to 'push on' the official trade union movement, and several amalgamations took place.

Intervention of the Government in affairs in the Soviet Union was prevented largely by the promptings of the 'General Councils of Action' which threatened a General Strike, and although it appeared likely, as in 1913, that Britain was veering towards a revolution based on direct action by the unions, the events described earlier involving the miners' strike of 1921 and the collapse of the Triple Alliance took the edge off the revolutionary appetites among the workers' leaders. The ensuing slump in trade which saw unemployment go over a million and trade unions lose about a third of their members, also pushed back the 'direct action' brigade.

As the slump worsened wage cuts became inevitable in most industries. As despair gained root in the hearts and minds of ordinary people, the unemployed workers' movement itself dwindled to small numbers, and the Communist Party fell into insignificance as the trade unions' leaders accepted constitutional methods for alleviating the situation.

It is puzzling that the Communist Party at this time did not achieve either the degree of influence or the membership which the extent of revolutionary views seemed to justify. At one time in 1921 membership reached 10,000 and the weekly paper had a circulation of 60,000, but in 1928 the membership was down to between 3,000 and 4,000.

The influence of the Communist Party has, however, always been greater in industry than in the broad political field, and this was as true in the 1920s as it is today. Small in number as they are, they have always been in the forefront of the battle, particularly strong in the shop stewards' movement, and with energies and dedication which are envied by other political parties.

In the 1920s, although the Labour Party voted against allowing the Communist Party to be admitted as an affiliated organisation, the relationship between the two political parties was friendly, and up to 1928 the Communist Party never put up candidates against the official Labour candidates, and only contested seats where there was no Labour candidate. The Communist Party were less isolated and more respected in these early years than they have been at any time since. In the 1924 General Election they ran eight Communist candidates and polled a total of 55,345 votes, which is more than they polled at the 1970 election.

In view of the consistently low polls of the present day Communist Party candidates, the votes for Saklatvala at Battersea —15,096, and Stewart at Dundee—8,340, must seem like the political halcyon days as far as they are concerned.

1928 – THE INTERNATIONAL SAYS OPPOSE LABOUR

The friendly atmosphere began to evaporate in 1928 when the Communist International decided that all over the world the Communist Parties should run candidates against the Social Democratic or Labour Parties.

The first election at which this decision was implemented was at a by-election in North Aberdeen in August 1928, when Wedgwood-Benn (Labour) was elected with a total of 10,640 votes, and the Communist candidate Ferguson was second bottom of the poll with 2,618.

With a few exceptions the decision to oppose official Labour candidates has been a blight on the Communist Party's hopes of even securing a small toehold in the House of Commons, and they have never got back to the 1924 electoral popularity which was impressive if viewed against the short life of the party at that time.

SHOULD THE COMMUNIST PARTY HAVE BEEN FORMED?

The dismal record of the Communist Party in elections does pose the question as to whether the Communist cause would have been better served by working within the Labour Party. The decision to form the CP was by no means unanimously applauded by all

Communists at the time. Lenin for one believed that the British Communists should have linked up with the Labour Party. In a debate at the Second Congress of the Comintern in August 1920, dealing with the tactics which should be used by Communists in Britain, he said: 'The correct tactics are affiliation to the Labour Party . . . but we cannot say that this concerns England alone. . . . The method of the old International was to leave such questions to be decided by the separate parties in the countries interested. This was fundamentally wrong.'

Lenin's advice was not heeded and perhaps not surprisingly, because in other writings and speeches he had already made clear his contempt for those who were leading the Labour movement in Britain. In his publication *Left-Wing Communism* in May 1920, he scathingly attacked Arthur Henderson, who was a much respected figure in the movement at that time, and stated:

If I, as a Communist, come out and call upon the workers to vote for the Hendersons, against Lloyd George they will certainly listen to me. And I shall be able to explain in a popular manner not only why Soviets are better than Parliaments . . . but I shall also be able to explain that I wanted to support Henderson with my vote in the same way as a rope supports the hanged.

Lenin's advice to Communists involved in industrial matters is also enshrined in the same book:

It is necessary to combine the strictest loyalty to the ideas of Communism with the ability to make all necessary practical compromises, the 'tack' to make agreements, zig-zags, retreats and so on . . . to resort to all sorts of devices, manœuvres and illegal methods, to evasion and subterfuge, in order to penetrate into the trade unions, to remain in them, and to carry on Communist work in them at all costs.

With these guidelines from Lenin in May 1920 despite his later statement at the 1920 Comintern, it is small wonder that the Communists in Britain did decide to form their own party. But during the remainder of their existence they were to rely heavily on advice from the Soviet Union, and in fact a resolution sent to Stalin by the British Communist Party in May 1924 said in one final passage, 'We hopefully await guidance and instruction from your Party.'

The decision by the Communist International to spur the British

CP into action against the Labour Party certainly started a political antagonism in the trade unions, and the inflammatory speeches at the 10th Congress of the Communist Party of Great Britain in January 1929 created a chasm between the Labour Party and the Communist Party which still yawns today. When J. R. Campbell at this Congress said 'It is our sacred duty to oppose the Labour Party and rouse the workers against it', he was, in fact, setting the British Communists off on a road which was to lead to a political wilderness.

Influential figures in our movement then and since have been CP members and have been respected, but deep down workers cannot draw close to a Party which seeks to disrupt a political grouping like the Labour Party which is a mass, working-class-based party. Changing from within would have been understood by ordinary men and women, but attacking from without the people upon whom working people depended for their advancement, is not easily forgiven by those who only have a peripheral interest in politics.

Chapter 9

1926 – the General Strike

'The trade union leader can do nothing with the idea of a
revolutionary general strike, this is, in his eyes, an eminently
political affair, involving ultimately the taking over of
Government by the Labour Party.'
  Max Beer: *History of British Socialism* (1940 edition)

Although the revolutionary movement went 'off the boil' in
1921–3, the Labour Party continued to make electoral progress.
In the General Election of 1922 the Labour Party polled 4,236,733
votes, and this rose to 5,487,620 in 1924. In the 1923 election the
Labour Party had polled 4,348,379 votes, and in January 1924 the
first Labour Government took office under Ramsay MacDonald
as Prime Minister.

As the Labour vote in the Commons was 193 to the Conservatives' total of 258, Labour depended on the 157 Liberal votes to
carry through a programme. Because of the virtual veto of the
Liberals, what Labour could do was limited, and this Government
was puny as a result, only enacting minor reforms. True, John
Wheatley put through an excellent Housing Act and some of the
most objectionable parts of unemployment relief were removed or
ameliorated, but workers in dispute for better conditions and wages
found that it was 'as you were', because Government opposition
to their claims disappointed Labour supporters, who expected at
least some assistance from their own Government.

It is perhaps fitting that this account of the 1924 Labour Government should follow the account of the early years of the Communist Party, because it was an attack on the Communist Party
which caused the election in 1924. Mr J. R. Campbell, the acting
editor of the Communist Party's weekly paper *The Workers'*

Weekly, wrote an article called 'Don't Shoot' in which he advised any of the British troops involved in strike duties not to fire at workers even if ordered. The Government saw this as an act of sedition and prosecuted Campbell. This action was disastrous and quite inexcusable, and it raised a 'hornet's nest' which evolved around the preservation of editorial comment and freedom of speech.

This incident caused the House of Commons to censure MacDonald for his so-called weakness in giving in to the clamour for the case to be dropped. Eventually, after more personal attacks on MacDonald, he dissolved the House and although the Labour Party polled 1,139,241 more votes than in 1923, the Tories returned 413 MPs to the Labour Party's 151, the Liberals limping back with 40 seats.

The Tory Government started their period of office in 1924 brightly, because the state of world trade was good at the time, but Churchill's money policy in putting Britain back on the gold standard meant that all British export prices were higher, and as a consequence Britain's industrial position was weakened and the workers felt the blasts of unemployment once again.

LABOUR MOVES TO THE LEFT

The election defeat of the Labour Party had its effect once again in the trade union movement, which returned to the direct action solutions of 1913 and 1920–1. At the Trades Union Congress at Hull in 1924 only a few weeks before the collapse of the first Labour Government, the Congress had carried its most militant and Socialist programme yet. Resolutions asking for public ownership and control of national resources were carried, along with others ranging from participation of workers in the control of industry, a working week of forty four hours, and a legal minimum wage. New powers were also given to the General Council to act in industrial disputes, and here the machinery was initiated which little more than eighteen months later was to organise the General Strike of 1926.

Looking back at the period from 1919 to 1926, it is possible to trace an increasing feeling of class consciousness within the Labour Party. The trade unions at this time, (except for a convalescing period after the 1921–2 defeats of the miners and engineering workers) certainly made it clear to the Labour Party

TO-DAY — UNEMPLOYED

THE LABOUR PARTY. VINCENT BROOKS DAY & SON LTD

PLATE III

PLATE IV

that they did not intend to be just followers of the party, but wanted to be informed supporters. The class nature of the Labour Party in opposition and its public appeal is vividly illustrated by the selection of posters which are illustrated in this book. Though fifty years old they remain vivid and effective. Some are tragic in their simplicity, but all of them are a far cry from any political strategy of appealing to the middle class at the time. The appeal was straight to the mass of the working class, and it was thought that those in the middle class who were sympathetic to Labour would come with us without posters or appeal. This was the logic of Labour's publicity in the early 1920s, and I for one am still emotionally moved when I see them, and believe the strategy is still right for today.

The movement by 1925 had moved significantly left, and although the Labour Party made four gains at by-elections, the main attention of the political activists in the trade unions was being concentrated on industry, and once again, as in 1921, it was the mining industry in which the fuse was burning!

The mine owners in 1925 were saying that the industry was losing money and that wages would have to be cut. The agreement which was settled during the term of the Labour Government in 1924 had patched up the deep underlying grievances that existed between the miners and coal owners, had run for its period of twelve months and was then terminated by the coal owners on 30 June 1925. After negotiations and a Court of Inquiry, followed by an inquiry by the Coal Commission, a report was presented to the Government on 6 March 1926. The fourteen conclusions of the Commission were accepted by the Government, but the employers hedged their acceptance around with so many 'ifs and buts' that it was impossible to state specifically what concessions they were prepared to make. The issues were also clouded because the mine owners insisted on a longer working day and in some mining areas were asking for cuts in wages of £2 2s 0d per week.

THE BUILD-UP TO THE STRIKE

During the months from July 1925 to April 1926 the Government had continued the mining subsidy without which the mine owners said they could not afford to finance the industry. The Government were, however, also preparing for a showdown with the Miners' Union if it became necessary. The extension of the

F

had averted such a confrontation at a time when the
nent was unprepared for conflict. Those nine months
were intended to give them time to put the country's supplies in a
position where a dispute would not be a catastrophe for the
nation.

The climb-down of the Government in July 1925 had, of course,
been interpreted by the unions as indicating that the threat of a
strike had borne fruit and that the recipe for success in the future
was the mixture as before. Never was a situation so misread as the
1925–6 conflict.

The Miners prepared for another strike if it was necessary and
issued a strike notice in April 1926. The mine owners were still
insisting that the industry could not be made profitable without
wage cuts and a longer working day. The Miners countered with
the well-known slogan, 'Not a Penny Off the Pay, Not a Minute
On the Day'. The simplicity of this presentation of the argument
certainly caught the imagination of the trade union movement
who were solidly behind the miners.

On 30 April the lock-out notices issued by the coal owners
terminated and the mines and pits all over the country stopped.
A special trade union conference of Executives had taken place
on 29 April and pledged full support for the Miners' claim and
approved strike action to any extent thought necessary by the
TUC General Council. This conference also asked the Prime
Minister, Mr Stanley Baldwin, to secure the withdrawal of the
lock-out notices.

The last day of April 1926 was a long day in the history of the
trade union and Labour movement. The unions' negotiators
(Industrial Committee of the TUC) met at noon to try and discover
some formula to avert a strike, for it was now obvious following
the Executives' conference the day before that the stage was set for
battle. Baldwin had had discussions with the mine owners the
previous evening and that morning, and at just after midday he sent the employers' final proposals to the House. These
proposals were received at the House of Commons by the
Industrial Committee of the TUC and the leaders of the Miners'
union, and the brutality of the proposals really staggered the
negotiators. The employers' terms sent by the Prime Minister were
for wages to be reduced to the 1921 level and for hours to be increased by 20 per cent.

Baldwin put his imprimatur on these proposals by stating that if these were accepted by the union the Government would set up a Commission *not later than 31 December 1929*, which would examine whether the state of the industry had improved enough by that time to allow the working day to be shortened to its 1926 length of seven hours.

THE PREGNANT HOURS

It is possible to picture the scene here and to inhale the atmosphere. The lock-out notices were due to expire in a few hours, the conference of union Executives, which had the day before pledged support and strike action if necessary, was awaiting the result of the meeting with the Prime Minister. The Miners' leaders and the Industrial Committee must have known almost as soon as the envelope was opened that the terms were atrocious. Not only did they demand abject surrender, but the offer from Baldwin of a Commission in three and a half years' time was really 'rubbing it in'.

Further attempts were made to persuade the Prime Minister to get the lock-out notices withdrawn, but they were unsuccessful. The Miners' Executive rejected the terms as 'not being worthy of consideration' and this decision was delivered to the Prime Minister.

Negotiations continued into the night with the Government trying to persuade the Miners' leaders to accept the wage reductions as a start, in return for which the Government would try to arrange a suspension of the lock-out notices to allow the negotiations to continue on the length of the working day. The Miners rightly refused.

The Government had one more gambit up its sleeve and asked the Miners to accept a declaration on the necessity for wage cuts made by the Coal Commission which had reported in March 1926. The answer by the Miners, while rejecting the need for reductions in wages, was that they were prepared to consider all the industry's difficulties when the Government had started the reorganisation scheme proposed by the Coal Commission and accepted by the Government. Although the Industrial Committee of the TUC felt that this assurance was at least enough to get the lock-out notices suspended, if not withdrawn, the Government Ministers were adamant that a wages reduction was necessary during the period of reorganisation.

Baldwin intervened at this point to say that he was not convinced that there was any chance of furthering the negotiations at
the moment, and that to carry on was to invite a second deadlock
which would leave them nearer the brink than the first. The Prime
Minister's intervention at this crucial point in the negotiations at
the end of a long, hard day, convinced the trade union negotiators
that the Government had decided a conflict was unavoidable.

Outside the House of Commons things were also 'hotting up'.
The trade unions fell upon a copy of a poster which was issued by
the 'Organisation for the Maintenance of Supplies'. This body
which aimed to help the Government if a strike did take place,
stated in this poster that the Government had declared a 'state
of emergency' and called on patriotic citizens to enrol to help out
in the emergency.

The printers refused to print the poster and Baldwin said he
knew nothing of it, but admitted that a proclamation declaring a
'state of emergency' was in readiness, though it had not been
issued.

This statement of denial by Baldwin had a delicacy of games-
manship which Stephen Potter would have envied. Without
breaking off negotiations he had indicated that the contingency
plans had been laid and that he was prepared for the worst.

As midnight was chiming the trade union negotiators were on
their way across London to the Memorial Hall to report to the
conference of trade union executives.

THE PLANS ARE APPROVED

Earlier that evening a sub-committee of the TUC had prepared a
scheme for a national stoppage of work. After the verbal
report of the breakdown in negotiations this draft was issued to
each union, and arrangements were made for a conference at the
midday following.

At that next meeting the Chairman, Mr Arthur Pugh, called
the 'strike roll' and all, except a few small unions comprising a
total of 50,000 members, declared their readiness to strike in
support of the Miners. The Miners agreed to leave the conduct
of the dispute in the hands of the General Council of the TUC, and
the unions at the conference agreed likewise.

The plan of action prepared by the TUC sub-committee was
approved. This set out arrangements calling industries on strike

as required. The following were the terms of the original resolution.[1]

These industries were to strike:

Transport, including all affiliated unions connected with transport,
i.e. railways, sea transport, docks, wharves, harbours, canals, road
transport, railways repair shops and contractors for railways, and
all unions connected with the maintenance of, or equipment,
manufacturing, repairs and groundsmen employed in connection
with air transport.

Printing trades, including the Press.

Productive industries (*a*) iron and steel
                        (*b*) metal and heavy chemicals group
(including all metal workers and other workers engaged in
installing alternative plant to take the place of coal).

Building trade – all workers engaged on building, except such as
were employed definitely on housing or hospital work together
with the workers engaged in the supply of equipment to the
building industry.

Electricity and gas – the unions connected with the supply thereof
were to co-operate with the object of ceasing to supply power, the
Executives of the unions being required to meet for the purpose of
formulating a common policy.

Sanitary services were to be continued.

Health and food services were not to be interfered with and the
trade unions concerned were instructed to do everything in their
power to organise the distribution of food and milk to the whole
of the population.

I have given the terms of the original resolution in full because
it was not a case of 'All Out'. Some thought had obviously been
given to the advisability of continuing essential services and
ensuring food supplies. In addition to the resolution the General
Council issued instructions for the supply of food, milk, medical
and other supplies to hospitals, clinics, sanatoria, welfare and
infant centres, nursing homes, maternity homes and schools. It

---

[1] *The British Labour Party*, edited by H. Tracey.
The Memorial Hall resolution laying out the plans for the General Stike and
the other official letters quoted in this chapter have been taken from *The
British Labour Party*, a book which had thirty-two contributors and was
edited by Herbert Tracey. Tracey was the TUC Chief Publicity Officer in 1926
and wrote the General Strike section of the book himself. As the TUC Publicity
Officer he no doubt had access later to the official correspondence which
passed at the time.

was obvious that the General Council did not wish to alienate
public opinion by unnecessary hardships for the infirm or by lack
of food or services apart from transport.

NEGOTIATIONS: 1 AND 2 MAY

Although the trade unions had made their plans for strike,
efforts still continued over Saturday and Sunday, 1 and 2 May, to
try to find a settlement. The TUC representatives went to Downing
Street on the Saturday night and again met Stanley Baldwin and
other Ministers, when another formula was hammered out. This
formula from Baldwin, although a bit ambiguous, said that if
negotiations could continue and the lock-out notices were
withdrawn, the TUC were confident that inside two weeks a
settlement could be reached on the lines of the Coal Commission
report.

The Government and the mine owners, however, insisted that
some flesh should be placed on this skeletal statement, and as
the Miners' leaders had gone back to their areas to prepare the
resistance to the lock-out and were not due back until Sunday
night, there was no further progress on Saturday.

On the Sunday night the Trades Union Congress representatives
again met at Downing Street, and after various drafts to try to
clarify what was expected from the unions in line with Baldwin's
formula on the previous night, a four-line formula was arrived
at. It read as follows:

> We would urge the Miners to authorise us to enter upon dis-
> cussion with the understanding that they and we accept the
> report as a basis for settlement and we approach it with the
> knowledge that it may involve some reduction in wages.

This proposed settlement showed how far the TUC were in
retreat from the earlier confident attitudes of a few months
previously in June 1925 when they and the Miners were preening
themselves on their fortitude and predicting that the wage
reductions demanded by the mine owners would be buried by
their solidarity of action. With the strike now at their elbow (it
was due to begin at midnight on Monday, 3 May) and the
knowledge given them by Baldwin that the Government had
already prepared emergency measures, the TUC now wanted to
come back from the brink.

Later the TUC representatives argued that they had not in fact accepted this as a basis for settlement, and that it was only taken down as a note of what had been said during the discussion. The Government, however, certainly regarded it as having been an agreed formula for a settlement and told the TUC that they expected them to urge the leaders of the Miners' union to accept it.

BALDWIN THE GAMESMAN

As it happened the formula was never put to the Miners, who arrived at Downing Street just before midnight, not because the TUC had decided it was unacceptable but because of an event from a quarter outside the immediate arena of dispute.

The printing workers in the *Daily Mail* offices had started their strike a day earlier than had been arranged, and Baldwin sent a message to the union representatives in Downing Street before they began to discuss the 'formula for settlement'. Baldwin's message was straight and to the point. He asked the TUC to condemn the 'overt acts' which 'were a gross interference with the freedom of the Press' and also said that the strike notices which had been issued by the unions must be withdrawn immediately. If this was not done the Government stated that it could not continue the negotiations!

The TUC representatives regarded this as a provocative ultimatum and tried to tell the Prime Minister, but there was no one from the Cabinet in Downing Street to take their reply. The TUC issued a statement in the early hours of Monday morning and the General Strike started at midnight on the same day.

I have dealt in detail with the build-up to the strike because I believe the continued retreat from their first positions on the dispute gives some idea of the morale of the TUC negotiators, especially during these crucial meetings on 1 and 2 May. The preparations made by the Government and the two occasions when Baldwin showed his readiness to force a showdown are ample evidence that the Government were prepared to fight right from the start. The willingness of the TUC to negotiate and to discuss the possibility of wage reductions, even after the General Strike notices had been issued, must also have been seen by the Government as an indication that the TUC had no stomach for the fight that lay ahead.

THE STRIKE THAT FAILED

The days that followed have been well chronicled in our history. The strike was well supported by the first wave of workers called on by the TUC. Initially about 2,655,000 were on strike, including the locked out miners. The engineering industry were not due to strike until 12 May, and the strike was called off before they became involved.

During the strike religious leaders on 5 May drew up a 'concordat' for a return to work as follows:

(a) Cancellation on the part of the TUC of the General Strike.
(b) Renewal by the Government of the offer of assistance to the coal industry for a short definite period.
(c) Withdrawal on the part of the mine owners of the new wages scales recently issued.

There were no takers for this solution and neither unions nor Government responded.

Speeches by Sir John Simon saying that the strike was illegal and unconstitutional were said at the time to have caused flutterings in the TUC dovecotes. These misgivings increased when Justice Astbury, in giving his verdict restraining the 'Sailors' and Firemen's Union' from calling members out on strike without a ballot, also gave his opinion that the national strike was illegal and contrary to law, and that those inciting it were not protected under the Trades Disputes Act of 1906.

NOT A 'TRADE DISPUTE'

These opinions alleging illegality were presumably formed because the unions unconnected with the mining industry were on strike in a matter which was not a dispute in the terms of the Act between them and their particular employers. Some TUC leaders did, however, believe with justification that sympathetic strikes were not illegal under the Act and that Justice Astbury and Sir John Simon were reading the Act wrongly.

Legal thinking has not changed very much in nearly fifty years on this matter, as this same legal point was raised again in 1971 when the AUEW called its members out on two one-day strikes against the Industrial Relations Bill. Although the union's decision in 1971 was constitutionally carried out according to its rules, the legal opinion given here was that the law giving the right to strike limited this action to disputes between workmen and employers and did not extend to the kind of protest strike which took place in the engineering industry on 1 and 18 March 1971.

On 8 May Mr Baldwin, the Prime Minister, said on the radio (called the 'wireless' in those days) that the trade unions must be resisted because they were trying to force the Government and the community to bend to their will. The unions replied saying that they did not aspire to overthrow the Government.

THE SAMUEL INTERVENTION

On 9 and 10 May talks were started between the TUC and Sir Herbert Samuel who, while ostensibly acting on his own responsibility, had the ear of the Government, and on Monday, 10 May, a proposed settlement was drafted. This was then discussed with the Miners' leaders who wanted some alterations and, following a meeting between Sir Herbert Samuel and the Miners' leaders at which the Miners declared themselves satisfied with the memorandum which Samuel was to present to the Government, the General Council on 11 May decided to end the strike.

It was a strange settlement, because Sir Herbert Samuel had impressed on the unions all the way through the negotiations that he was acting on his own and not for the Government or the coal owners, and the letter sent by him to the TUC indicates this most forcibly. Sir Herbert Samuel's letter to the TUC Chairman said:

Dear Mr Pugh,

As the outcome of the conversations which I have had with your Committee, I attach a memorandum embodying the conclusions that have been reached. I have made it clear to your committee from the outset that I have been acting entirely on my own initiative having received no authority from the Government and can give no assurances on their behalf. I am of the opinion that the proposals embodied in the memorandum are suitable for adoption, and are likely to promote a settlement of differences in the coal industry. I shall strongly recommend their acceptance by the Government when the negotiations are resumed.

Yours, etc.

Herbert Samuel

The TUC leaders were therefore in a position whereby they had, verbally at any rate, committed themselves to calling off the

General Strike on the basis of a plan by Sir Herbert Samuel which (as Samuel was careful to point out) did not have the approval of either the Government or the coal owners, though it is true that the Prime Minister in public speeches had been taking a line which could have been interpreted as being amenable to the proposals in the 'Samuel Memorandum'.

These public statements of Mr Baldwin found a place in the TUC's reply to Sir Herbert Samuel. The TUC reply stated:

Dear Sir,

The General Council having carefully considered your letter of today, and the memorandum attached to it, concurred in your opinion that it offers a basis on which the negotiations upon the conditions in the coal industry can be renewed.

They are taking the necessary measures to terminate the General Strike, relying upon the public assurances of the Prime Minister as to the steps that would follow.

They assume that during the resumed negotiations the subsidy will be renewed and that the lock-out notices to the miners will be immediately withdrawn.

Yours, etc.

Arthur Pugh (Chairman)
Walter M. Citrine (Acting Secretary)

The Miners' Executive, however, rejected the Samuel Memorandum as a basis for a resumption of their negotiations because it implied a reduction of wage rates. They were also rightly annoyed that proposals affecting negotiations on the Miners' problems had been apparently finalised without them being consulted by the TUC General Council. The Miners' view therefore was that they were not accepting the TUC–Samuel proposals, but if the TUC wanted to call off the General Strike it was their (the TUC's) responsibility. In stating their position here the Miners had no doubt in mind that they themselves had agreed that the TUC would be in full charge of the General Strike.

The TUC leaders duly went to Downing Street on 12 May and officially terminated the strike. The decision was blazed forth in the Government's emergency newspaper *The British Gazette* as unconditional surrender by the unions. This view was endorsed by the rank and file, and cocky employers sought to victimise and intimidate employees by attempting to impose harsh 'return to work' conditions. These were largely resisted, but many non-strike agreements were concluded as the whole movement swallowed the bitter bile of industrial defeat.

THE BITTER HARVEST OF DEFEAT

The trade union movement suffered an immediate decline in membership as breakaway unions were formed which promised workers that they would not take them into foolish strikes, and house unions run by the employers also flourished in the sterile soil of disillusion.

The miners most of all felt the keenest sense of betrayal and their own lock-out dragged on for another seven months. The hot summer of 1926 did nothing to boost the need for coal, and with even nature conspiring against them they accepted the coal owners' terms and went back to work on lower wages and longer hours and on district agreements.

REACTIONS IN DEFEAT

With the surrender of the miners on 5 November 1926 (Guy Fawkes Day!) the defeat was complete. The period was a traumatic experience for the trade union movement. Men and women re-examined their ideals and political allegiances. They drew different lessons, and those who were only 'card carriers' opted out of the movement altogether for a time.

Some unpalatable lessons had to be digested. Nye Bevan, in his book *In Place of Fear*, said of the collapse of the General Strike and the defeat of the miners: 'The trade union leaders were theoretically unprepared for the implications involved. They had forged a revolutionary weapon without having a revolutionary intention.'

Many agreed with the views expressed by Nye and he himself at that time started to reappraise the theories of Syndicalism which he had learnt from Noah Ablett and James Connolly in the balmy political days of 1910–13. Many blamed the chicken-heartedness of the TUC General Council and still hold the opinion that if the TUC leaders had been resolute and not so ready to compromise the fight could have been won.

TUC UNPREPARED FOR THE ULTIMATE

I do not believe that history bears out the latter view. I believe that the weakness of the trade unions in the General Strike was that they had so much economic power that it did represent a threat to the Government, and that any Government worth its salt would have had to face up to the challenge or quit.

The difference between the two sides, the Government and the unions, was that at the crucial stage in the negotiations prior to the strike on the evening of 30 April, Baldwin adroitly revealed in answer to the TUC's question that he had, in fact, everything ready for the emergency if it came. The TUC on the other hand had not planned beyond the successful organisation of the strike. If they had at least planned what they intended to do in the event of a stand down by the Government or a breakdown in law and order, the outcome may have been vastly different. I am not arguing that it would have been a good thing for the nation had such a situation emerged in 1926, but if they had shown that they had thought of these possibilities this would at least have placed the TUC in a stronger position.

The trade unions had learnt the main lesson however, that the use of the General Strike was too revolutionary a weapon for the limited purpose which they had in mind, and that once it is threatened (if the challenge is accepted, as Baldwin accepted it), then in a democratic country it is destined for defeat.

DIRECT ACTION TAKES A KNOCK

The Syndicalists too had received a sharp blow to their ideology. Both in 1921 and in 1926 the idea of a mass strike by all workers had been central to their 'direct' approach to changing society – if the country is immobilised then leaders would arise to carry on the next phase of action to take over industry itself and run it for the workers.

Those who thought that a General Strike was a potential rival to orthodox political action had not planned for the time when such action reached a breakdown in the existing society. Revolutionary situations need rebels, and rebels were thin on the ground in Britain, as G. D. H. Cole said in *The World of Labour* in 1913.

The trade unions have to take men as they find them, and revolutionary methods only succeed for long with revolutionary people. In England, the rebel is a very rare phenomenon. Trade unionists as a whole have very little revolutionary spirit. They will bear the slaughter house meekly, provided the market does not demand the slaughter of too many at once; they will lie down gladly in their thousands in the green pastures of Liberalism and Reform. Meanwhile profits will go up and real wages will fall. Capitalism has not yet to die in its last ditch.

Although a trifle over-expressed, Cole's view of the revolutionary 'timbre' of the British trade unionist, written in 1913, turned out to be true in 1926 and has proved true to the present day. Today in Britain the 'direct action' camp is back in business. Their resolutions through one means and another find themselves on trade union and Labour Party agendas. The start of a liberation policy is still seen by some at the point when the Trades Councils take over education and the police. The modern Syndicalists are, however, themselves sadly split into many groups. In 1971, one of these groups, called the 'Hammer and Anvil', with a total membership of five, disintegrated when a sub-committee of three divided over a statement of policy to be presented to the other two. Some of these groups are, however, influential and at least two of them, the 'Socialist Labour League' and the 'International Socialists', find the cash and the enthusiasm to publish a newspaper. Both are well produced and well read also by many trade union leaders and members.

I sense a revival in these small Socialist groups who regard the Communist Party as being establishment-orientated and the Labour Party as being unworthy of their fire of criticism. This revival no doubt coincides with the frustrations experienced in the 1960s, but they too, even today, are faced with the problems which faced the Syndicalists in the 1920s. 'Direct action' in their political vocabulary means 'strike', and in our kind of democracy this means taking on the State which means ultimately that those taking part in the strike must realise and appreciate that the strike action is intended to revolutionise society.

Look around the mass of trade unionists and trade union leaders and answer truthfully if you see them entering knowingly on such a path.

No – the answer to changing society in our country is orthodox political action, but one problem is as common to orthodox action as to the situation which arose during the General Strike. How do we achieve a transfer of power? Orthodox and revolutionary movements must have this answer in their haversacks. Neither the Syndicalists nor the Trots, nor the Labour Party have this answer at the moment, but we will be looking at all the ideas on this in the Labour Party haversack shortly, so I shall finish this important chapter in our industrial history with two final observations on the General Strike.

THE SUBTLE BALDWIN

The first concerns the capable handling of the General Strike by Baldwin, the Prime Minister. He was a master of political inertia and at some stages in the negotiations this was exactly what was required from the Government side.

Baldwin, it is said, presided over a capitalist decline in Britain, but as Bevan said in *In Place of Fear*: 'There was no capitalist way of preventing the decline, and the most that can be said against Baldwin was that being a Conservative he could not get out of his economic dilemma by applying socialist policies.'

Bevan's rating of Baldwin as being one of the most subtle of the Conservative prime ministers is certainly borne out by his handling of the General Strike. Like a good chess player he never used an excess of force but only applied enough at the right time in exactly the right place. Nye, however, also said that Baldwin's actions strengthened his Marxist beliefs. 'When the gentle Baldwin bows to accept the orders of the ruthless property interests of the State,' Bevan said, 'how can we contest the Marxist claim – nothing has weakened the Marxist doctrine of class war.'

One other interested observer looking in from abroad was astonished by the Government's handling of the General Strike. He was J. V. Stalin. In talks later with H. G. Wells – 'A Verbatim Record' published in the *New Statesman* in 1934 – Stalin said:

The first thing any bourgeoisie would have done in the face of such an event, when the General Council of trade unions called for a strike, would have been to arrest the trade union leaders. The British bourgeoisie did not do that, and it acted cleverly from the point of view of its own interest. I cannot conceive of such a flexible strategy being employed by the bourgeoisie of the

United States, Germany or France. In order to maintain their rule the ruling classes of Britain have never foresworn small concessions and reforms.

From reading that I get the impression that not only governments of the bourgeoisie would have chucked the union leaders into jail, but be that as it may, Stanley Baldwin's handling of the strike receives an unsolicited and indeed unexpected testimonial from Joseph Stalin.

MODERATE OPINION – STRENGTHENED

So far we have analysed only the left-wing reactions, but the majority of the trade union leaders and members had markedly opposite views. The failure of the strike and the consequent setback of the trade union movement was seen by them as a justification of the doubts that many of them had when they first embarked on the strike. Their reaction was to draw in their political horns and to resolve never again to embark upon a confrontation of unsure outcome such as that represented by the General Strike.

Changes in the future will be made through the ballot box and this means rallying behind our constitutional instrument of political change – the Labour Party. During the General Strike negotiations the Labour Party had been a passive spectator – afraid of the consequences of victory – half pleased that the bid had failed, but ready, only too ready, to pick up the political pieces.

The moderate leadership of the unions was strengthened by the General Strike. They stood for no more 'high falutin' '. 'Syndicalist', 'taking on the State' lunacy and the workers were in a mood to hear them loud and clear. The General Strike has left a legacy of political attitudes in the trade unions which permeates trade union political thinking even today. The trade union-constitutionalist – 'no industrial action for political ends' man has his roots firmly bedded in the 1926 strike. He speaks for a majority in the Labour Party even now at a time when the party is moving left. The modern 'nineteen twenty-sixer' has a place in a future chapter when we examine the contending streams of political thought in the party today.

Chapter 10

Unemployment, War and a Labour Government

'The saddest object in civilisation and to my mind the greatest confession of its failure, is the man who can work, and wants to work, and is not allowed to work.'

Robert Louis Stevenson, 1850–1894

'DOWN' BUT NOT 'OUT'

The working class is never down for long, and the reactions of Tory backwoodsmen to the collapse of the strike which forced Baldwin's hand and led to the Trade Disputes Act of 1927 in themselves provided a catalyst which reactivated the trade union movement to regain its former confidence and industrial poise. This Act, which was introduced by the Government to illegalise strikes of a general character and to prevent coercion of the Government, showed that the words of Sir John Simon and Justice Astbury had been heeded by the Tories. The fight against the Bill united the movement faster than anyone would have thought possible, and against the backcloth of the General Strike the resilience of the movement surprised even its adherents. The parallels between the industrial relations arguments in 1927 and those which re-emerged in 1971 will be studied in a later chapter on industrial relations.

Against a background of mounting unemployment and slump in the USA, the dole queues also stretched out in miserable crocodiles in every town and city in Britain. The sterility of the unemployment of the time is caught by Stephen Spender's verses:

Moving through the silent crowd
Who stand behind dull cigarettes
These men who idle in the road
I have the sense of falling light.

They lounge at corners of the street
And greet friends with a shrug of shoulder
And turn their empty pockets out
The cynical gestures of the poor.

Now they've no work, like better men
Who sit at desks and take much pay.
They sleep long nights and rise at ten
To watch the hours that drain away.

I'm jealous of the weeping hours
They stare through with such hungry eyes.
I'm haunted by these images
I'm haunted by their emptiness.

By 1931 unemployment had risen to 3,250,000 and in 1929 a Labour Government had been elected and beaten by the crisis. The infamous Coalition Government followed in 1931 which reduced the Labour Party to a rump in the MacDonald-Baldwin National Government. In this election Labour lost 213 seats and took their place in the new Parliament with 55 seats.

The history of that sorry period for the movement is writ large in the minds and hearts of those who were old enough to suffer and understand it at the time. 'Political Treason' was the charge against Ramsay MacDonald, Snowden and Thomas, levelled by an angry Labour and trade union movement. 'Treason', according to Talleyrand, 'is a matter of timing, and depends on whether or not your followers will follow you.'

They did not follow MacDonald, and a man who had given his life to the movement tarnished all he stood for in a few short weeks. Baldwin lifted him, used him, and laid him away like a rubbing rag when he had outlived his usefulness to the Tory majority in the National Government.

In the movement's crisis time in 1931 Arthur Henderson emerged as the leader who 'saved the soul of the Labour movement'. Henderson accepted the leadership and it was a period for

G

the Labour movement which saw them blamed for the economic crisis and painted in the press as those who had led the country into trouble and then 'chickened out'. MacDonald and Snowden were depicted as men of principle who stayed to see the crisis through. Henderson, who was remarkably restrained in his criticism of MacDonald and Snowden, did reply to these Press attacks on one occasion when he said:

> We are accused of deserting the sinking ship and leaving Mac-Donald and Snowden standing like Casabianca on the burning deck. . . . We did not desert the captain. It was the captain who brought in the pirates and deliberately scuttled the ship. We were prepared to balance the budget without unemployment cuts.

During the October election of 1931 Henderson was ill and stood to be defeated at Burnley by a loud-voiced Admiral Campbell, whose knowledge of politics was minute. Four months later Henderson was President of the Disarmament Conference. Henderson led the party for only a short time and handed over to George Lansbury. Henderson's death in 1935 coincided with Lansbury's resignation as leader of the Labour Party because of the party's decision on rearmament, and 'Clem' Attlee became leader in 1935 which was an election year which saw Labour returning with 154 seats, 95 more than in 1931.

Before the curtain falls on Arthur Henderson in this book, it is worth recording the breadth of his interest and experience: an iron moulder, a branch secretary and a National President of my own union, an MP, a member of four Cabinets and a Foreign Secretary and also Secretary of the Labour Party. Finally, one must add his international work on disarmament as Chairman of the Disarmament Conference, and in the League of Nations. His long career was unsullied and he died truly a Labour man in every sense of the word, and his *own* man. Success meant less to him than doing what he thought was his duty. Arthur Henderson's contribution to trade union political thought was intelligence allied to integrity and absolute sincerity.

The 1930s were dominated by economic crises and unemployment. Curiously enough, while the unemployed were rotting in a society which struggled unsuccessfully to find economic answers to the problem, the real wages of those fortunate enough to be at work rose. The Japanese invasion of Manchuria in 1931 was followed by other acts of naked aggression. War was in the air.

Mussolini's invasion of Abyssinia in 1935 was followed by Hitler's occupation of the Rhineland in 1936 and by the Spanish Civil War in the same year. The Nazi-Fascist incursions continued with the annexation of Czechoslovakia in 1938 and culminated in the invasion of Poland on 1 September 1939.

The Labour movement were so incensed by Chamberlain's ineptitude that although strongly supporting the decision to stand up against German-Italian aggression, they also stated that they could not accept any invitation to join the Government. Nine months later, however, in May 1940, they were to become part of the War Coalition Government under Winston Churchill. Chamberlain's non-interventionist and appeasement policies had been jettisoned by the Tories and Labour were now free to give their vital support in mobilising the nation against Fascism.

The decisions of the Labour Party Conferences during the 1930s had given the party a direction in foreign affairs which had enabled them to take a decision to join the Coalition without splitting the movement. Hugh Dalton, who was Chairman in 1937, said in his opening address:

These last six years the world has rattled back to barbarism at breakneck speed. The greatest need today is for a return to honest courage in our foreign policy and for another Labour Government in Britain to reverse the helpless slide towards supreme catastrophe.

Dalton saw the danger of appeasement in Europe and the leadership were backed throughout this period by Conference decisions which, although in favour of non-association with the policies of Chamberlain, also favoured co-operation with all parties under a different policy and leader to prosecute the war. The TUC were equally forthright in defining their attitude. War was declared on 4 September during the Congress at Bridlington, and the following declaration was carried:

This Congress believes that the Nazi Government, having chosen for its people the way of war, must be resisted to the utmost. It must be opposed by all the forces that the civilised nations can concentrate for its defeat and overthrow. The defeat of ruthless aggression is essential if liberty and order are to be re-established in the world. Congress with a united and resolute nation enters the struggle with a clear conscience and steadfast purpose.

The attitude of the Communist Party was not so clear and was very far from steadfast. At first they supported the war, but when Russia signed the Nazi-Soviet pact with Hitler they changed their minds and opposed the war. When Hitler finally attacked Russia however, the war became a workers' struggle against Fascism and they were solidly behind the war effort! Political gyrations of these dimensions certainly weakened support for the Communist Party then and since.

The effect of the war on the trade unions was soon evident. The National Arbitration Order of 1940 made awards under this Act binding and strikes arising from these awards illegal. The efficacy of this legislation is discussed in a later chapter. The membership of women in the unions grew as they were admitted to engineering and other jobs previously exclusively reserved for males. The TUC were consulted by the Labour Ministers in the new Coalition who had been given almost all the industrial Ministries. Ernie Bevin was Minister of Labour, Attlee was Lord Privy Seal, D. R. Grenfell was Secretary of State for the Mines, Fred Montague was Minister for Transport, Hugh Dalton was Minister for Economic Warfare and Herbert Morrison was Minister of Supply. Under the new Emergency Powers Act there was power to direct labour and the operation of this fell to Ernie Bevin who could not have carried out his immense task without the active co-operation of the TUC.

The capable way in which the Labour Ministers dealt with their key responsibilities was a big factor in the landslide victory for Labour in the 1945 election. For the first time in any British election patriotism was not the exclusive property of the Conservative Party. Labour Ministers and the Trades Union Congress had fought hard for victory so that when Churchill went on his 1945 election tour the crowds cheered him as the war leader, but rejected his political party. The servicemen's vote was also crucial, and for the first time a large number of them voted. In 1918 only 25 per cent of those in the forces had voted, but in 1945 over 60 per cent voted. Two million servicemen and women voted by proxy. Labour had a majority of 145 seats over the other combined parties. Attlee was the new British Prime Minister. His first task was to organise the economy to take the returning servicemen into industry.

THE TRADE UNIONS AND THE 1945 LABOUR GOVERNMENT

In their election manifesto *Let Us Face the Future* Labour had set out their post-war plan for rebuilding Britain. The task of reconstruction which faced them was an awesome one. During the war Britain had suffered damage to railways, docks and factories valued at £15,000,000,000. Over four million houses (one in every three) had been destroyed. £152,000,000 of gold reserves had gone, and half the merchant fleet had been sunk. How in the face of all this was a Government to get Britain going again without at least temporary unemployment – a repeat of the unemployment which faced the returning troops from the 1914–18 war?

The Labour Government did all this. There was no mass unemployment. There were hard times, food shortages, fuel shortages aggravated by the hardest winter for many years in 1947. The 1945 Government's election programme was based largely on the Labour Party's short-term programme produced in 1937. It was described then in the NEC documents as a list of urgent measures of 'Socialism and Social Amelioration' which would be carried out by a Labour Government during a full term of office when returned by the electors. *Let us Face the Future* contained all the 1937 measures and the 1945 Government carried them all into practice, and more besides.

It nationalised mines, railways, electricity, gas, civil aviation, steel, road transport, cable and wireless, and the Bank of England. It introduced Social Insurance Benefits, Family Allowances and a new National Health Service. It raised pensions, workmen's compensation, altered the law of common liability in accident cases, introduced distressed area legislation and exercised a degree of control over the economy which was far greater than many left-wing socialists were advocating. John Strachey, far to the left in 1940, produced a Popular Front programme *Programme for Progress* which would have settled for much less than the Attlee Government in fact achieved.

But things did not all go well, and the trade unions were finding their new role of co-operation with the Government not as easy as they had thought. The first major clash took place in 1948, when the Chancellor, Stafford Cripps, in a White Paper, 'Statement on Personal Incomes, Costs and Prices', argued that prices must be stabilised if exports were to rise, and called for a standstill in the level of general incomes unless it was accompanied by a corresponding increase in the volume of production. Wage increases were only justified outside this criterion if they were necessary to attract labour to an under-manned industry.

In March 1948 the TUC called a meeting of trade union Executives where after a long discussion it was agreed to support the policy of the Government with a few provisos on low paid workers, differentials, and a policy to check profits and prices.

In January 1950 the TUC called another meeting of trade union Executives, spurred on by the recession in the USA in late 1949, and the devaluation of the pound by the Labour Government. This time the TUC General Council asked for support for a more stringent wage freeze and the card vote, although in favour, was very close. Four and a quarter million voted in favour of the freeze, and three and three-quarter million voted against. The writing was on the wall that the unions were not going to stand for the freeze for much longer. The strains were very evident in February 1950 when the Labour Government was re-elected with a small majority of six, and by midsummer the revolt of the unions was in full spate. The final break came at the Trades Union Congress in September of the same year when a composite resolution against Government policy on the freeze in incomes was carried against the General Council.

The other piece of legislation which was sticking in the union gullet was the National Arbitration Order 1305, which made arbitration compulsory and since 1940 had, in fact, removed the right to strike.

The crunch on compulsory arbitration came in the summer of 1950 when maintenance engineers in some London Gasworks struck against an Arbitration Award of $1\frac{1}{2}$d per hour, and under the emergency powers were eventually, after appeal, fined £50 each. Other cases followed, including a prosecution of six London dockers which failed, and after this the NAO was ditched and the Industrial Disputes Order, which allowed for voluntary arbitration, took its place. Comment is made in a later chapter on industrial relations about the operation of both of these instruments brought in by successive wartime and Labour Governments to deal with industrial problems. None of the compulsory measures was, in practice, successful and the trade unions had come through a new and not very pleasant experience.

In October 1951 the Labour Government stood for election

once again, and this time, although the Labour vote increased by nearly a quarter of a million votes, the Tories had twenty-six seats more than Labour. Six years of Labour rule had ended, and the trade unions had experienced their first real taste of what co-operation with a government of their choice really meant. On the two fronts where Government policy conflicted with the traditional activities of the unions, the strains had proved too great. The freeze policy of 1948 had interfered with collective bargaining and no effective controls had been devised to freeze prices or to stop dividends and profits being distributed later. Wage increases that could have been won in 1948–51 were forfeited forever, but the dividend limitation and profits standstill simply meant that this buried treasure could be dug up and distributed to shareholders when the economic situation allowed or, as in this case, when the Government of the country changed.

The second front of Labour Policy which ran head-on into trade union traditions was, of course, the virtual removal of the right to strike. Quite apart from the lack of effective action to prosecute claims against employers, the absence of strike action as an outlet for the expression of industrial feelings led to a frustration in the trade unions which was bound to erupt as the economic problems piled up. The Labour Government had carried out the programme upon which it was elected, but it was the situations for which it had not planned that caused the split between it and the unions.

These breakdowns between the industrial and political wing of the movement emphasised the need for more detailed planning and prior agreement about the precise measures which are bound to be necessary in controlling the economy. More public ownership would not have prevented the breach, although many left-wing socialists pinned their anti-Government arguments on this course. What the split did reveal was that economic planning for a socialist Government in Britain could not be built solely on resolutions at Labour Party conferences. The depth of the planning necessary was, I believe, realised by some of the political and industrial leaders after about three years of Labour rule. By then the worsening economic situation and external pressures had made necessary some kind of action to promote exports and keep down costs. The decision of the Government was unilateral and depended more on loyalty than on logic. The unions did not know the precise economic answers to the situation and reacted instinctively in defence of their rights. It was this combination of circumstances which brought Labour's electoral eclipse.

The movement would learn from this -- or would it?

Chapter 11

Thirteen Tory Years and then Another Labour Government

'As the Fifties ended and the new universities proliferated –
with the needs of technology providing the driving force –
the issue was yet further complicated and restated in terms
of the supposed conflict between science and the humanities.
Were we aiming to produce machine directors, servicers and
minders – or the educated nation the 1944 Act had
promised? Efficient functions, with the schools offering
mainly "career tickets" – or whole men and women?'
  Harry Hopkins: *A Social History of the Forties and Fifties
  in Britain*, 1963

The Tories in 1951 took over a vastly different kind of country
from the pre-war Britain. Labour certainly had its troubles in the
six years 1945–51, but the transition from war to peace had been
achieved and the spectre of unemployment which haunted all
Labour leaders in the 1930s had never appeared in the post-war
reconstruction. Indeed, full employment had been achieved over
the lifetime of the Labour Government and this had made a big
difference to the general behaviour of British employers. No talk
of wage cuts, even when the Government felt that costs should be
not only stabilised but reduced. Until 1971, in fact, it looked as
though unemployment was no longer a major social evil and that
the more sophisticated problem of inflation was the evil that
needed controlling.
  The economic crisis faced by the Labour Government in 1951
was a culmination of crises in 1947 and 1949. The removal of
wartime controls in the USA in 1945 produced rocketing prices

there which, at a stroke, almost reduced by half the loan which Britain had received from America. By 1947 the position had worsened and controls were placed on the home market sector of goods and building. In 1949 the wage and price controls described earlier were introduced and the recession in the USA forced devaluation in Britain in the autumn of that year. But these crises were due more to external than internal reasons, and Labour had, by its 'fair shares' policy during the period of shortages, its implementation of the Beveridge Report on Social Insurance, and its introduction of the Health Service, made Britian a fairer place in which to live.

Externally, too, the economic position started to improve by the end of 1951. As the USA slackened off her stockpiling of raw materials, the price of these fell with a consequent improvement in our import bill. By 1953 our imports were costing us about £300 million less, and this was money in the kitty. Goods now began to come on to the home market in greater quantities than in the previous fourteen years and unemployment was below 2 per cent, so that there were customers with money to buy. Between 1951 and 1959 average consumption per head in Britain rose by 20 per cent. The Tory posters screamed their message 'Tory Freedom Works'. The public believed it and returned the Tories at the election in 1955, and again at the 'Never Had it so Good' 1959 election.

THE AFFLUENT FIFTIES

Great Britain had entered her affluent period, with the 'admen' harnessing the new selling force of television to titillate the appetites of hungry, acquisitive consumers. The Conservative Party had taken up the economic doctrines of Keynes and focused attention on the technicalities of growth and investment and 'shares for all'. Labour's appeal for fair shares and the inequity of the distribution of the proceeds of growth fell on the deaf ears of an electorate who were now persuaded that fair shares meant the kind of share out which they had experienced immediately after 1945.

The Tory Governments of 1951, 1955 and 1959 embraced some of the techniques of planning, and carried out large investment programmes in the nationalised industries. They subsidised agriculture, fixed farm prices, reorganised the aircraft industry, and introduced plans to weld cotton into a smaller, more efficient industry. A far cry from traditional *laissez-faire* Conservative policies. The Tory actions in the fifties were, however, to direct political controversy into an economic debate, a debate about how to control the economy instead of *whether* to control it. As international trade expanded the prices of raw materials and our imports continued to fall. Temporary crises in 1955 and after the Suez adventure in 1957 were regulated by monetary adjustments, cuts in investment, increases in the bank rate, curbs on hire purchase – all the old familiar devices that we have come to know and resignedly detest over the years.

A PERIOD OF NEW POLITICAL THINKING

On the industrial front the Tories ended the Industrial Disputes Order of 1951 and also, despite union protests, abolished the Industrial Disputes Tribunal and the principle of voluntary arbitration. The effect of these changes on the unions is discussed in a later chapter on industrial relations.

The trade unions' political thinking during this period of changing values was influenced on the left by Nye Bevan, and in the middle by Tony Crosland's *The Future of British Socialism*, which was published in 1956. John Strachey, who had been with his *Necessity for Communism* in 1936 the darling of the Left Book Club, and the 'left', published a book in 1958 called *Contemporary Capitalism*. This followed the reasoning of Crosland and declared that capitalism now was not capitalism as he had described it in the 1930s, and that the 'fighting programme of mass struggle' which he had called for in *The Coming Struggle for Power* would not now be required.

Bevan struggled for the soul of the party and the unions, but apart from an inspiring holding operation at the post mortem Labour conference in November 1959, he never commanded a majority of minds or votes at any time during this period, nor indeed until his death. The 'modern social democrats' took Crosland's approach to their hearts, and the Labour Party's economic thinking in *Industry and Society* in 1957, and in *Signposts for the Sixties* in 1963, was directly influenced by his political analysis in *The Future of British Socialism*. Some of Crosland's arguments are examined in the next chapter, 'Which Political Way for Labour?', so it will suffice here to say that in 1956

Crosland stated in modern terms what many were feeling as a result of their political and social experience in the forties and fifties.

THE UNPOPULARITY OF THE UNIONS

One of the by-products of the 1950s was the growing unpopularity of the trade unions. They had never been loved by all, but at least in the 1920s, 30s and 40s there was among the general public a kind of respect and a recognition of the task they were undertaking in industry. But throughout the 1950s the Press and television put a bad face on almost every national dispute in which trade unions were involved. They were portrayed as narrow-minded, rapacious and uncaring in their regard for what the Press called the 'national interest'. In 1959 George Woodcock, the TUC General Secretary, admitted in an article in *The Listener* that the 'image' of the unions was bad and that the movement was more unpopular than it had been for many years.

The atmosphere of the 1950s no doubt had much to do with the trade unions' unpopularity. The affluent society of the late 1950s was breeding in the higher wage brackets a worker who was behaving differently. Between 1950 and 1956, 50 per cent more money was spent in Britain than in the previous six-year period. In 1947 there was little demand for washing machines, but by 1957 one middle-class family in three had one, and one out of five working-class families. Spending on electric, electronic and durable goods rose nearly six times faster than other consumer spending. By 1955 the *average* household expenditure had reached £19 per week, and four years later in 1959 it was £25 10s 0d. The prosperous areas were, and still are, the Midlands and the South East. The *Daily Herald* gave statistical proof that between 1955 and 1959 the skilled and unskilled manual workers emerged as the biggest spenders on a whole range of goods traditionally regarded as middle class products. Hire purchase boomed between 1953 and 1958 when instalment credit doubled in those five years. The advertising industry sucked in university graduates, and in his book *A Social History of the Forties and Fifties*, Harry Hopkins said:

These were the years in which the advertising men finally succeeded in shaking off that old barker's straw hat and assuming the black homburg to which their central position was now seen to entitle them. They no longer sold an article but generated an atmosphere, propagated a philosophy and projected a vision of the good life.

THE WORKERS' CHANGING ATTITUDES

The difference in working-class behaviour and attitudes in the 1950s came out in many ways. There was 'hogging of overtime' in the factories. Some workers had more hours on their card than the factory cat! Many took another job in the evenings. Trade unions found it difficult to control overtime working and put reasonable restraints on PBR. Wives were working for what was called 'pin money', but in reality it was for those shiny consumer durables. An opinion poll in 1958 reported that more than half of the population regarded themselves as middle class. What many were in fact saying in this poll was that they did not regard themselves as *working class*! It could be said of course, that the majority of these were, according to some definitions of class, properly working class, but proving even to those concerned that they were in fact working class is a rather pointless exercise if they regard themselves already as middle class. What they think of themselves will decide how they act! If they think they are middle class they will act as middle class, politically as well as socially.

Technology also was changing the worker. The old industries, where they were not declining, were being modernised and more machines meant less jobs in trades where workers had been the backbone of trade unionism. Inflated by the boom in consumer spending, the service and distributive industries flourished and the close communities of workers with strong ties, which still exist in certain industries, were no longer regarded by the new trade unionists as patterns which had to be followed. Lay-offs in the car industry in the Midlands were greeted not with solidarity and sympathy for those pushing their claim, but with intolerance and a much expressed view that the unions should be doing something about the lay-offs.

The high social expectations, the new attitudes and standards of solidarity were fertile soil in which the Tories, aided by the mass media, were able to encourage a growth of anti-trade unionism. Some workers in traditional, solid groups were still more likely to strike than others, notably miners and dockers, but others had their eyes fixed on some object of domestic importance, and like the crest of hills, there was always one more on the horizon when one was attained.

Michael Shanks said in 1961 in *The Stagnant Society*:

> The trade unions therefore are failing to adjust themselves to the changing pattern of industry and society. This gives them an increasing dated 'period flavour'. The smell of the music hall and the pawnshop clings to them and this more than anything alienates the middle classes and the *would-be* middle classes from them. To be a trade unionist is to align oneself with those at the bottom of the social ladder at a time when the predominant urge is to climb it.

I do not agree that what Shanks said is true, but I do agree that he has described fairly accurately what a lot of people felt to be true of the unions in this period. The *would-be* middle classes referred to by Shanks would, of course, include those workers who regarded themselves as middle class.

To the Labour Party in the late fifties the unpopularity of the unions was a serious political handicap. Even Bevan said in his distinctive way: 'The trade unions cannot win an election for Labour but they can lose one!'

A 'REHABILITATION' CAMPAIGN

I believe that over the last ten years the trade union movement has at least broadened its appeal to all who work for a living. The spectacular advance in the recruitment of non-manual workers is freeing the movement from the slogans and banners of the past, but there is some way to go yet before we are rehabilitated in the minds of the public. A vast campaign is needed to focus attention on the positive work done by the unions – a spotlight on the basic honesty and absence of corruption in the British movement which sets it high in international trade unionism. Let the public, whoever that may be, realise that without the 'fifth estate', as Winston Churchill called the unions, industry would rapidly descend into an anarchic, dispute-ridden morass if trade union disciplines, agreements and codes of behaviour were withdrawn from our economic life. The trade unions may not be popular, but they are indeed necessary.

CLAUSE FOUR CONTROVERSY

The trade union image in the 1959 election was doubtless one of the factors which sparked off the Clause 4 controversy. At the post-mortem conference in Blackpool in November 1959, Hugh Gaitskell, in his speech as leader, said that one of the reasons for the defeat of the Labour Party was the out-of-date image created by Clause 4 of the constitution of the party, which committed it to common ownership of the means of production, distribution and exchange.

This argument, and the subsequent action of the NEC which left Clause 4 untouched and clarified what it meant in a declaration of principles, was really the reaction of those in the party who were seeking to express outside public criticism of the outmoded appearance of the Labour movement to what they thought was a new kind of electorate. The argument was foolish and unnecessary and is examined later in the chapter on ownership and control, but the fact that Gaitskell felt this had to be argued out at that time was a political blunder, which for me cast doubts on his judgement and his basic *rapport* with the rank and file of the party.

The trade unions certainly found their political voices again, and Gaitskell and the Clause 4 abolitionists, although receiving a good show from the press and television, were routed by emotion as well as by good common sense. The Clause 4 controversy need never have happened. It had not been a factor in the 1959 election. If it had been, Labour, with the same constitution, would not have been elected in 1964 and 1966. The public, despite the importance given the matter by the papers, treated the argument with indifference, spiced with a dash of bewilderment. The members of the party, however, fought among themselves like political tigers, and in a few weeks a political party which had been healthy and united in the election was transmogrified into a dialectical shambles. Those who had worked so hard during the election did not deserve to see the party disintegrating after it, from self-inflicted wounds.

The politicians who 'wrung their hands' in the press after the election, saying that the policy of the party was wrong, were not only politically and philosophically in error – their action was tactically disastrous! You can hardly tell an electorate one week that your policy is good and then, because your view is rejected, tell them the next week that the policy was all wrong. Simple political facts like these were overlooked by those who 'went in to bat' against Clause 4 in 1959.

However, it is important to appreciate that the new thinking of the 1950s by Crosland and others, plus the poor regard which the public had for the trade unions, were the twin launching-pads of the Clause 4 critics. These critics eventually settled for the NEC declaration, and I do not think they will again attempt to scale the Matterhorn of common ownership. Not constitutionally at any rate!

THE 1964 LABOUR VICTORY

It was 1961 before the unions were to have a real industrial 'dust-up' with the Government, and this came when the Government introduced a pay pause which was opposed by the TUC and all the unions. Three 'wise men' were also installed at this time to oversee the economy, but their combined wisdom did not reduce the balance of payments deficit which was the reason for the wage freeze.

The freeze quickly thawed and in 1963 the Christine Keeler story, plus the economic troubles, sent the Tory Government's popularity plummeting. The *Daily Mirror* referred at this time to 'Sex rearing its lovely golden head', but I doubt whether Prime Minister Harold Macmillan had the same laudatory view of the scandal which rocked the Government.

Macmillan gave way to Sir Alec Douglas-Home, and 1963 finished with the trade unions and Labour Party in good heart, following Harold Wilson's technological speech in Scarborough in October. This speech, which was the most modern given by any politician for many years, certainly had an effect on the nation, particularly upon the middle class. Harold Wilson succeeded in convincing the public at this time that Labour had changed its cloth cap for a slide rule, and the old-fashioned image which the Party had been saddled with during the whole of the fifties was dispelled almost in an afternoon. Wilson's speech also left lots of questions unanswered, but proposed that the way forward was to be based on economic growth and that the skill of the technician was to be harnessed in the service of the community. The precise policies to achieve those ends proved much more difficult than the speech had forecast.

The election, when it came on 16 October 1964, saw Labour

returned as the Government with a small majority of 4 seats, gaining 56 seats on a 77 per cent poll. On 31 March following they went to the country for a fresh mandate and gained 48 seats for a majority of 97 seats. The poll was lower than in 1964, with 75·9 per cent voting. The fall in the numbers voting at the 1966 and 1970 elections is disturbing from the viewpoint of Britain's democracy, and there is an electoral harvest awaiting the party that can get below the skin of indifference and apathy which is at present afflicting one person in every four in our society.

THE 1964–70 LABOUR GOVERNMENT

The six and a half years of Labour Government were turbulent, both politically and industrially. Labour came to office in October 1964 and discovered that it was facing a balance of payments deficit of £864 million. Unemployment was also higher than normal. Nine hundred thousand had been unemployed in 1963, and although the 1964 pre-election boom had reduced this, the underlying trend was not good. Inadequate investment in industry, housing, education and the public services over the previous years had made Britain a weak country economically and socially. Nearly two million people were living below National Assistance levels, and the old age pensioners had been shabbily treated by the Conservatives.

It is no task of this book to chronicle in detail the problems and achievements of the Labour Government during this period. They made mistakes, but they also achieved much. When they left in 1970 they handed over to the Tories a balance of payments surplus running at over £600 million a year. They had by 1969 increased spending on social security, health, housing and education by over 70 per cent, compared with 1964. Earnings in 1969 were 37½ per cent higher than in 1964 and prices during the same period went up by 23½ per cent. Between 1964 and 1970 the Labour Government concentrated on productivity, efficiency and industrial output, whereas the Tory period of government from 1959 to 1964 had been characterised by a concentration on rent, profits, tax evasion, capital gains and foreign investment. This was the difference between the two Governments.

Labour's defeat in June 1970 was due less to their record than to the split between the Government and unions, which demoralised the Party for over two years, and the patching-up of the differences

H

and the pick-up in the economy came too late to keep them in office. The six and a half years were truly frustrating years for the trade union movement. In the 1945–51 period the Government had a fund of goodwill which came from a realisation of the extent of the post-war reconstruction task which had to be carried through by the Government. The 1945 Government was also the first majority Labour administration, and so the policy road was clear, with no precedents to stand out as sore thumbs of past experience. This was far from true in 1964. There had already been grumblings at the 1963 and 1964 conferences about the role that Labour's prices and incomes policy would play in the economy, and analogies were being drawn with the Cripps wage freeze of 1948–50. These misgivings were calmed by the statement made by Frank Cousins at the 1964 Conference that the Transport and General Workers' Union would go along with a prices and incomes policy provided that it meant the planned growth of wages. This ambiguous papering over of the argument was only a temporary salve on the sore which was to erupt in a much more violent form in 1967 and 1968.

The row over the operation of the incomes policy and the later conflict between the unions and the Government on industrial relations, were the main events which influenced trade union political attitudes during the 1964–70 Labour Government. Both of these raised fundamental issues about how far the State should intervene in both fields, and what kind of a compact the unions required from the Government on economic and social progress as the price for co-operation.

In two later chapters the prices and incomes and industrial relations policies of the Labour Government are examined in some detail. Nevertheless, one general point must be made in concluding this chapter. There is no doubt that the 1945–51 Labour Government had more determination and hence more success in facing up to their economic problems. Looking back at the record of the two Labour Governments there is ample evidence that the post-war Attlee Government did change society in this country, and that the people accepted these reforms. It is true that the country voted Tory during the fifties, but even the Conservatives were percipient enough not to disturb basically the social fabric of the Welfare State, the Health Service and the State ownership of the basic industries introduced by Labour. In contrast, the 1964–70 Labour Government, while exhibiting more technical expertise, was less successful in attaining its objectives. It did have a limited success in improving industrial efficiency, and eventually achieved a sound balance of payments position. It also improved the Social Services, but at the end of the Government there was little to show that changes had been made in the inequalities existing in our society. Human values in 1970 were every bit as materialistic or even more so than they were in 1960.

In 1968 and 1969 there was an alarming breakdown of communication, not just between the Government and the public, but between the political and industrial wings of the movement. This was the real kernel of the discontent in the trade union movement. The union movement was not only unaware of the reasons for certain measures but also conscious of not being consulted as part of the process. This was partially corrected in the latter part of 1969 and 1970, but the malaise had bitten deep and confidence in the Government was never quite the same again.

This situation must not be allowed to occur again in the movement. A machinery of consultation must be developed now and in the next few years so that future policies can be agreed upon and understood by all the Labour movement. More specific suggestions will be made around this aim in later chapters, and it is at this point that we leave the historical examination of trade union political development.

Chapter 12

Which Political way for Labour?

'We have here a country and a people.
The problem is, given a country and a people, to find how
the people may make the best of the country and themselves.'
Robert Blatchford, 1851–1943

It has been necessary to make our trade union historical and
political safari over the last century in order to prepare ourselves
for an analysis of the streams of thought that now contend within
the unions. On the way through these historical facts we have
sought to satisfy queries as to why the unions should be in politics
and aligned with the Labour Party. From the experience of
the Osborne case the present restricted financial role of the
unions, and the democratic need for a strongly financed party of
the workers, we have adduced that trade unions should be
allowed to expend money for political purposes from their general
funds. The Registrar, I believe, will be grateful for this suggestion.

Our examination of the 1910–13 'direct action' period in trade
union history, and our study of the General Strike in 1926 and
its aftermath, have enabled us to form an opinion of what kind
of political action is likely to promote a socialist society in
Britain. Our early look at socialist political theories in the
nineteenth century and the new theories advanced in the last
thirty years both in Britain and from abroad, has equipped us to
look in some detail at the present theoretical thinking of the Labour
Party and the unions.

This examination is essential, because we cannot hope to unite
on future policies unless we get our theories clarified. There is
little point in starting a discussion on specific policies if a sizable

group in the unions or the party believe that the pure socialist answer to all problems is nationalisation and workers' control.

'Moderates' say that these are clichés and slogans, and are used as a defence against thinking out our modern socialist position. This could be so. But if these two instruments are the answer, then it is time we fed them into our programme; whilst equally, if they are not the answer, then it is time we spelled out why not, and stated our alternative.

The events covered by the early chapters of this book certainly vividly illustrated that, in the formative period when trade union political thought was being shaped, unionists did argue about the philosophy and political direction of the movement. Have we lost the habit? One of our greatest needs at the moment in the Labour movement is for us to redefine our objectives for the future in terms that make political sense in the 1970s. If the trade unions claim to have a major role in defining Labour policy then they must be prepared to put forward positive objectives and specific policies instead of only reacting to the policies produced by the political wing of the movement. It is as much the fault of the trade unions as the politicians that, as each Labour Government is elected, it is singularly unprepared and lacking in knowledge about the measures required to make sense of the brave speeches and resolutions that we marshal through at our Annual Conferences.

If there are trade unionists standing aside from the argument at present because they believe in direct action or because they are Marxists, then we should, in our advanced stage of political development, be percipient enough to range these arguments against the others that are widely held within the party and see which among them makes political sense. I see no alternative to such an examination unless we propose forever and a day to build on the policies of expediency rather than on the rock of socialist belief.

THE 'MODERN SYNDICALISTS'

We therefore start our look at the contending theories for the soul of the Labour movement by examining some small groups which have already been mentioned and then at the main contenders – the Marxists and the moderates.

In Chapter 9 I have already summarised the arguments against the small socialist groups who sponsor the cause of direct action. They are growing and have an appeal to young socialists which should not be underestimated. Their views still strike young people in search of a philosophy with the same piercing clarity which Nye Bevan spoke of in his youth. Their message is revolutionary and simple, but as has been argued at some length in discussing the General Strike earlier, a revolutionary weapon needs a revolutionary people and this is not a picture of the British working class which I recognise. I have a deep respect for many of those who devote themselves to the cause of their minority views with an enthusiasm and intensity which is not rivalled in other socialist groups in the party, but they are the wrong horses for the wrong course. If they could spin both universe and time the globe would maybe stop at a place and a time which would make their theories and course of action relevant to the circumstances and thinking of our people, but they can't and it won't.

So we leave the modern Noah Abletts and James Connollys as far as this examination is concerned, but rest assured we will continue to hear from them. In some important, strategic parts of industry they are as active as ever and even in control. Their view that agreements with employers are only 'temporary truces' means that they are set on a constant collision course. These 'modern Syndicalists' are elected to their positions by the workers who must feel that they do a job of work for them on industrial matters. Whether the gains from militant bargaining equate the time the workers lose on local revolutionary exercises is a matter on which only the workers can pass judgement. At present in such places they vote for the 'direct actionists' with both hands and feet. When their feet are sore they may start using their heads and hands in a different way. It's up to them!

THE MARXISTS AND A CHANGING SOCIETY

We now turn to the main contenders for the soul of the Labour Party, the 'Marxist' versus the 'moderates'.

Firstly, we look at the views of the large group of Marxists who have dominated the political left wing of the party since it was formed seventy years ago. In the early chapters, which traced the development of socialist thinking in Britain, we have already described the electrifying effect Marxist theories had on socialists at that time. The successful social revolution in Russia in 1917 and the opportunity this provided for putting Marx's theories into practice naturally drew socialist adherents closer to what was for them the only living example of socialism. Of course, Russia was a Communist state and followed the theories of Marx and Lenin, spiced earlier with a dash of Trotsky, and later with an excess of Stalinism. But it was clear early on that Britain's socialist thinkers did not all feel obliged to call themselves Communists or join the Communist Party after 1921 simply because they were Marxists.

John Middleton Murry, himself a Marxist but never a member of the Communist Party, summed up his view of the British Marxist. In his book *The Necessity of Communism* (1932), he said:

To believe in, to pursue, to give oneself to Communism in this country does not mean to become a 'Communist', it means to devote oneself to the task of making the Labour Party Marxist and revolutionary once more. The English Communist is the man who works with those and for those who aim at a real social revolution, at the complete eradication of the capitalism system. It is the revolution that matters, the name of Communist does not. It seems to me fantastic to suppose that in this country we should ape the manners of the Russian Revolution; it seems to me natural to suppose that the experience of the next few years will be such as to make Communism appear to a decisive minority of Englishmen completely reasonable. In England too, we can expect to be allowed to put the Communist case in season and out of season without hindrance. How long that freedom will continue I have no idea. It depends upon how quickly the fundamental Marxist version permeates the Labour Party, which is the natural instrument. If the Labour Party becomes radically Marxian instead of parasitic and sentimental, why, then, the cause is as good as won. And the condition of the permeation of the Labour Party is the increase of those intellectuals to whom Communism is veritably the one religious faith.

Middleton Murry was an intellectual of his time, speaking to other intellectuals, but his firm belief that Marxists should be in the Labour Party for the reasons he gave forty years ago are accepted today by the vast majority of Marxists in this country. Murry's views in the book quoted burn brightly with his intense belief in the political developments which Marx had forecast.

Labour Party Marxists, most of them at any rate, also regard Marxist theories as being the only answer, but have they stood the test of industrial economic and social changes in our society in Britain?

In examining Marx's beliefs and holding them up against today's backcloth, I want to make it clear that I regard Marx as a dedicated genius and a man who under conditions of severe poverty and hardship gave us a brilliant analysis of how nineteenth-century capitalism worked. More than that – his theories were dynamic. He did not stop short at the analysis but went on to describe in detail how capitalism would evolve. So his theories not only show with a brilliant clarity how things were, but also (a much more difficult task) how they would become. The fact that his philosophy has not come true is not because Marx's brain was at fault, but because certain factors evolved which he could not possibly have been expected to foresee. The effect of capitalism on the British working class did not turn out as Marx had prophesied, and therefore the class has not behaved politically as Marx thought it would. The reasons why this is so are many and complex, but this does not destroy the service which Karl Marx gave to the socialist movement by his work. Only an intellectual dwarf would sneer at his failure to foretell in the 1850s what capitalist Britain would be like in the 1970s.

Harold Wilson said that 'a week is a long time in politics'. Well, 120 years is a long haul for a political prophet who is assessing changing factors in industrial development, social change and political behaviour.

What did Marx predict and how have his predictions been wrong?

Briefly, Marx believed that because of the inner contradiction of the capitalist system, the mass of the people would become so poor ('the pauperisation of the masses', as he called it) that the system would collapse and there would be a revolutionary change in society.

THE POLARISATION OF THE CLASSES?

An essential element in Marx's theories was the reality of class and the struggle between the classes in society. Marx believed that this class struggle was the great reality – the greatest moving force in history that transcended all others. He believed that each stage in the social development of a country was marked by the predominance of a particular class which ruled.

It was Marx's definition of class which set him apart from other thinkers. Tony Crosland in *The Future of British Socialism* deals with what he calls 'determinants of class' and says that 'most sociologists adhere to an "objective" theory of class determination; that is they assume that social class is more or less automatically determined by certain objective and identifiable criteria, normally of an economic character'. The criteria which Marx used to determine class was the relationship of the individual to the control, ownership and power of production. So Marx's definition was almost technological as well as being economic.

In a capitalist society, said Marx, there are broadly two groups of people. Those who own the means of production and give orders and those who take the orders. He did realise that there might be a small group of intermediate individuals between these two, but did not regard their presence as interfering with his general argument. Marx called those who owned the *bourgeoisie*, and those who did not the *proletariat*. His theory was that as capitalism developed it would cause a concentration of production into ever-larger units and that the small producers who were independent or not connected with the large units would be stifled and would fade away. Thus 'small business' would disappear. He also believed that as capitalist firms became larger many of the intermediate positions which certain 'staff' workers had during the early development of capitalism would become obsolete and that these workers who previously had related themselves to the owners because of their position in the firm, would find themselves among the ordinary workers – the proletariat.

Marx saw this as a continuing, dynamic process with the units of production building up into huge combines and gathering more power in society as it grew. As an ever-increasing mass of workers became subject to the will of capitalist combinations, so this inevitably would increase the size and strength of the proletariat. Finally, as the people polarised into only two classes, the bourgeoisie and the proletariat, the increasing misery of the proletariat (the 'pauperisation of the masses', already mentioned) would overthrow the capitalist system, take over society and run it for themselves.

It will be seen from this brief description of Marx's view of the

evolution of capitalist society that it rests on the assumption that
with technological progress and increasing mechanization, power
would be in larger masses and that this development would not
be confined to industry, but would also take place in other sectors
of capitalism, such as banking, finance and insurance. Marx also
held that in time, huge trusts and finance institutions would, in
fact, control these larger masses of production. Even in agriculture
Marx thought that the size of farming units would also grow,
and that the small farmers and the peasants would be faced with
the same relationship to those who owned the large farms, as their
proletariat brethren in the towns and cities.

As I write these prophesies of Marx about capitalist evolution
I can almost hear a murmur of agreement from my Marxist
friends, who will be nodding and saying 'Yes, all these things
have happened' – and truly some of them have. But some have
not happened, whilst other things *have* happened which nullify
the ultimate logic of the argument by Marx. Although capitalist
development in Britain has meant larger concentrations of control
over production, the control of these enterprises has also changed.
Some of the ownership has passed to the kind of trusts etc.
described by Marx, but side by side with this in many industries
there has been a wide spreading of ownership to small and bond
shareholders who get their dividends but have no say at all in the
control of these businesses. This has happened, and the company
records are to be seen as proof of the diffusion of ownership,
whilst the non-attendance at shareholders' meetings are ample
evidence of the fact that those who run industry today control it
without owning it. More about satisfying the shareholders later,
and the factors that govern large enterprises!

Marx also did not visualise (how could he?) that instead of
fewer intermediate jobs being created between the owners and
the proletariat, as the scale of the enterprises grew, the reverse
has been the case. Some jobs did disappear, but the intermediate
positions as a whole have increased in number. Today large-scale
firms attract an ever-growing number of technicians, supervisors,
personnel management, administrators, job evaluators and others.
The workers and their leaders are continually complaining that
their firms are top-heavy with management. Workers can see them,
and it is also proved by the employment statistics. The importance
of this development is that the majority of those who could be
loosely called a managerial and technical group, are what Marx

called 'in the service of capitalist society'. They *relate* not to the proletariat but to the bourgeoisie!

Outside industry, too, there is a growth in the numbers of professional workers. This growth is much greater than in other proletarian occupations because the mechanics of technology displace fewer of the professions than other workers. Most of these identify themselves not with the working classes but with the middle classes, and the middle classes are difficult to divide into bourgeoisie and proletariat.

In agriculture too, the concentrations of production have not proceeded as swiftly as Marx predicted. The small farmer is still complainingly with us and certainly not to be regarded as a member of the proletariat.

So the 'polarisation of the classes', as Marx expounded it, has not taken place. Not only have the managerial, technical and professional workers grown as a group relatively faster than other occupations, but even the number of small businesses is not declining. It is true that large capitalist firms, mergers and take-overs are killing off some small businesses in some industries, but small business *as a category* is still with us and is surviving. This may appear surprising, but the facts are that certain kinds of small business do thrive in a continuing period of technical advance and different patterns of social behaviour (which have also changed since Marx's day) have led to a growing proportion of small businesses.

In the introduction to his book *Studies in Class Structure* (1955), G. D. H. Cole explains that small shopkeepers still exist in growing numbers and that our policy of building houses away from town and city centres is a factor in this growth. All housing schemes have provision for these rows of shops at regular intervals, which are almost all taken by small independent traders in contrast to those in city and town centres which are allied to the major chian stores.

The large-scale production of cars and increasing Britain's car-owning population have been fertile conditions for the growth of small garages. The increasing plethora of household electrical gadgets and the social march of television have again been an ideal field for the mushrooming of small electrical firms. The number of small builders engaged in repair work for the increasing ranks of owner-occupiers or in working for major firms has also grown.

Big restaurants have not squeezed out the small restaurants or cafés, and those which serve 'carry out' meals have shown a particular increase in number as more women have gone out to work. The rise in living standards has led to more meals out, particularly at weekends, and the small restaurants have picked up their share of this increasing trade.

As Cole points out, the only countries where small business *as a category* has decreased over the last century are those which have decided that they are not to be encouraged as a matter of policy. Thus in the USSR and the Communist East European countries small business has declined but not disappeared, though this is not due to the evolutionary process described by Marx.

One other defect in Marx's theories was his statement that it was the advanced industrialised nations that were ripe for change and that the industrial worker would be the leading protagonist in changing the capitalist system. This has not happened. So far, most progress in gaining acceptance for Marx's views and leading on to the Communist society has been in the agrarian countries where the peasantry have been the front runners of social change. The revolutions which have occurred up to the present have taken place in backward, not advanced, capitalist countries.

We can therefore conclude that 'the polarisation of the classes', which stands at the heart of Marx's evolutionary exposition of the development of capitalism and its ultimate effect on their political behaviour, has not taken place in Britain as he predicted. If the lot of the workers in advancing capitalist societies had been one of increasing poverty then sheer frustration and anger would have led, if not to revolution, certainly to more agitation and political discontent with the capitalist system. But Marx's 'pauperisation of the masses' has not come true. Even those who suffer from 'ingrowing political pamphlets' can hardly deny the rises in living standards of the ordinary people which are attributable to three main factors. Firstly, the rise and increased power of the trade unions; secondly, the readiness of a capitalist establishment to make concessions; and thirdly, the growth of the 'social conscience', which gradually led to minimum standards of subsistence for even those left behind by the system. All these factors have meant that since the 1850s, when Marx made his prognostications, the living standards of the proletariat have improved steadily.

One of the reasons given by Marx for the increasing poverty expected among the workers as capitalism developed, was that there were inner contradictions inherent in the capitalist system which caused slumps and crises in ever-recurring cycles. Contradictions there certainly are in our kind of society, but the frequency of the slumps and their severity has been nothing like Marx thought. There were no crises from the 1840s until 1932, and even the depression in Europe did not bring the downfall of capitalism – it brought Hitler to power and then war in 1939. In the USA Roosevelt's New Deal strengthened the trade unions, who in turn made the 1930s bearable and the course in America became reformist rather than revolutionary. In Britain and, indeed, in the other countries mentioned, the only revolution was that the doctrines of Keynes became weapons enabling capitalist economies to avoid catastrophic unemployment which took the edge off social discontent. Since the 1930s there have been a few uncomfortable lurches in capitalist countries but no collapse. Looking at capitalist economics today, it would only be a very rash person or one partially blinded by political blinkers who would predict the collapse of capitalism from the contradictions outlined by Karl Marx.

In saying this it is not intended to argue that the resilience of capitalism means that it should not be changed, but it does mean that if we understand its resilience we are better equipped to discover the best ways to change it, or get rid of it altogether.

So people have not become poorer due to capitalist crises and slumps as Marx had predicted, and neither have their living standards declined either relatively or quantitatively. Over the years there has been a shift in the share out of wealth in favour of the workers, albeit more slowly than we desire. In addition to the shift in direct income there has also been a tremendous increase in the indirect incomes of workers by the increasing value of the 'social' wage made up of social security benefits, access to the National Health Service, clinics, etc.

Marx's pauperisation of the masses has not taken place yet at any rate. Some Marxists say 'give it time', but 120 years is a very long time and no other theory that I know of would be kept on ice for that length of time if it did not look like being proved true. It is one thing to believe stoutly that Marx may be proved right at some time far in the future, but it is quite inexcusable to take up political attitudes to today's political and social problems on the premise that everything Marx said is true today or may even become true in our lifetimes.

Saying that Marx has not yet been proved right does not, however, mean that we have to accept the view of capitalism which the upholders of the present system would have us believe. Their view is really economic nonsense. The Conservatives try to justify the scale of capitalist concentration by efficiency arguments which are rarely borne out by reference to the prices paid by the consumer or by any social operation of the capitalist system via the doctrine of 'consumers' sovereignty'. Free enterprise, it is said, really operates by the will of society. The people indicate what they want to buy and what services they require and a benevolent capitalist system provides these goods and services at the right price. The producer satisfies his customers by supplying them and his shareholders by maximising profits. Private enterprise thus competes for the goodwill of the consumer both by carrying out their present desires and by intelligently anticipating what they will need in the future. Everything therefore in a free enterprise society it is proposed, finds its own point of balance. If prices are too high, the firms concerned suffer in competition with those who are more competitive. The mechanism of the market automatically performs any necessary adjustments without interference from politicians. Inefficient capitalists go to the wall and the consumer gets a fair deal all the time.

This convenient explanation could be called 'capitalist economics for the under fives' because it clearly does not begin to answer questions about the power of large-scale business organisations or whether the capitalist producer ever tries to 'rig' demand. By apparently elevating the importance of the ordinary man and woman in dictating what the capitalist enterprises produce, the apologists, of course, argue that the customer is the dominant partner in our society and that free enterprise is subservient. They also maintain that since shareholders own the companies and in fact elect the directors it is this large group who run free enterprise. So the free-enterprise, market-operated, self-regulating, consumer-orientated society is, in fact, wonderfully democratic provided we do not look too closely at these basic assumptions.

Strangely enough this view of capitalism is kept afloat by some of the socialist opponents of capitalism. I have heard them argue often at trade union conferences that the capitalist system is wrong because it is full of cut-throat competition and that the only function of the monopolies is to exploit the consumer and make profits. They turn the free enterprisers' version of economics

on its head and then argue that all we have to do is to turn the
lot upside down – sack the shareholders, set up a public
monopoly, put an end to competition – and everything will be
fine.

There is some truth in both of these assumptions. But the real
truth, based not on opinion, but on what is actually happening to
capitalist society, is that neither Marx nor the free enterprisers nor
the socialist critics I have mentioned have accurately described
how capitalism is working today. Until we do define this phenomenon, we cannot effectively set about finding the right answers to
change it.

Large public corporations and large private firms are more
remarkable for their similarities than for their differences.
Shareholders, as has been mentioned earlier, have very little
control over the firms that they are supposed to own. The
managers and technicians who actually run industries have more
on their minds than returning the maximum profit to the shareholders. They have their own future and power to spur them on.
The size of the organisation and the power that goes with it, the
prospects for promotion and their own security, are their powerful
incentives.

This means that, although management must ensure that
shareholders do receive an adequate return they fall far short of
distributing the maximum profit or dividend which could be
paid if maximising profit were the be-all and end-all of capitalist
production. Indeed, if this were so, many firms would not be in
the sectors of industry that they are in at the moment. They could
obtain bigger profits by investing their cash elsewhere. James
Burnham, in his book *The Managerial Revolution*, says that
'profits do not accrue to the management but money retained
for investment (and not distributed as profits in the form of
dividends etc.) does remain at the disposal of those who run the
firm'. So shareholders must get reasonable earnings on their
holdings, but the managers will see to it that their future is shored
up by an adequate share of capital for investment. This was borne
out quite graphically in the years 1948–50, when the Labour
Government introduced a wages and dividends freeze. The shareholders wept, and the managers, while shedding a few outward
tears in sympathy, were inwardly smiling because it meant that
their aspirations for more investment in their firms would be
more likely to be satisfied in such a situation.

Keynes, in his book *The End of Laissez-Faire*, was probably the first to recognise this factor when he said:

A point arrives in the growth of a big institution at which the owners of capital, i.e. the shareholders, are almost entirely dis-associated from the management, with the result that the direct personal interest of the latter in the making of great profit becomes quite secondary. When this stage is reached the general stability and reputation of the institution are more considered by the management than the maximum of profit for the share-holders.

Today the sheer size and complexities of the larger firms and the fragmentation of shareholding makes it absolutely impossible for the shareholders to have a say in deciding the major issues. Those who do the day-to-day running of the enterprise have all the answers and, apart from ensuring a conventionally adequate return for the shareholders, it is their own interests, their own desires, which are paramount in the minds of managerial decision-makers.

One more important factor about the attitude of management in the large firms. What frequently troubles them most is the possibility of take-over. This brings uncertainty and a new management elite to whom they must adjust and accept. The maximum retention of profits in the company for development keeps companies out of the hands of the banks and finance companies and so free from outside interference. Not many take-over bids are accepted against the board's advice, but not many are rejected if the board recommends acceptance. The fact that shareholders do not control the companies they own does not mean that we have abolished the conflict between management and worker, but it does mean that decisions are not taken by remote meetings of shareholders who have no knowledge of the industry. Neither does the non-control of the shareholders mean that shareholdings do not matter in a capitalist society. They do matter, and shareholders, if they are wise, devote their attention elsewhere in the market and in politics to ensure that the structure of taxation does not move against unearned incomes. Our task as socialists is to see that wealth is redistributed and that industry is controlled and made accountable to the community.

This part of the argument has been designed to show that, contrary to what Marx said, it is not always necessary *to own in order to control.* In some cases it is necessary and desirable, but in other cases there are other and better ways of achieving a socialist answer.

In addition to the power of the managers and technicians, there is one other important factor which has some bearing on the control of the large-scale private enterprise. This factor springs again from the 'nature of the beast'. The dominant firms in our economy in Britain have four main characteristics:

they are large;
they have stability – almost a permanence;
they are controlled by professional managers;
they are able to finance their own development.

The five largest companies in Britain in 1968 had a combined annual turnover of £6,000 million. The leading thirty companies have an annual combined *budget* which is well in excess of the National Exchequer. These figures illustrate the scale of such firms, but even these, big as they are, are small beer compared with the giant international companies. This scale and the scope of their operation means that their capital commitments are enormous and not easy to alter once made. To design and sell a complicated piece of equipment requires a large amount of money initially. It also requires a specialised work force. Lastly, it needs time. The time factor is extremely important. Years can elapse between the initial designing of an article, and the appearance of the first production item ready for sale, depending on its complexity.

These three factors mould the behaviour of large scale companies and the larger the companies are, the more these factors bear on their behaviour. John K. Galbraith, the American economist, describes these factors as constituting the 'technological imperatives' which are shaping modern large capitalist enterprises. Galbraith, in his books *The New Industrial State* and *American Capitalism*, postulates that the age of free enterprise and free markets has been destroyed not by socialism, as Marx predicted, but by technology. Galbraith shows how the commitment of large capital sums, manpower, knowledge and time, are dominating the actions of large companies. Taking the history of the Ford Motor Company, Galbraith illustrates the point by showing that in 1903 when Henry Ford produced his first car he did it with $30,000 and 125 men. The first car was sold three

I

months after the company was formed. Of course there was no competition, no big market survey, no mammoth advertising campaign and not much difficulty about making design alterations after the first models were produced to suit the customer. That was in 1903 when cars were only starting to be produced in quantity. It was in fact an early stage in what was later to be the capitalist mass production of motor cars.

Contrast the 1903 experience of Fords with the production and sale of the Ford Capri, which was sold in Britain for the first time in 1969. The Ford subsidiaries in Britain and Germany combined their resources in 1962 and from there carried through a programme of seven years' development work which required a prior commitment of £20,000,000. Design studies on the Capri began in 1962. In 1965 Detroit gave it the green light, and by July 1966 the project was firmly committed to production. By August 1968 the advertising strategies were agreed upon, and in January 1969 the car was announced to the general public. The advertising *launching* in Britain alone cost £150,000, and the other continuing publicity expenditure has to be added to that.

Stan Ellen, the Vice-President of Ford of Europe Manufacturing, said, 'We are rolling dice for £20 million – the car has got to sell.' With a mammoth commitment like that – it sure has!

The importance of this size of commitment in money, machinery and manpower is that once it is under way it has a momentum of its own which has little to do with capitalist economics or the free market. The company and its managers are no longer free to behave as 'private entrepreneurs'. The commitment dictates the behaviour of the management. Intelligent workers in those firms know this and trade union leaders who negotiate with large firms also know this to be true. It was the 'technological imperatives' which made Fords in the 1971 strike reach a settlement which was over twice as much as their 'final offer' before the strike started. Vauxhall, B.L.M.C. and Chrysler also ignored the bleating of the Government for the same compelling reasons.

Marx would not have known a 'technological imperative' if he had seen one. Although he foresaw the concentration and size of enterprises, he did not see that this would alter the behaviour of the companies to bring about a new stage of capitalist development. This comparison between what Marx thought would happen to capitalism, and what has and is actually happening, shows that although he explained clearly how the capitalist system worked in a technical sense (his theory of surplus value, for example, cannot be faulted), what Marx did not do was to forecast correctly the forces in society which would be operating later in an advanced capitalist country.

A summary then of our analysis shows that we have had no 'polarisation of the classes', but instead a proliferation of middle-class occupations and professions in which workers neither think or act socially or politically as the proletariat. Nor have we had a 'pauperisation of the masses', because capitalist society, tempered by the power of the unions, has lost the cutting edge of discontent and left revolution as very much an outsider in the political stakes of Great Britain. The very fact of capitalist concentration has moved the power of control away from those who own to those who are concerned with running the industry and who are seldom shareholders of any standing. Finally, because of the other forces – the 'technological imperatives' which also determine the decisions which large-scale capitalist firms must take – all these facts, and facts they undoubtedly are, mean that Marxism is far from being the Mount Sinai of socialist political theory.

One final point before we leave our analysis, which concerns many who regard themselves as Marxist in the trade unions and who are members of the Labour Party. How many of these accept Marx's 'dictatorship of the proletariat' as the intermediate stage in Britain on the way to the ultimate socialist society? Not many, I suspect. Many of them do accept that in our country it may be possible to achieve a peaceful transfer from capitalism to socialism without the need for the 'dictatorship of the proletariat', which in the USSR and other Eastern European countries is assuming a permanence which no 1920s British socialist would have calculated or wanted. According to Lenin, however, those who believe in a peaceful transition have no right to call themselves Marxists. In volume 21 of his book *State and Revolution*, defining the difference between the Marxist and the 'pseudo-Marxist', Lenin says:

Only he is a Marxist who *extends* the acceptance of class struggle to the acceptance of the 'dictatorship of the proletariat'. Herein lies the most profound difference between a Marxist and a mediocre petit (and also a big) bourgeois. On this touchstone a real understanding and acceptance of Marxism must be accepted.

Many of those who call themselves Marxists in the unions would not satisfy this stringent, unequivocal criterion laid down by Lenin. They have in fact more in common with Eduard Bernstein who, in his *Prerequisites of Socialism* in 1899, expressed views which are much more akin to the self-styled trade union Marxist than those of Marx himself. Bernstein, branded as a 'revisionist' by the true Marxists, is regarded as an arch-enemy, and A. Lozovsky in his book *Marx and Trade Unions* heaps the ultimate in Communist epithets on him by referring to the *Prerequisites of Socialism* as 'the holy bible of modern social democracy'.

Some of us do not disagree with the status Lozovsky gives to Bernstein's classic criticism of Marx's forecasts, but differ from Lozovsky's low opinion of his theories. Many of us find Bernstein's works standing up better to the changing nature of our society than the main conclusions of Marx about capitalist society. Bernstein's belief in industrial democracy, the growing into socialism peacefully by reforms and democratic processes, the democratisation of industry through the trade unions, and the development of social security, are all much more plausible objectives for a socialist of our times than those advanced by the Lenin-Marxists.

In this long but by no means exhaustive look at the teachings of Marx it has occurred to me that some may say that I have unfairly presented what the modern Marxist believes today. However I have looked at some leading Marxists who have repostulated the doctrine in recent years, and have found that the means towards socialism for them are still purely Marxist. In 1963 J. R. Campbell, who was then Chairman of the Communist Party's Economic Committee, wrote in *The Challenge of Marxism*:

The ownership of the means of production in any society determines for what purpose they will be used. In capitalist society the purpose is to realise the maximum profit for the owners of the means of production. The fundamental law of capitalism is to squeeze the utmost surplus value from the workers by hand and by brain.

This definition by Campbell shows no updating of Marx. The statement is simple, clear, but entirely wrong in its conception of how capitalism works at present. If the problem is stated incorrectly then there is no chance of coming up with a correct answer.

'IF NOT THE MARXIST WAY – WHICH WAY?'

If modern capitalism does not operate as Campbell believes, and if, as we have seen, the operation of the system does not have the effects on the labour force which Marx predicted; further, if ownership does not mean control, then it follows that contemporary socialists should not be confined to State ownership of all industry as the only way forward to a socialist society in Britain. If control and not ownership is the answer in some sectors, should we not be addressing ourselves to the problem of transferring power from the large corporations to the community? Public ownership still has its place in this transition, but it is certainly not in its monolithic form an exclusively correct answer. Public ownership has been joined by economic planning in the political arsenal of the thinking British trade unionist. Modern technology and new, sophisticated means of economic analysis are providing us with alternatives in planning which are nearer to the correct industrial and political solutions to our problems in present day Britain.

Modern technology has eroded the free market principles of early capitalism, and large corporations have to plan to live with the scale of commitment demanded by the growth of this technology. Our economy is subjected to the power of the large corporations and to the *plans* of those who control them.

The traditional weapon of Labour's economic control has been through public ownership and this will, if extended, achieve some of the aims of British socialists – the control to some extent of the use of natural resources in the interests of the community. But ownership alone is not the final key. Transferring industrial assets from private to public hands does not by itself create a new economic system, for what really matters just as much is who the new planners are, what their plans are, how their plans are made, and how they are made accountable to society.

So ownership can provide us with half an answer – possibly the quantitative half – but the qualitative half, which decides what kind of society we live in, depends on factors other than ownership.

ANALYSING THE 'MODERATES'

That brief synopsis of the task facing socialists who are anxious to understand and cope with problems which actually face us, instead of shaping up to imaginary and outdated problems which exist only in political musings, brings us to the other main group of socialists in the trade union and Labour movement – the so-called 'moderates'.

I would be the last to claim that all those who are classed as moderates are rabid disciples of Bernstein – most moderates have no fixed theories – but lumped in the moderate camp are those who have a clear philosophy about the correct socialist policies which should be followed to achieve socialism in Britain. So, in the 'moderate' group we have an alliance of the cautious, the constitutionalist, the follow-my-leader and the modern social democrat who has a philosophy.

The 'moderates' are therefore a mixed bunch, and it is only possible to guess at some of the attitudes which have persuaded them to act cohesively as a unified majority of the Labour Party and also (until the recent changes of leadership in the larger unions) in the trade union movement itself. The 'cautious' moderate is probably cautious by nature. He wants to change our society but believes in industrial and social reforms being introduced which do not disturb the *status quo* too much. He does not object to a succession of reforms, but prefers the changes to be slow and gradual.

Members of this group, particularly those who are active in the trade unions, are not flamboyant characters and are certainly not 'uptight' on political theory. If they were, they would also be active on the political side as well as in the union. Those interested in theories usually find a ready ear or a kindred spirit, not at a trade union branch meeting but at the CLP, even if it is only in 'Any Other Business'.

The 'cautious' moderates are influenced by the 1926 strike. They have either been in it, read of it, or listened to those who were involved. They have passed judgement, as a result of 1926, on how they intend to change society. They have evaluated the progress in Britain since 1926, seen the rise in living standards, looked at other places where changes have been more violent and less beneficial to the working class, and have opted for the kind of change which will not result in hardship to their class. It is difficult to erect a philosophy around such a 'matter of fact' conviction as they have, but conviction it is. Their contribution to the trade union movement is immense. These are the 'grass roots' of the active trade unionists. This is the bulwark of branch committees up and down the country. These are the unsung, who do the work of the union and on whom the spotlight seldom falls.

The second element in the grouping of 'moderates' is constitutionalist by nature. 'Constitutionalists' have been weaned on trade union rules and agreements. They have a hallowed respect of decisions and of those elected to lead. They enjoy a good exposition of standing orders or the constitution better than a sparkling oratorical performance from the rostrum. These 'constitutionalists' never support a reference back, and in conference or branch usually support the officials and the platform.

This may sound like a caricature of a kind of person, but such are to be found in every shop and in every branch. Their constitutionalism extends to opposition to unofficial strikes in their own shops at one end of the spectrum, to a denunciation of industrial action for political ends at the other extreme. They are not born 'constitutionalists'. They start off in trade union work because they have a strong sense of responsibility and the dormant constitutionalist in them gradually takes over. It may well be sometimes that a decision taken on constitutional grounds avoids delving into the political niceties of the argument, and some of them find this a convenient and easy way out of controversial situations without taking sides or offending those on both sides of the main argument. Nothing can be done, according to them, without rules and definitions, and rules must be kept. These are usually the disciplinarians in the unions and the party who have little time for those who offend the code of the movement. They, too, have been influenced by the 1926 strike. They did not like the 'untidiness' the strike revealed constitutionally, and have decided that the direct industrial challenge is not their way of changing society. It's Parliamentary democracy for them. Socialists they are deep down, but they are constitutionalists first and foremost.

The third element among the 'moderates' are those who only broadly accept the analysis and criticism of Marxism contained in this chapter. They have come to this conclusion not because they are cautious or constitutional by nature, but because they are philosophically convinced that the means of achieving socialism in Britain are not those expounded by leftists and Marxists.

Most of them at some time in their political thinking have been Marxists – but they have read on. The political events influencing their thinking have been, in chronological order, Marx, Bernstein, the trade union experiences of 1913, 1921 and, most important, the General Strike of 1926. They have accepted some of the economic doctrine of J. M. Keynes, also of the 1926–30 vintage, and since then have agreed broadly with the updated British socialist analysis by Tony Crosland in *The Future of Socialism* (1956). They understand how modern capitalism works, and even comprehend Galbraith's 'technological imperatives'. They respect Marx but do not accept his predictions.

They do not lack conviction about the need for social and industrial change, but they see the problems not as they are seen by the Marxists, but as they really are! Their answers to socialising the economy are a mixture of ownership and control. Their appeal in the trade union movement is to those who are perceptive enough to take the evidence of how society works from what they see around them and the ascertainable facts about society which are known to be true, rather than from woolly text-hewn tracts and pamphlets. They are conscious that as 'revisionists' they are open to attack. Their position is much more difficult to state than the left wing case. They are an influential element in the trade union movement and in the Labour Party, and the movement has broadly followed the thinking of these 'latter-day' Bernsteins since the 1926 strike.

These are the thinking social democrats. It is against them that the worst epithets are hurled by the left wing inside and outside the Labour Party. They have tried in formulating Labour Party policy to lay stress on the real problem in Britain, which is the transition from capitalism to socialism. Nye Bevan saw this immediately after the collapse of the miners' strike in November 1926. It was then that he realised that he must look again at what he had learned from the Syndicalists. Michael Foot, in the first volume of his life of Aneurin Bevan, describes how at this time Bevan said that the British working class must think out deeply what it meant by a transference of power *and how to prepare for it more deliberately*. Bevan did not see eye to eye with the 'moderate' point of view, but at least they were agreed on the problem, which both believed was more complicated than simply transferring everything to the State. In the words of Michael Foot in the same book, when Oliver Jones 'said to Nye Bevan after the 1926 defeat that it looked as though there was nothing left but to join the Communist Party, Nye replied, "Oh no. All it means is that we shall have to fight harder".' Nye started then to think about the transition in Britain from capitalism to socialism, and so must we.

In the analysis of the political views of the contending groups within the party, I have, I believe, given enough factual information to throw some doubts on the accuracy of the political way charted by Marx, and in the course of this analysis we have looked at how modern capitalist industry operates, and in particular at the problem of ownership and control. With this in mind, the remaining chapters of this book will attempt to define what action Labour should follow in certain controversial areas of policy.

The book is not long enough to permit a look at all policy areas, but the four areas selected, i.e. public ownership; industrial relations; prices, incomes and inflation; and the problems of organising the movement for power, are key areas where little clarity is being exhibited at present.

Chapter 13

Control and Ownership –
A Policy for Labour

'He owns me, who owns the means whereby I live.'
William Shakespeare, 1564–1616

In our analysis of Marxism we rid ourselves of the argument that the only way to control private enterprise was to institute public ownership of the enterprise. This means that we can now set out to define the criteria of socialist public ownership which should be applied in Great Britain and which industries these are likely to affect.

In defining the sectors of public ownership let us keep firmly in our minds that State ownership does not automatically lead to what we would call a 'socialist society'. As stated earlier, if we want to control and use the community's resources for the benefit of all, we must look also at the problem of making such public enterprises accountable to the nation. What we are therefore concerned with are the three problems of ownership, control and accountability.

Technology automatically gives power to those who lead large industrial enterprises, whether public enterprises or private. The challenge to social democracy in this country is to devise means whereby the interests of the community are paramount against the expertise and push of these large firms. We have to ensure that the power wielded by major public and private enterprises works for and not against the kind of democratic principles which will embrace a socialist Britain. Public control is not sufficiently guaranteed by saying that the public industries are accountable through the Minister to Parliament. This is a bureaucratic answer which means little in practice. 'Whipped' MPs will usually accept a Minister's defence of a corporation which is under fire, and we here are concerned not just with the flare-ups and crises that occur from time to time, but also with continuing democratic control throughout the working life of the industry or company.

THE CONTROL OF INDUSTRIAL DEMOCRACY

The main way this can be done is by an extension of industrial democracy. It is time that the power and influence of the workers and unions is recognised and used for positive objectives. Effective participation by the workers in the development of British industry is a necessary extension of our socialist beliefs. It also holds the prospect of bringing home the 'economic bacon'.

Workers do have a kind of control of industry at the moment – control exercised with their feet! It is very necessary that the workers should have power to obstruct in their own interests measures which they do not like, but it is indefensible that in the 1970s this negative power should be the only one we have in influencing major decisions in industry. Hammering out a policy to provide a positive, effective policy on industrial democracy, is a job for the trade unions.

Development of industrial democracy will lead to better industrial relations and less disputes. It will also mean a much wider area of accountability and control by the community. Properly applied it will result in the development of the worker as an individual, and it should also lead to greater efficiency and a bigger national cake for all to share. As long as the power of the worker is artificially confined, however, it must inevitably be used only in reacting to the decisions of management, in which workers have had no say except by the crudest pressure of industrial action.

It is ludicrous that when a works gate closes behind a worker in the morning, the portcullis of managerial functions falls with a thud on his rights as a citizen; that when a worker punches his cards he also knocks for six some of the basic elementary rights which he has outside the factory. Outside the gate he has the right to influence how his local authority and his country are run, but once inside he has no rights to influence the decisions which affect the most important part of his life.

A share in decision-making in industry does, of course, mean rolling back the present frontiers of managerial function and then extending 'government by consent' in industry. This extension of the rights of people who work is the very essence of democracy. It makes them whole men and women.

THE FORCE OF TECHNOLOGY

Industrial democracy is also necessary for reasons other than the democratic fulfilment of workers. The force of technological change is also banging on the factory gate. Job insecurity and the need for flexibility of labour require an overhaul of the present procedures by which industrial decisions are reached.

Technology in many ways degrades the formerly creative worker, and job satisfaction drops when men and women are relegated to being machine minders. Industrial technology may decree that they are minders of machines. Our task is to ensure that they do not have minds like machines! We can ensure this by allowing them to take part in running their industries.

The expertise, technical and otherwise, which resides in all workers must be used for the good of the common pool. Increased efficiency is bound to result when this reservoir of knowledge is tapped. The latent productivity which lies idle at present in the minds of our labour force may be one of the answers to growth which has eluded successive governments to date. This pool of knowledge cannot be released without a change in the master-and-man relationship in industry.

INDUSTRIAL DEMOCRACY – MAIN INGREDIENTS

The case for introducing industrial democracy is easier stated than the method of achieving it! The way *not* to achieve it is by talking about joint consultation as being something separate from negotiation. Joint consultation was a flop. At best it was a dangerous talking shop, at worst it divided the workers into consulters and negotiators. Shop stewards contracted out because they were suffering from 'industrial schizophrenia'. Their role as negotiators conflicted with their role in joint consultation.

The first requirement for success is to combine both consultation and negotiation in a single-channel procedure, so that when we sit down as workers to discuss how machines are manned, how overtime is worked, the dismissals procedure, or the shop or factory investment programme, we can, at the same time, discuss the rewards, monetary and environmental, flowing from these objectives.

Secondly, the necessary changes must be made in company law so that there can be a disclosure of information concerning the activities of the company which will enable sensible management and bargaining decisions to be taken. This is absolutely vital if the dialogue in decision-making is to be based on fact.

Thirdly, the workers' representation must be firmly based on the trade unions; and fourthly, the trade unions must work out in detail the structure of management-worker representation at shop, plant, and where necessary, at national level.

We cannot run industry like a branch meeting and decide everything by a show of hands. Checks and balances must be built into the joint management committees at some levels. Interesting experiments are taking place at home and abroad to guide us as to what is likely to be the most successful way of developing a trade union policy on this subject. We have to decide whether these schemes are applicable to Britain and capable of general development.

CHANGES IN THE ROLE OF THE UNIONS

I realise, of course, that some unions are lukewarm to the extension of democracy in industry. They claim that single-channel bargaining will weaken the unions and make them creatures of management. These views demand some respect, but it must be recognised that a revolutionary change in the way decisions are made in industry does compel changes in the role and organisation of the unions. These changes must be weighed against the advantages. Of course it will involve changes in the union's role, especially in collective bargaining, but which should we place first in our consideration – the embalming of the present role of the unions, or the interests of the workers? If the changes are fundamental to the development of workers' rights, and constitute a major step towards social accountability and control, then surely some change in present trade union functions is a small price to pay. Surrendering the present trade union role for an ineffective policy of industrial democracy would be a bad bargain, but not if the alternative were a policy with democratic teeth which bit into managerial functions and gave the workers a really effective say in how their firm would operate.

I believe the movement is convinced about the need for industrial democracy, and the time between now and the next General Election should be spent by the unions in putting the flesh of specific policy on the skeletal principles which are spoken of and approved of so often in the forums of our movement. Industrial democracy must be seen to be a key and integral part of any programme which aims to bring the economy under socialist control.

THE ROLE OF PUBLIC OWNERSHIP

Ownership, however, is also essential, but State ownership can be even more autocratic and uncaring than private ownership, and so public enterprises must also have industrial democracy to leaven their operation and to provide social accountability. I realise that to some socialists, ownership by the State is the end-all and be-all of their belief. While such faith may be touching, it is also very naive in the light of the facts from countries abroad and from the nationalised concerns in Britain.

I suppose it all depends on what your individual definition of socialism is. If it means the nationalisation of the means of production, distribution and exchange then we are confusing one part of the means with the socialist ends. By this criterion the USSR is a more socialist country than, say, Yugoslavia or Sweden! If our decision means the enforced State control of economic life, then Hitler's Nazi Germany was socialist!

In neither of these cases, USSR now, or Germany then, would the end result, the kind of society produced by these economic means, be regarded as socialist by the overwhelming majority of socialists in Great Britain. The truth is that nationalisation, planning and control have proved adaptable to more than one purpose. This takes us back to the old axiom that it is unwise to confuse the means with the ends.

SOCIALIST VALUES

The ends themselves relate to socialist values, which must be the moral integers of our kind of socialist society. Some of these values are a protest against the past and present excesses of the capitalist system. The others are economic, idealistic and even ethical.

Tony Crosland summarised the social and economic values in *The Future of Socialism* as follows:

1. A protest against the poverty and squalor which capitalism has produced.
2. Wide and humane concern of the need for Social Welfare, and concern for those in need or oppressed.
3. A belief in equality and the classless society with emphasis on the workers' rights and status.
4. The rejection of competitive antagonisms in line with the ideal of fraternity and co-operation.
5. A protest against the inefficiency of capitalism as an economic system, particularly in its tendency to produce mass unemployment. Mass unemployment is equated with inefficiency.

Crosland's socialist values are timeless. They are without jargon and cliché. He defines the values without falling back once on the vague word 'socialist' itself. G. D. H. Cole in his book *A Short History of the British Working Class Movement* said that the heart of socialist values was 'a broad humane movement on behalf of the underdog', which is exactly the basis of the first three of Crosland's values. Crosland's first and last values are protests against the capitalist system on social, moral and efficiency grounds, and the others are what all socialists would want to see in a society free from the built-in antagonisms of capitalism. Only two of Crosland's values are negative, the remainder are positive.

From this slight digression we have arrived at a statement of values which would be the pillars of a socialist policy. In none of them have we mentioned means, because we have been concerned with defining ends. To talk about public ownership as an end or as a definition of socialism is to erect a mental block which obstructs a socialist view being focused on the values which should direct our actions. With a clear understanding that we are talking about the methods which have the best chance of ushering in the socialist values and aspirations defined by Crosland, we can now look at the role of public ownership in Britain free from charges of revisionism or of being the polluters of the pure milk of socialism.

WHAT ARE THE COMMANDING HEIGHTS?

This philosophical introduction to our examination of the role of public ownership is essential because the Clause 4 controversy in 1959–60 rightly showed that the rank and file of the party did not take kindly to a constitutional dilution of the articles of socialist faith upon which the Labour Party and trade union movement stand. Clause 4 was preserved, and the famous Clause 10 of the declaration by the NEC of the Labour Party, amplifying the party objects, now states:

> The Labour Party is convinced that their social and economic objectives can only be achieved through the expansion of common ownership, substantial enough to control the commanding heights of the economy.

It is the yardstick of the above declaration of the objects of the Labour Party that will guide my reasoning on how much public ownership is necessary. True, Clause 4 is more general in its language, but Clause 4 was never interpreted by any as meaning everything would be State owned, and since no socialist in Great Britain desires a monolithic society, there is no departure from British socialist principles in discussing a role for public ownership which falls short of 'nationalising the lot' and which does admit of a place for private enterprise in our kind of socialist society.

In a political democracy like Britain the case for public ownership has to be argued with an electorate who have yet to be persuaded that it is a good thing for the economy. Arguing in favour of public ownership means listing its practical advantages over the capitalist form of ownership. As a result, we need to start formulating our policy on this issue, not merely by putting the case for public ownership but also by stating the principles which will guide us in applying public ownership to the manufacturing and commercial sections of the economy. I will, therefore, begin this discussion, not with a shopping list of companies or industries to be nationalised, but with a statement of the *criteria* for public ownership.

BASIC INDUSTRIES AND PUBLIC UTILITIES

The stability of the bed-rock of the economy rests on the well-being of its public utility services and of the basic industries. Many of these, because of the element of public service are not placed to make the same level of profits as manufacturing industry or other service industries outside the public sector. Their attraction to private investors is non-existent, but their continued development and efficiency are vital to the rest of the economy. For these reasons the 1945 Labour Government nationalised coal, water, steel, electricity and gas, the railways and parts of road and civil air transport.

The 'public utility and basic industry' criteria for public ownership are still as strong today as they were in the past, and there are good reasons for adding to those already nationalised. The next Labour Government should take into public ownership the port transport industry, which would complete the services link up between land and air, and should give this industry the capital development necessary to handle efficiently the trade of a nation like ours which lives on imports.

North Sea Gas should also be taken into public ownership, preferably as part of a National Hydrocarbons Corporation which would be in a position to market not only the gas but also its valuable by-products.

One other industry which merits attention on the public utility criterion, is the building industry; but here, because of the proliferation of small businesses, nationalisation is impossible. In this sector the next Labour Government should form a National Building Corporation to set the pace and the standard for house building in Britain. Social need demands that this vital commodity should be brought under more direct Government control. The tragedy of successive Labour Housing Ministers has been that as the building of homes is split evenly between Local Authorities and private builders, the ministers have very little control over half of the house building in the country.

Action is imperative on the public ownership of the Port Transport and North Sea Gas industries and the establishment of a publicly owned corporation in building to fulfil the 'public utility and basic industry' criteria laid down many years ago.

SELECTIVE OWNERSHIP – KEY SECTORS

The second criterion is that of 'efficiency'. In today's terms this means looking at those sections of industry which hold the key to growth in our economy. No complete industry needs to be nationalised under this criterion, but there is a need for selective public ownership of some of the major firms in the technically advanced industries.

Selective public ownership is necessary in machine tools, motor

K

and commercial vehicles, the development of automatic transfer machinery, the aircraft industry, whilst major firms in industries like chemicals and plastics, which have an increasingly important role to play in our exporting future, should also be considered for public ownership. A viable shipbuilding industry is also part of an efficient Britain, and here again selective ownership in carefully picked yards is bound to be a more efficient prospect than financing the private ship builders' failures in an industry which is subsidised in all other shipbuilding countries.

PUBLIC ENTERPRISE AND REGIONAL DEVELOPMENT

The third criterion for public ownership is related to regional development. Most of the problems in the less prosperous regions of the country stem mainly from an imbalance of declining heavy industries, such as coal, heavy engineering and shipbuilding. Private investment is slow to move into these areas, and here the carrot or stick measures of control by Industrial Development Certificates or financial grants given as investment grants, tax allowances or employment premiums, must be complemented. This can be accomplished by the twin measures of selective public ownership in the crucial areas of employment, and also by new public firms set up in specially selected industries. These need not be major complexes but there could be as many as required, linked to public concerns such as the Post Office, Gas and Electricity Boards, etc., and operating as production units for these particular fields of activity.

MARKETING PUBLIC RESEARCH

Another fruitful if small area of public ownership is the manufacturing of the marketable research coming from the Department of Scientific and Industrial Research. If public money produces the ideas, there is no reason why publicly owned enterprises should not be set up to manufacture and market the results.

DEPENDENCE ON GOVERNMENT CONTRACTS AND PUBLIC SERVICES

In applying the criteria for public ownership, attention must also centre upon those industries which rely mainly on Government contracts for their existence. This particularly refers to the defence industries and also other industries which are almost wholly involved in supplying the nationalised industries. The outstanding example of an industry which leans heavily on the State for its livelihood is the pharmaceutical industry. The cost of drugs within the National Health Service now makes some action here imperative. Various reports have indicated the wide disparity between the price of 'made up' drugs and the proprietary brands. It is really indefensible that this part of the nation's health bill should not be under public control. On the grounds of cost control alone, selected parts of the pharmaceutical industry should be brought into public ownership.

But that is not the only reason. The research and laboratory techniques and facilities which could be developed within a public pharmaceutical industry, directed towards the common good and putting the nation's health instead of profit as first priority, would be a powerful agent in our fight against the killer diseases of the 1970s.

A STAKE IN THE ENTERPRISE

In line with our belief that there should be no public money given to companies without an equal ratio of public accountability, it must follow that in all cases where aid is granted the State should acquire an appropriate equity shareholding in the company concerned. This is particularly necessary in the operation of loans and aid within the terms of the 'late' Industrial Expansion Act, and this provision was, in fact, one of the alternatives on 'restitution' in this Act when loans were granted.

PUBLIC HOLDING COMPANY

One other important development in extending public ownership which is long overdue in Britain, is the setting up of a State holding company on the lines of the IRI in Italy. The purpose of such a company would be to collect together all the State holdings in its portfolio and manage these in the public interest. We already have enough of such holdings in this country at present to justify such a holding company, and with the additional interests likely to accrue from the policies outlined in this chapter, such a company would be a valuable addition to our 'public ownership' arsenal as well as a step towards socialising the capital market.

THE BEHAVIOUR CRITERION FOR MONOPOLIES

Finally, in our list of criteria come the 'monopolies'. Those which should be publicly owned are not so easy to define. They certainly cannot be selected on size alone because on this basis many of the State owned firms are already monopolies. They have, for instance, a monopoly control of the market and the exclusive production of the article or service concerned. Coal, Gas, Steel, the Railways are all examples of State monopolies.

The yardstick for taking a monopoly into public ownership must be concerned rather with how it behaves in the economy. If a monopoly is exploiting the consumer, or the society in which it operates, then for the sake of control it should come into public hands. Such a criterion would indeed be a deterrent to monopolies which ignored the public interest or sought to influence unduly the political direction of our society, or which in any way misused the economic power which they undoubtedly possess.

One of the monopolies which comes into the reckoning for public enterprise is insurance, where collapses in recent years such as that of the Vehicle and General Insurance Company certainly have highlighted the strong case for a State guaranteed insurance company in the field of motor vehicle and general insurance. The law in this sector, unlike the voluntary aspects of insurance, decrees that a person driving a vehicle must be insured. It is therefore eminently arguable that the State should provide this service and give the insurer a choice of public or private insurance. Such a choice would be in keeping with the obligation of the insurer to the community at risk from his vehicle, and also fair to the individual, by providing him with a 'non-collapsible' policy.

A PROGRAMME FOR LABOUR

These would be the criteria upon which I would build a programme of public ownership in Britain. Each single criterion can be argued without use of dogma, as being for the good of the community. The combination of nationalisation, selective public ownership, competitive public ownership and a Government stake in firms with public investment, is a varied array of forms of ownership which are diversified enough to avoid the pitfalls of State monopoly.

This delineation of criteria also shows that, having rejected

Marx's conclusions, there is no need to turn our back on public ownership as one of the necessary means of controlling a socialist economy. I say 'one of the necessary means' because there is a lethargy in socialist thinking which tends to believe that when you have said 'nationalisation' you have spoken in one word the creed of socialism. 'Nationalisation' is often for socialists a convenient by-pass around some problems that do require new thinking, because they are new problems!

THE CONTROLS OF INTERVENTION

For this reason I would like to end this chapter by returning to the central issue of control. We have so far dealt with two forms of control, industrial democracy and public ownership, but there are others.

The other controls should be directed towards making all companies, public and private, more accountable to society in general. Companies must be made to tell more of what they are doing. They must be made to justify their pricing policies, future investment and their forward decisions on manpower and production. We must open up this dark sector of our economic life because planning is difficult without this information, and also because the lives and future of many people depend on these decisions and they have a right to know what is afoot. On the basis of this knowledge it then becomes possible for measures to be taken to complement, or if necessary to permit intervention in these decisions if it is considered to be publicly desirable.

Some of these controls are already with us. Tax allowances and investment Grants already partially direct investment policy. Industrial Development Certificates (an effective intervention), Regional Employment Premiums, and Special Investment Grants partially determine the location of industry. Guaranteed orders where appropriate in shipbuilding and aircraft can control the future of these industries, and a whole host of measures (including the planning machinery, nationally and regionally, industrial training levies and policies, Corporation Tax, SET) are all measures which can be extended and refined and are even today having more effect on the direction of private and public industries than ever before in our economic history.

These last controls are perhaps the most lasting economic contribution made by the 1964–70 Labour Government. These measures are the most 'interventionist' which we have seen, operating from outside industry itself.

CONTROL – EQUALITY AND REDISTRIBUTION

In this chapter a programme of ownership and control has been outlined. It is far from exhaustive and many important issues have not been examined. Apart from the industrial democracy proposals the argument about equality and redistribution has not been seriously raised, yet both of these are bound up with a control of the economy which will lead to a greater economic independence of the individual. A greater degree of public accountability inside industry through industrial democracy, through public ownership, and through interventionist controls working from outside industry, will mean inevitably a reduction in the disparities of income and opportunity, and a faster progress towards the elimination of poverty in our society. By controlling the commanding heights of the economy we will have increased the sum of human happiness in Britain.

Chapter 14

Industrial Relations

(a) A Look Back at Labour Legislation
(b) A 'Labour' Industrial Relations Policy

'In making labour a part of everyone's life and the whole of
nobody's life, lies the ultimate solution of industrial
difficulties.'

H. G. Wells

Controlling the direction of the economy either through public
ownership or through other controls does not automatically
ensure that production will flourish and that harmony will
prevail in society. A happy, efficient society depends mainly on
its framework of law, its judiciary system guaranteeing fair play,
and also upon the development of the working environment of
the individual in such a way as to ensure that the antagonisms
which do inevitably arise in industry, where there is a conflict of
interests, do not degenerate into a bitterness and discontent
which seeps through into the social life of society.

A LOOK BACK AT INDUSTRIAL LEGISLATION

Most of the black periods of our history have stemmed from
industrial discontent, either collectively as in the 1926 General
Strike, or from isolated incidents such as the Taff Vale and
Osborne cases. Because the way industry behaves can cause
governments to shake and sometimes fall, all governments in all

countries have sought at some time in their history to contain industrial strife by legal means.

TAFF VALE, OSBORNE, SOUTH WALES AND CLYDESIDE

This happened in Britain with the Taff Vale case in 1900, and as already mentioned, the effect of the legal judgement against the Railwaymen was to almost double trade union membership in a single year. Hardly the result which was expected! This judgement, although stopping strikes for a year or two, also diverted the trade unions more into political action to seek a remedy.

The Osborne judgement in 1909 mobilised the trade unions into political action to find a legal answer to financing MPs, which eventually resulted in the reversal of the judgement by Act of Parliament and the introduction of the new Trade Disputes Act (1913).

Even in times of war legal sanctions in industrial relations have met with resistance and have been discredited. In 1915 in South Wales 200,000 miners stopped work only thirteen days after the Munitions of War Act had made strikes illegal, and the Government, influenced by Arthur Henderson, negotiated a settlement rather than invoke the new powers in the Act.

Within weeks of the South Wales dispute another broke out on the Clyde which, after fines had been levied on the strike leaders, eventually blew up into a major political storm. This dispute was partially settled only by resort to the 'Defence of the Realm' regulations which resulted in the removal of six of the Clyde Workers' Committee to other parts of the country. This action by the Government was resented angrily by militant workers in other parts of the country, especially around Manchester, and this feeling lent impetus to the formation of the shop stewards' movement.

The ultimate result of these three sets of legal intervention, Taff Vale, Osborne and the South Wales and Clyde 1915 disputes, was to strengthen trade union membership, to invigorate trade union political action, and lastly to lay the foundations of the shop stewards' movement. None of these results was desired by those invoking the law, but they happened despite, or even because of this. The history of our Labour movement is peppered with instances of legal repression producing exactly the opposite effect from that desired by the establishment.

TRADES DISPUTES AND TRADE UNION ACT – 1927

Another historical analogy is the 1927 Trades Disputes Act which followed the collapse of the General Strike and the miners' lock-out in 1926.

The 1927 Act set out to limit the right to strike by making illegal any stoppage of work which had any object other than the furtherance of a trade dispute. This was aimed at illegalising the 'sympathy' strike. The 1927 Act also illegalised any strike which was aimed at coercing a government or causing hardship to the community, and made it an offence to finance such a strike.

But the most controversial change in the law by the new Act of 1927 was the substitution of 'contracting in' in place of the 'contracting out' provisions in the political funds of unions. Under the 1913 Act members who did not 'contract out' of paying the political levy had been automatically political paying members. The 1927 Act completely reversed this procedure and because of this change, the affiliated membership of the Labour Party fell by over a million in 1928. This section of the 1927 Act picked out the trade unions for special treatment and of all the organisations in the country the trade unions were the only ones subjected to the humiliating restrictions that 'contracting in' imposed.

Once again the invoking of legal strictures against the unions led to action being intensified in other ways. The political and industrial restrictions in the 1927 Act led to trade unions taking an increasing interest in the running of the industries with which they were concerned. Workers began to aim at a share in the control of their firms and this started the Mond-Turner conferences which were the forerunner of the 'industrial democracy' movement.

As well as boring a way into managerial functions, the trade unions in 1927 were also united by the repressive 1927 Trade Disputes Act in a way that would have seemed impossible a year previously. The collapse of the General Strike had left the unions disillusioned and weak, but the need for united action against the 1927 Act welded the workers together in a very short period of time. The new Act, imposed by a hostile and arrogant Government at a time when the unions were 'down', was seen by the workers as a signal that the Government intended to cripple them both industrially and politically while it had the chance.

But the unions again showed their resilience. The 1927 May Day Manifesto set out their opposition to the new legal measures in a manner which is curiously apposite to the 1971 Industrial Relations Act. The campaign in 1927 against the Act was as vigorous as the TUC's campaign in 1971. The arguments by the unions were similar, as will be seen from the following text of the Manifesto:

The 1927 May Day Manifesto

Long established rights and legal powers, won by the Trade Unions by years of struggle and sacrifice, are imperilled by the Government's Trades Disputes and Trade Union Bill. A dangerous attack has been launched upon the workers' organisations by the powerful employers' associations and reactionary class influences which control the Tory Government.

Their aim is to deprive the workers, by Act of Parliament, of their strongest weapons of defence against exploitation and oppression. The Trade Unions are to be fettered by legal restrictions upon the right to strike, the right to picket, the right to use union funds for union purposes, the right of trade unionists to associate with one another and to act together in pursuit of a common policy by lawful means.

The blow is aimed at the fundamental principle of Trade Unionism – the principle of combination by the workers who share a common experience of toil and hardship, exposed to the risks of unemployment, of wage cuts, of unjust and oppressive conditions of labour, no matter in what industry or trade they are employed.

Those who have grown wealthy and powerful by exploitation of the producers, hate and fear the unity and discipline of the Trade Union Movement. They know that the strength of the organised workers is their solidarity, their loyalty and devotion to the organisations they have created. They seek to destroy these organisations, not by frontal attacks which the mass of wage earners can understand and repel, but by mean and malicious attempts to undermine the spirit that has united the workers.

The Government's Bill offers incitement and encouragement to trade unionists to betray their fellow members and to bring divisions and dissensions into the Unions.

It exposes to the peril of criminal prosecution, to fine or imprisonment, those who take part in any strike or stoppage of work which can be declared illegal within the meaning of the Bill.

It places in the hands of the police, of magistrates, of judges, the power of deciding whether workmen who cease work in protest against injustice or unfair treatment from employers are to be punished. It disables the Trade Unions from using their funds or their power of effective action to defend their own members when such legal decisions are given.

Remember the Taff Vale case!

Remember the Osborne judgement!

Remember the pronouncement of Mr Justice Astbury!

In countless instances it has been proved that the law can be trusted to penalise the workers and to paralyse the action of their organisations when industrial disputes arise. This Bill increases these legal dangers for the Trade Unions a thousandfold.

The Bill denies to workers in the Civil Service freedom of association with their fellow workers outside the service. The Civil Service Unions are not to have the assistance of other unions in their efforts to improve conditions of employment under the Crown, and are not to be allowed to assist their fellow trade unionists outside the service, although the conditions in other employment are used as an argument against Civil Service workers.

The Bill strikes a heavy blow at the political rights of the Trade Unions. It is intended to injure and impoverish the Labour Party by making it difficult for the Unions to collect political subscriptions from their members. It does more. It strikes at the whole of the political activities of the Trade Unions.

To disable the Labour Party the rich men who have dictated the terms of the Bill are attempting to prevent the Unions from collecting the political contributions their members have, by ballot, decided to make for the lawful political objects the Unions are entitled by Act of Parliament to pursue.

The Party of the rich is trying to cripple the Party of the poor. A rich Party financed by secret funds derived from the sale of honours and from large subsidies subscribed by wealthy men, is trying to disable a poor Party which carries on its work by modest contributions from Trade Unionists.

The Trade Unions make no concealment of their political funds.

The Labour Party collects its funds in the light of day. The Parties opposed to the Trade Unions and the Labour Party are financed from secret sources they dare not reveal. They have millions at their disposal.

Are the adversaries of Labour to have the right of obstructing the collection of political funds by the working people, to interfere with the arrangements of the Unions for gathering the pennies of their members in order to maintain the Labour Party while the rich men may make large secret contributions to the organisations engaged in fighting the Labour Party and to dis- able the Trade Unions?

Workers! Your enemies use every unfair weapon against you. Meet their unscrupulous, mean and malignant attack by resolute and united opposition! Rally round your leaders! Your loyalty to your Party is the Party's guarantee of defeat for your enemies and triumph for your cause.

The 1927 May Day Manifesto may be a trifle declamatory by modern comparison, but it sets out a powerful argument against the legislation then, and much of it is equally applicable to the 1971 Act.

The 1927 Trades Disputes Act was ultimately repealed by the 1945 Labour Government and this put the legal position back to the Trade Union Act of 1913. The 1964 Labour Government enacted a small Trades Disputes Act in August 1965 which gave workpeople and their representatives protection against suit for intimidation which they thought to be necessary if negotiations in industry were to proceed freely.

The 1971 Act, however, brought back many of the attitudes, if not the exact words, of the 1927 Act, and put the unions back to the Taff Vale legal position as far as liability on their funds is concerned. This is particularly so for those unions who have decided not to register under the new Act.

THE DIFFICULTIES OF ENFORCING THE LAW

This brief historical rundown of the attempts at legislating to contain industrial disputes certainly confirms the arguments of the unions that legislation of the kind introduced by the 1971 Industrial Relations Act is likely to be counter-productive. Each time in the past that industrial relations legislation has been intro- duced there has been industrial unrest, and situations have arisen which have plunged the law itself into disrepute.

One of the main problems confronting legislators is that if the law on disputes is broken it is likely to be broken *en masse* by the workers concerned, and this means that if the law is to be enforced some punishment must be invoked either against those who have broken the law or against those who have led the illegal action. Ultimately, despite the gamut of provisions laid down in the 1971 Act, this can mean a defiance of the law either by the impossibility of disciplining large numbers of workers who are in conflict with its provisions, or by action by large numbers of workers in support of those who have been disciplined because of illegal industrial acts, as the case of the dockers' solidarity action on behalf of their jailed stewards clearly demonstrated in the climb-down of officialdom in mid-1972.

THE STORY OF 'BETTESHANGER'

Either way the law has difficulty in operating. Also of historical importance in this connection was the Betteshanger Colliery dispute in Kent, which led to a mass prosecution of a thousand workers in 1941. These prosecutions were undertaken in line with the National Arbitration Order – a wartime measure which made strikes illegal if an award was made under the Act. The evidence given by Sir Harold Emmerson, GCB, KCVO (Permanent Secretary to the Ministry of Labour in 1941) to the Commission on this case is really like an extract from a 'Ruritanian' industrial dispute.

All the thousand workers had to plead guilty or else they would have had to be tried separately. The union co-operated in the pleas of guilty and accepted on behalf of the thousand workers that the decision on a few test cases should cover the lot.

Emmerson's evidence states that the Court proceedings went smoothly, with a carnival atmosphere permeating the proceedings. Bands played the processions to court and women and children cheered them on their way.

The three union officials involved were sent to jail, one for two months and the other for one month, the three sentences including hard labour. Thirty-five were fined £3, or one month's imprisonment, and the remaining 962 were fined £1, or fourteen days in jail.

The strike, however, continued. The only men who could call it off were in jail! The Secretary for Mines, along with the President of the Miners' union, Ebby Edwards, went to see the men in jail and five days later an agreement was signed in the prison between the colliery management and the Kent Miners' union.

Although the settlement gave the workers almost what they wanted, and in fact reversed the NAT Award, the workers would not resume work until the officials were released. The Secretary for the Mines led a deputation to the Home Secretary for the immediate release of the officials.

After eleven days in jail the officials were released. The Ministry of Labour, according to Sir Harold Emmerson, was filled with gloom and apprehension. They had been able to prosecute only because the 'criminals' had co-operated, but only nine men had paid the fines! The Clerk of the Justices was preparing almost a thousand commitment warrants to put those in jail who had not paid, which incidentally would have stopped the pit for another month, and because of lack of accommodation in the local jail would have either meant transporting the miners to other jails to do their stint, or putting them away a few at a time on a rota system!

The colliery management offered to pay the fines for the workers. The Ministry said no – on no account were they to do this. The Court eventually were told not to enforce the fines.

The Betteshanger story could have been written by Lewis Carroll. Only the Mad Hatter was absent, or was he? Here the actual enforcement of the law in an industrial dispute ended with the workers gaining their point and the law again in disrepute.

LEARNING FROM THE PAST

The experience of the past therefore tells us that legislation is not the answer to industrial dispute and is indeed counter-productive. The effect of legislation in industrial affairs has consistently produced a reaction and a result opposite to that intended by the legislators. It could therefore be argued that if this has been past experience then the unions should be supporting legislation as a means of increasing solidarity and opposition to the present Industrial Relations Act.

This may well be a course of action which historians could advocate, but in all the cases mentioned in this summary of the inefficacy of industrial legislation, workers have suffered in the *short term*. The Taff Vale judgement did set the movement back for a time, the Osborne verdict did affect the finances of the Labour Party for a while, the Betteshanger affair also caused worry and some hardship to those involved.

In the long term all were counter-productive, but a trade unionist or a politician lives in the short term, and while it is correct to argue that industrial legislation has been counter-productive in the past, it does not follow that we can afford to ignore the hardship and setbacks which previous legislation has caused on individual workers or the movement.

Unions have been and are opposed to the legislation of the Tory Industrial Relations Act of 1971 because of the short-term effects on union members. There is little doubt that the new Act will run into trouble in its enforcement provisions for unfair industrial practices, for precisely the same reasons as have been mentioned in this chapter. The unions believe that eventually it will be shown to be ill conceived and will once again produce the opposite results to those desired by the Government. But in the short term it could lead to industrial chaos which would for a time lower the living standards of workers. The unions' opposition to the new legislation therefore has been entirely logical, and the argument concerning past unsuccessful legislation is also correct because it is directed to those who believe that the new Act is a lasting answer to our industrial relations problems.

Thinking people are bound to ask, sometime in the future, why the Act was pressed through Parliament in the face of the opposition of the unions, whose co-operation is necessary for the success of any industrial relations policy. The Tory Government will be hard put to find an answer which makes sense, other than once again to blame the unions for not co-operating with legislation which they dislike, because it is directed against their basic interests and that of the work force as a whole.

It is not the intention here to dissect the 1971 Act in detail. The unions' case against the main provisions of the Act has been stated in detail in many publications, including the TUC's own pamphlet 'Reason'. The unions have remained united in their opposition to the Act and opposed to the philosophy and the analysis on which the Act is based. They all believe that the Government has asked the wrong questions about industrial relations, and has therefore come up with answers which are industrially harmful, irrelevant and unworkable.

Unions may be divided about the tactics they employ in opposing the effects of the Act, but this disunity should give no solace to those who want to 'cut the unions down to size'. No responsible trade union leader has been simply 'bloody-minded' in his opposition to the Act. Deep down his day-to-day industrial experience has told him from the start that this Act would embitter industrial relations, and in modern industry where production levels depend on mutual agreement between employers and workpeople could only cause a deterioration in our industrial performance and a weakening of our economic strength.

No trade union leader contemplates the effect of necessary action on members and the community without concern, but the industrial die has been cast and unions have responded accordingly. The only bright spot in the whole murky mess has been that many employers have agreed with the trade union diagnosis of the Act and have regularly signed local and domestic agreements which, in fact, 'contract them out' of the main provisions of the legislation. The large scale introduction of these 'Tina Lea'* clauses with the agreement of management, once again bring the law into disrepute. Common sense has superseded the legal measures of the Act.

Those who believed that the Act would pull their industrial chestnuts from the fire are heading for a political as well as an industrial roasting, for the Act is now shown to be industrially chaotic and ineffective. The public is bound to ask why these effects of the Act were not foreseen, and those who instigated it will be in bad public odour.

Opposing the 1971 Industrial Relations Act, criticising the legal interventions in 1900, 1906, 1909, 1915, 1927, and illustrating the ineffectiveness of the enforcement of the law in such industrial disputes as 'Betteshanger' in 1941, does not mean we believe that industrial relations should be left exactly as they are. There can be improvements and there should be a policy for creating a more balanced state of industrial affairs. The mainspring of this policy must, however, be the voluntary acceptance of changes by both sides of industry.

Legislation has a part to play, but not in the restrictive role which has been designed for it so far, in all the attempts at industrial reform in the last seventy years.

The Labour movement has the expertise and experience to put forward a policy which makes sense and which stands a good chance of being acceptable. The remainder of this chapter is devoted to outlining what this policy might be.

* *Tina Lea: This is not a legally enforceable agreement!*

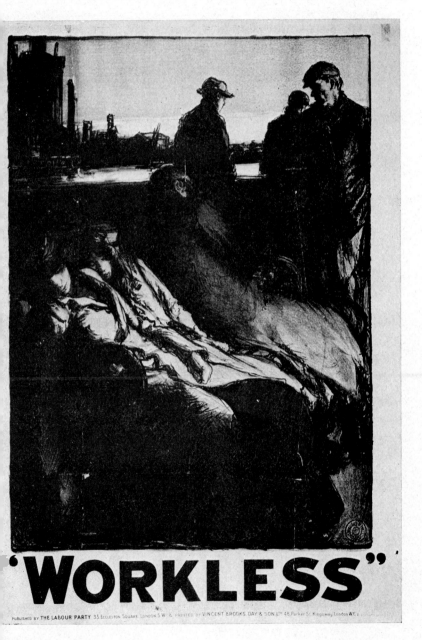

"WORKLESS"

PUBLISHED BY THE LABOUR PARTY 33 Eccleston Square London S.W. & Printed by VINCENT BROOKS DAY & SON L?° 48 Parker St. Kingsway London W.C.

ATE V

"FORWARD! THE DAY IS BREAKING!"

Published by The Labour Party, 33, Eccleston Square, London, S.W.; and printed by Vincent Brooks, Day & Son, Ltd. 48 Parker St, Kingsway, London W.C.

A 'LABOUR' INDUSTRIAL RELATIONS POLICY

Constructing an alternative industrial relations policy means asking the right questions about modern industry and then finding the right answers.

A reasonable starting point for such an analysis is to relate one's own industrial experience to some of the studies and surveys which have been conducted into industrial relations and then to decide which of these has come to grips with the problems as they really are either in whole or in part.

Having been involved at shop level as a shop steward and a branch official for ten years, and as a National Official and General Secretary for seventeen years, I have no doubt in my own mind that the 'Donovan Commission' (the Royal Commission on Trade Unions and Employers' Associations, 1965–8) is the report which deals with things as they are and does not assume a kind of industrial backcloth which is never in fact there. There are gaps in the Donovan Report, but the factual material and most of the conclusions reached are nearer to the truth than in any other report.

One of the main criticisms of the 1971 Industrial Relations Act must be that it is founded on the Conservative policy statement, *A Fair Deal at Work*, and little or none of the Donovan thinking found its way into the 1971 Act. A team of experts who sifted evidence and exchanged experiences for three years were entitled to have some consideration taken of their conclusions—but the Tory mind had 'gelled'. The fixative had been the political milage they hoped to get from an Act that dealt with an industrial situation which only existed in Central Office handouts and Conservative weekend speeches.

Ask any objective person in the field of management, unions, press or industrial relations, about the validity of Donovan and they will all say that Donovan asked the right questions and got most of the right answers.

With the guidance from Donovan on what the industrial problems really are, and what solutions are likely to be successful, we can now proceed to fashion an industrial relations policy for the 1970s which makes sense, which will work and which will benefit those in industry and the nation as a whole.

L

THE ROLE OF LEGISLATION

Does accepting that an industrial relations policy must be voluntary mean that legislation has no part to play in it? No – there is a place for legislation, but not in the robes of a legal framework as in the 1971 Act.

The Tories see voluntary collective bargaining working within a legal framework as being the answer to a more ordered situation. The trouble here is that voluntary bargaining cannot be contained within a legal framework! The mutuality that must exist cannot thrive inside legal restrictions. Voluntary bargaining must be *free* to be workable – it leads sometimes to disputes, and these disputes are a logical end to some rounds of bargaining. To say that voluntary and free bargaining will apply until the 'crunch', at which point those involved in making the claim (which is usually the workpeople) will have to take a parliamentary-defined path to remain within the law, is in fact to have the law intervening in the bargaining process itself.

There is a role for legislation, but it is not as an electrified fence to be erected around an industrial compound. To be successful, legislation must be confined to that aspect of industrial relations which needs definition and, indeed, which is capable of definition.

GUARANTEEING BASIC INDUSTRIAL RIGHTS

There is such a sector within industry today and in which legislation already plays a minor part. I refer to safety regulations, contracts of employment, redundancy payments, etc. Here legislation defining minimum conditions of behaviour has been successful, and this role could be extended to include other matters.

I would define this role for legislation as 'guaranteeing basic industrial rights', with the law operating to define the minimum conditions of employment and also making participation in decision-making in industry free from legal obstacles.

Legislation should be extended to make a wider 'contract of employment' for each individual worker. The new contract would include some of the existing requirements and some new minima as follows:

(*a*) Details of Job: Job description
                                             Minimum rate

	Bonus or PBR calculations
	Overtime and shift premiums
(b) Conditions of Employment:	Hours of work Termination of employment Redundancy procedures Redundancy payments Dismissals procedure (other than redundancy)
(c) Grievance Procedure:	Domestic procedure Outside procedure
(d) Health and Safety Regulations:	Relevant regulations to department or industry

Legislation should be enacted requiring all the above information to be given to the worker at an induction session prior to starting in a new job. Such legislation would lay down minimum conditions on all of the definable conditions of employment, such as termination of employment, redundancy payments, holidays, whilst on other points the legislation could contain examples of 'model clauses' which should be followed.

The model clause is particularly important in 'Redundancy procedures' and here, as well as laying down the general principles to be followed in redundancies, the displacement caused by mergers and rationalisation should receive special attention. Such redundancies should warrant protection and payment going far beyond the present minima in the Act and should be graded according to age and service.

Dismissals procedure is another aspect of industrial relations which is best dealt with by the 'model clause' approach'. In many large firms today the dismissals procedure for unsuitability has provisions for two verbal warnings in the presence of the shop steward followed by one written warning before action is taken by the management. An appeals procedure is built-in at all three warning stages and a blot-free record for a certain period removes any previous warnings.

Industrial misconduct is an inflammable cause of dispute and is also dealt with on a similar basis, so that the quick flare-up of supervision and worker is the start and not the end of the enquiry into the circumstances of the dismissal.

Under such circumstances workers know 'where they stand' on these issues, which do inject an element of fairness and reasoned judgement into these troubled situations involving redundancy and dismissal, and lower the industrial temperature.

HEALTH AND SAFETY

Considering the number of working days lost through sickness and accident it is surprising that the economic effects of this have not received more attention from successive Governments. Legislation requiring a decent standard of medical facilities to be available in all medium and large factories is long overdue. Small factories should also be legally required to link up in group schemes to provide treatment facilities. The facilities required are not just a First Aid box but an adequately equipped medical room with a full-time, trained person in charge.

These requirements would benefit employers and work people alike, for the firms which have installed such services have all reported substantial cuts in lost working time due to the treatment of minor injuries alone. Legislation on this would therefore be both humane and economic.

Conditions and health hazards in factories need the constant supervision of an effective joint management–worker safety organisation. Legislation should require Safety Committees to be compulsory and the size and composition should be stipulated for the differing sizes of factories. Workers' safety delegates should have the right to visit the scenes of accidents and to ask questions. On Factory Inspectors' visits the safety delegate should accompany him and should have access to reports.

Let us tackle the real problems of suffering and days lost in this sensible way. A crusade on healthier and safer factories is a more noble approach to better industrial relations than a crude list of unfair practices and penalties!

DISCLOSURE OF INFORMATION AND INDUSTRIAL DEMOCRACY

The third logical field for legislation in guaranteeing basic industrial rights, is directed towards extending industrial democracy. The reasons for this have been developed in an earlier chapter, but the legislation would be needed to bulldoze through company law to remove legal obstacles to the workers' being given the necessary information to conduct intelligent collective bargaining and a real say in decision making.

The Government should set the lead in extending industrial democracy by introducing 'industrial democracy projects' in publicly owned industries and in Government factories.

INDUSTRIAL REPRESENTATION ACT?

The minimum requirements for democratic participation in making decisions in industry could be set out in an Industrial Representation Act which could define the basic essentials upon which industrial democracy could be founded. This Act could be reasonably based on the main points already outlined earlier, such as:

single channel bargaining;
disclosure of company information;
areas covered by joint decision-making;
workers' representation – trade union based;
operation at shop and factory level.

These three fields of basic industrial rights – minimum employment conditions, health and safety, and industrial democracy – could be adequately defined and efficiently guaranteed by legislation. Such action would provide a solid and balanced foundation on which the remainder of an industrial relations policy could be erected.

Let us now start to build up from the shop floor the kind of policy which will improve relations in British industry.

FACILITIES FOR SHOP STEWARDS

The conditions under which a shop steward does his job of representing union members cannot be divorced from any study of industrial relations. Over many years the functions of the shop steward have grown and he has changed from being a collector of 'cons' to his present status of a workshop negotiator. He used to be a 'messenger', carrying grievances from shop floor to branch or district committee, but now industrial situations demand speedier answers and in most cases he has now been given the power by his union to settle disputes as they arise.

Although management often regards the shop steward as its own personal *bête noire*, it also realises that he is more likely to understand complex bargaining which is closely related to his hob than the full-time official from outside. In most unions the growth of the power of shop stewards has meant a corresponding decline in the next nearest unit of union organisation to the shop floor. In the majority of manual unions this was the branch committee or its equivalent, and the trend in most unions is to reorientate the negotiations previously done by the branch around the stewards and their committees.

Work groups today are also more dependent on one another than at any time in the past, and this fact has led to shop stewards getting together on joint committees to discuss common problems, exchange information and take united action. The shop stewards' movement which started on Clydeside in 1915 has now, by dint of the growth of collective bargaining and modern technology, almost achieved respectability. I say 'almost' because although almost all firms recognise shop stewards as individual negotiators and union representatives, many employers still do not recognise or negotiate with shop stewards' joint committees. These attitudes are changing however, and future industrial circumstances will force employers to recognise these committees, since union local organisation will be grouped officially around this unit of representation.

Some employers of course still regard shop stewards as a kind of necessary evil. They recognise them for negotiating purposes but make it as awkward as they can for the shop steward to do his job. This is an extremely short-sighted attitude, for shop stewards, harassed by lack of facilities and time and under financial pressure, are less likely to be objective about departmental problems.

If the shop steward has power and is important, the management would do well to give him the status that his position deserves. Far better to make it relatively easy for him to do his job and then be straight with him in negotiation, than impede him by denying him the essentials for his job and then have to wheedle him in other ways to keep production going. As a shop steward for about ten years in a shop of 300 members, working straight piecework and receiving very little aid from the management, I can speak with feeling about the importance of having some elementary provisions made by employers, so that I could have done the job more efficiently and at less cost to myself and family.

In the spectrum of industrial relations I place the provision of decent facilities for shop stewards very high in the order of importance. By itself it will not revolutionise industrial relations overnight, but it is an essential part of any comprehensive policy. The best firms are already making these provisions. The task is to make the 'present best' the future 'norm' in British industry.

Where do we start? We start by analysing the work of the shop steward and find it falls into three categories:

he is a workman within the factory;
he deals with the grievances of his members;
he does work on behalf of his union.

What kind of facilities and provisions does he need to fulfil his three separate functions?

1. Facilities as a Workman
The steward depends on his job for his living, and in modern industry this normally means that his living standards are based to some extent on piecework. His absence from his job on shop steward's work therefore frequently involves him in loss of earnings. Sometimes this is made good by his workmates, but he should not need to rely on a 'whip-round' for his weekly wage. The shop steward is used by the management as well as by the workers, so the management should allow him not only leave of absence from his job, but also payment for the time spent on negotiations at average earnings.

As a workman too he frequently places his job in jeopardy because his job as a shop steward propels him into arguments with the management, and this in times of stress leaves him vulnerable to dismissal.

Many firms are prepared at least to guarantee no discrimination in their treatment of stewards, but this works better in practice if the procedure for leaving the job to go on union work is clarified in an agreement and carried out formally by the shop steward and the supervisor in question whose permission must be sought.

These three provisions –

leave of absence from job under an agreed procedure;
payment of average earnings for time spent on industrial negotiations; and
some protection against discrimination –

are all essentials of the steward's function as an ordinary workman in the shop.

2. Dealing with Members' Grievances

The second function of a shop steward is what could be called the industrial relations side of his job, which involves taking up grievances of individual members, dealing with wages and conditions claims for groups of workers or for the whole department he represents, and honouring whatever membership he may have on joint stewards' committees in the larger factory or plant. Shop stewards are also frequently involved on other works or factory committees, including joint consultation and health and safety committees. Last, but most important, he is the 'link' man between the workpeople and the management and has to relay information on the results of negotiations both ways.

To carry out the 'industrial relations side' of his functions the shop steward must have the authority of his position recognised by management and requires some credentials from the union. This credential is not just the 'trappings' of office. Stewards change frequently and the possession of credentials indicates to both management and work people that he is the accredited person.

Defined areas of representation upon which his electorate is also based enables both steward and management to know the jurisdiction of his activities, and elections should be conducted properly with a secret ballot if required by the members.

'Representing the members' means for a steward having access to them and being able to speak to individuals or groups of workers as required. An agreed code of conduct should be worked out with the management whereby the steward can contact individuals during working hours in relation to complaints and arrangements should also be made for such meetings (e.g. meeting rooms, or specially provided places where groups of workers can meet with the steward at lunch breaks or after work).

Negotiations and communications require the use of typing facilities and duplicating services. We are not advocating that the management should provide secretaries for shop stewards, but management assistance in typing and duplicating shop stewards' notices and reports is vital.

Larger firms should provide office accommodation for shop stewards with filing cabinet, table and chairs and the use of a telephone, though not necessarily in the office. Notice boards should be specially provided at mutually agreed places for the display of shop, plant and union information.

Finally, on the negotiating side of the shop steward's duties, there is the need for training, and here the shop steward should be encouraged and paid by the management to attend union/management approved training courses.

These provisions –

proper credentials;
fairly conducted elections;
defined area of representation;
ability to contact workers;
Office accommodation, equipment, typing and duplicating services and the use of telephones;
special union notice boards; and
time off for training with pay –

are all vital facilities if the shop steward is to be an efficient negotiator and a competent information link between management and workpeople.

3. The Shop Steward's Work on Behalf of the Union

There is, of course, a connecting link between the industrial relations side of the steward's job and the duties he carries out for the union. His main duties in this field are collecting contributions and recruiting new members as they take up employment in his area.

Contributions are paid in three main ways:

(*a*) by collection in the shop;
(*b*) by deduction from wages by management;
(*c*) at branch meetings.

The shop steward is not concerned with instances where individuals 'pay in' at branch meetings, but he is involved with the other two methods.

Where contributions are collected in the shop the shop steward should be allowed to collect these in working time and should be paid by the management for any time lost.

More and more firms are today agreeing to a payroll deduction (called the 'check-off') of trade union contributions from wages. Some stewards object to this, wrongly I believe. I know that there is a suspicion among stewards that the 'check-off' system may be used in times of dispute as a weapon by the management, but if this took place the stewards should immediately cease the practice and go back to collection.

The check-off system, although breaking some contact of the steward with the member, does give the steward more time to attend to his members' grievances and relieves him of tedious recording and 'paying in' to the branch. It keeps down arrears and saves trouble arising from action being taken on those who make a habit of being behind with their contributions. Provided each individual signs his willingness to have his contributions deducted in this way and the stewards make it clear that they will not be deflected by threats to withdraw the facility, then the check-off is beneficial both from the aspects of time saving and contribution income.

More unions are now encouraging stewards to adopt the check-off, and more firms should agree to its operation.

RECRUITMENT

A careful eye on recruitment saves trouble both for management and the shop steward. New entrants to an organised shop should be directed to the shop steward and periodically, say every two weeks, the management should supply the steward with a list of the new entrants who have started work in his area. The steward should be allowed to talk to them, preferably in the induction stage of their employment.

These facilities by the management –

(a) provision for stewards to collect dues in working hours; or alternatively

(b) the operation of the 'check-off' system; and

(c) shop stewards' access to new entrants for trade union membership purposes –

are the modern recognition of the unions' constructive role in industry and facilitate the work of the shop steward on behalf of the union.

All these services are necessary. Some firms have all of them and many have some. Some, alas, have none at all.

The excellent Report Cmnd 4668, by the CIR (1971), shows that the provision of modern facilities for shop stewards is a 'must' in

important and varied sections of industry. Progressive managements are happy to provide these in the interests of efficient and
good industrial relations. When these facilities are agreed they
should be treated as a right and not as a charitable act and should
be incorporated in a special agreement between the management
and the union. This removes the temptation to discontinue them
when the 'going gets rough', as it does occasionally.

I have spent some time over basic terms in outlining these
aspects of an industrial relations policy. Both the guaranteeing
of basic industrial rights by legislation and the provision of
facilities for the shop steward are certainly tackling the problems
at shop floor level. This is an absolutely vital approach to industrial relations. Bad relations start not in the union Executive
boardroom, but on the shop floor.

Too many experts in looking at industrial relations have seen
disputes deadlocked at national level and have therefore started
searching for some national level solution. Disputes are like the
waves dashing on the Cornwall beaches. They start many miles
away from where they eventually finish and like waves, they start
with a ripple, which could have been calmed in this case by the
right atmosphere and conditions on the shop floor. With the base
of our industrial relations pyramid on sound foundations we can
start to build the other necessaries for a comprehensive industrial
relations system.

BALANCED PROCEDURE AGREEMENTS

Bargaining at shop floor level is usually within the framework of a
procedure agreement with various steps and stages by which
grievances, if not settled initially, are progressed through the line
management of the firm and eventually outside the works to local
or district conferences then, if still not settled, ultimately arrive at
national level.

Most industries have procedure agreements which have been
fixed nationally and, although these agreements do provide the
framework of a grievance procedure at shop level, most firms now
also feel it necessary to graft their own extended domestic
grievance procedures on to the initial stages of the national
procedure agreement. This should be encouraged because the
best settlements, both in terms of workers' gains and a healthy
industrial atmosphere afterwards, are made at domestic level.

Clear domestic procedures setting out the steps for raising and progressing grievances are essential and management representatives and workers' representatives should have recognised powers to settle at their appropriate levels.

One requirement is essential, both in domestic and national procedures, and that is a fair balance in how each side can apply sanctions as a grievance or a claim goes through procedure. It is ludicrous today, when the unions are supposed by some to have too much power, that if the workpeople have a grievance or a claim they must work normally until the procedure has been exhausted, and yet the management who wish to change working practices or payments can operate these changes forthwith. That kind of 'managerial imperialism' may have been acceptable in Abraham Darby's time, but in modern times such an imbalance is an industrial anachronism.

One cardinal feature of all procedure agreements, domestic and national, should be that the *status quo* must apply until all the stages have been exhausted. This provision, coupled with built-in time limits at each stage of procedure, would ensure that workpeople would observe the rules of procedure. There is no reason at all, given the will, why grievances and claims from workers and changes in working practices by management should not complete their journey through procedure in a maximum of six weeks. Industrial procrastination is the thief not only of time but of the men's credence in the efficacy of official action on grievances and claims. Let a man know that he and the management are both on the same footing while all changes are being discussed, and let him see that he will either have a settlement in six weeks or the right to impose sanctions to secure his claim, and he will stick to the book, because it will make sense to him.

A shorter and quicker procedure also takes the edge off the usual management argument that a *status quo* arrangement would mean inefficiency, because necessary changes would be delayed. Six weeks of negotiation would not cripple any firm and experience has shown that modifications mutually beneficial to both sides often burgeon in the process, provided that the procedure is not bearing unfairly on one side and distorting their view of what the management is trying to do.

Many large firms already have these two factors, the *status quo* and a time-limited procedure, in their agreements. The Industrial Society recommend both in their 'Model Procedure Agreement'.

It is time for the rest of British industry to move with them into the 1970s.

The Government can give a lead here also by operating such procedure agreements in publicly owned and Government industries. They could publicise these as the 'national norm' for dealing with industrial grievances. The ground now is fertile, let them sow!

DEFINING THE AREAS OF COLLECTIVE BARGAINING

Before leaving the shop floor, one other matter remains and that is to define the areas of collective bargaining which are appropriate to national and to local levels.

The Donovan Commission spelled out this problem and came up with sensible answers. It defined the national industry-wide bargaining as the 'formal' system of collective bargaining and the bargaining that takes place at shop and plant level as being the 'informal' system. This is a good description, because industry-wide bargaining has been polished and 'formalised' over the years, while local bargaining has been allowed to develop inform-ally on the basis of precedent, custom and practice.

The Donovan Commission recognised that these two systems are in conflict today and that this conflict is caused by industry-wide negotiations tackling areas of bargaining which cannot possibly give an equitable settlement to all the firms and workers covered by the national agreement. This is particularly true when general increases in wages are being negotiated. How can the amounts negotiated be regarded as satisfactory by all workers in firms as diverse as, for example, those in the engineering industry? It is a negotiating impossibility and the growing gap between minimum rates negotiated by national agreements and actual earnings negotiated by shop agreements is a living, statistical proof that in firms where the national negotiations are reckoned to be completely unreal the gap is filled with 'informal' bargaining at shop or plant level.

This conflict cannot be solved by extending the national nego-tiations and disciplining and restricting local negotiations. Such a course would make negotiations more unrealistic. The way to tackle the conflict is to rationalise shop and plant bargaining and to allow most of the dynamic negotiations to take place at the point of production whilst confining the national industry-wide negotiations to the business of negotiating minimum wage rates and conditions for the industry. There remains a large field of 'minimum' bargaining still untouched, particularly in relation to fringe benefits and minimum holidays. These need more realistic harmonisation with European countries.

Defining the appropriate areas of bargaining between national and local level would also enable unions and employers' associations to reorganise their staffing structures so that the talents and expertise of keen minds on both sides might be available a little closer to the shop floor than it has been in the past.

This redistribution of negotiating responsibility from national to local level and the consequent reorganisation involved to make it work efficiently is probably the biggest challenge facing the unions and employers at the present time.

The changes at shop floor level already proposed in this chapter do make this transfer of responsibility less difficult to operate in practice.

THE ROLE OF ARBITRATION

Despite the gallons of ink spilled in recent years on the subject of industrial relations, there is still little clarity on what the role of arbitration should be in industrial disputes.

Although arbitration has been used extensively by unions and employers at national level, it is used only on isolated occasions at local level. I believe that both unions and employers need arbitration services at some time, locally and nationally, but some thinking is necessary on how these services should operate.

NO COMPULSORY ARBITRATION

Recognising the need for an arbitration service is not to say that there is any place for compulsory arbitration imposed by a government, however well-meaning the aim might be. The argument against compulsory arbitration rests partly on the fact that those compelled to go to arbitration are not likely to accept the award with good grace; hence, the industrial aftermath of what is thought to be an unjust award, arbitrarily imposed, can often leave a legacy of poisoned industrial relations which is much worse than the effects of the original dispute.

The second argument against compulsory arbitration is more

fundamental. If a government decides to have compulsory arbitration as part of its policy in settling industrial disputes, as a government it is actually guaranteeing that in the claims which are referred to this body the arbitrators' judgements are giving workers affected the highest living standards that the economy can absorb at that particular time. They are also, conversely, undertaking that employers are not being asked by the same judgements to pay more than the economic situation permits. It is equally impossible to guarantee such settlements in voluntary arbitration, but the fundamental difference is of course that negotiators have agreed in the case of voluntary arbitration to settle in this way.

Even if the judgements did satisfy the economic criteria, no arbitration decision could guarantee that the workers would be willing to work for the employer on the conditions of the decision. Equally, no arbitration decision could ensure that the employers would be willing to employ workers at the level proposed by the arbitrators.

Until the State is in a position, either by reason of ownership or control of the economic factors which make up living standards, or has the necessary information to enable it to forecast the economic 'law of the situation', it is illogical and unfair for it to build in compulsory arbitration as a means of settling disputes. For these reasons compulsory arbitration has no part in this industrial relations policy.

One other important point about any kind of arbitration is that it is never satisfactory to begin an argument about the composition and terms of reference of an arbitration committee in the white heat of a deadlocked dispute. The principles governing an acceptable system of arbitration have to be set out calmly and objectively beforehand.

A MUTUAL ARBITRATION SERVICE

We need an arbitration service which is mutually acceptable to both unions and employers and capable of being used sparingly at local and national level. The principal requirements here are that the arbitrators are *personae gratae* with both sides and operate as independent agents. For these reasons I reject any arbitration service which is grafted on to the conciliation service of the Department of Employment. An arbitration service must be free of Government pressure, and the only way to ensure this is for the unions and employers to set up a service themselves.

Since all disputes are related to particular industries there is no merit at all in setting up a national arbitration board which would be remote and inflexible. Neither is an elaborate system of staffing and offices necessary. The prime necessity is to have acceptable, experienced people on call to adjudicate on disputes if necessary.

An arbitration service could be set up which fulfils the above requirements by unions and employers in their joint negotiating committees mutually agreeing on a number of acceptable arbitrators. The number would depend on the size of the industry involved and on the history of disputes. These arbitrators would form an 'arbitration service in waiting' and each of the arbiters would be paid a retaining fee each year. This retaining fee would be paid half by the union and half by the employer. The arbitrators would have to be in a position to deal with requests for arbitration as required, as arbitration would be a part-time function for them.

The list of arbitrators could be reviewed periodically by the unions and employers, with arbiters being 'retained' for a fixed period of, say, three years, after which their continuance on the list should be reviewed.

The arbitration list could be available to unions and employers for local as well as national disputes, and the areas of negotiations where arbiters could be called in would be settled mutually between both sides. Individual unions could also if necessary have their own arbitration service with employers in those enterprises where both sides agreed that arbitration would be helpful at times.

This mutual arbitration service, with an agreed panel of arbiters paid retaining fees by both sides, would be the nearest we could get to a fair system of industrial adjudication. Its use would be voluntary, but the decisions of the arbitration would be binding.

The cost for unions and employers would be small compared to the advantages which the idea offers. In time the arbitrators would not only acquire knowledge and expertise in the particular problems of each industry, but would also build up a working relationship and a status with both unions and employers.

THE WAGE-EARNER'S FIRST SAFEGUARD IS HIS TRADE UNION

VOTE LABOUR AND RESTORE TRADE UNION RIGHTS

The Capitalist Politicians have sought to cripple the Worker's Safeguard

The Agricultural Workers' Charter!

Raise the Wage-earners' Standard of Living

VOTE LABOUR AND SECURE

AN ADEQUATE MINIMUM WAGE
REASONABLE HOURS OF LABOUR
ABOLITION OF THE EVILS OF TIED COTTAGES
BETTER EDUCATIONAL FACILITIES
SMALL HOLDINGS OR ALLOTMENTS

PLATE VII

PLATE VIII

REINSTITUTE THE INDUSTRIAL DISPUTES TRIBUNAL

One other area where arbitration in some form has a part to play is in the field of minor claims relating to particular crafts and conditions. Between 1951 and 1959 the Industrial Disputes Tribunal fulfilled a useful purpose and for doctrinaire reasons this body was abolished by the Conservative Government in that year.

Trade unionists were angry at the ending of IDT. It had a reputation for fair dealing in its area of influence. The IDT delivered many judgements on the 'interpretation' of agreements and the cessation of its services over the last fifteen years has left a gap which has not been satisfactorily filled either by the 'Industrial Court' or the machinery of the Ministry.

In extolling the virtues of the IDT I recognise the reservations which employers had about this system of unilateral arbitration. Although both sides had the right to submit references to the IDT, in practice its services were used almost exclusively by the unions, whilst on the occasions when employers received awards in their favour it was difficult to enforce these awards.

These views of the employers were conveyed to the Government in 1958 when the Government was abolishing the Defence Regulation on which the Industrial Disputes Order was based, and despite the unions' opposition the view of the employers was accepted.

The Donovan report did not favour a return of unilateral arbitration on IDT lines because it felt the system was too one-sided to operate on a permanent basis. As a trade unionist, however, I feel here that the Commission took too much note of the weaknesses spotlighted by the employers and not enough of the number of industry-wide disputes (particularly on complicated differentials) which were settled by the Tribunal. The Commission does record that the IDT in its seven and a half years of existence gave over 1,270 awards. I know some were resented by the employers, but this is hardly reason enough for throwing overboard an industrial tribunal which was certainly not over-generous to trade unionists in its awards and was operating with a considerable store of acumen and knowledge.

In their evidence to the Donovan Commission the three largest unions in the country, the T & GWU, AUEW and the NUGMW, all said that they favoured the restoration of unilateral arbitration on the IDT model. I do not say that their support makes it right,

M

but to have a form of arbitration in these troubled times with which workpeople are broadly in agreement is surely a major consideration when deciding whether this kind of arbitration should have a place in industrial relations?

The argument for the restoration of IDT is justified and it should be reinstituted to carry out its former role.

RETAIN 'THE INDUSTRIAL COURT' IN FORMER ROLE

The Industrial Court, renamed the 'Industrial Arbitration Board' in the 1971 Act, also has an expertise and should be retained to continue its pre-Industrial Relations Act role. This role was to deal mainly with issues referred to it jointly by unions and employers for adjudication and with claims made by unions under Section 8 of the Terms and Conditions of Employment Act, 1959, which concerned the observance of recognised terms and conditions and the application of the Fair Wages Resolution.

These two bodies, the IDT and the former Industrial Court, are the only two *Government* agencies for general use which should be available at national level, but the Wages Councils and other bodies relating to particular sectors of industry, which are in operation now, should continue where required.

Having now decided on an independent acceptable system of mutual arbitration and the Government arbitration agencies which should exist for use in disputes if required, we are left with the important question of how far the Nation should provide some kind of conciliation service to reduce the need for disputes to be taken outside the normal procedures for settlement.

Even with an acceptable mutual arbitration system and the Government agencies, there is no doubt that the ideal settlement is that made within industry. Conciliation services are available at present as part of the Department of Employment's industrial services, but the central and controversial role taken by the previous Labour Government and by the Conservative Government in industrial affairs is bound to mean that trade unionists and employers see these services as grinders of the Government axe. As a result the conciliation services are becoming less used than previously, and this trend is likely to accelerate under the operation of the Industrial Relations Act.

A completely new service is needed in the field of industrial conciliation, divorced from Government departments, and most certainly not attached in any way to the Government Department which deals with industrial relations.

How could such a service be developed with the certainty that it would be used? I believe that such a service has four cardinal requirements:

1. The service must be independent.
2. It must be readily available.
3. It must not have powers of settlement.
4. The staff must have the confidence of both sides of industry.

A 'NATIONAL INDUSTRIAL MEDIATION SERVICE'

With these four requirements in mind it is possible to construct a service which will give Britain a 'fresh start' in 'mediation' on industrial problems. A National Industrial Mediation Service should be set up as an independent agency with a structure guaranteed by Act of Parliament. The mediators and staff would be paid by the State but not responsible to any Minister. The National Industrial Mediation Service (NIMS) would have as its object the duty to 'mediate' in industrial disputes, when required by both sides, and to help the two sides to arrive at a settlement. The NIMS would cover the whole of the country and for this the country would be divided into, say, fifty geographical regions with a Regional Mediation Service in each. There would be a National Mediation Office in addition which would be available for national industrial issues if required. Each regional office would have a Mediation Officer, and possibly an assistant and secretarial assistance. These officers would be appointed by the Government after mutual agreement had been reached at tripartite talks between the Government, the TUC and the CBI.

The qualities of the Mediation Officer are important. He should in every case have had actual experience (not just book knowledge) of industrial negotiations, have an ability to get along with people and to use his initiative and discretion. The latter qualities are impossible to categorise but are important in the kind of role which he will play in industrial mediation.

The Regional Mediation Officer's responsibility would be to 'get to know' his region, and the main people on the union and employers' sides who deal with industrial relations. He would be expected to assimilate gradually a knowledge of the main industries in his region and to have a knowledge of the main agreements. He would follow closely the conditions of employment in his region and would have power to call the two sides together when he felt that a serious dispute was in the offing. In the course of mediating, he would be able to ask that the parties to the dispute would not take industrial action while the negotiations were in progress, but he would not have any power to enforce this request.

The mediator would exist to help both sides to reach an agreement themselves, not to impose his ideas of a settlement on them. He must have wide powers of discretion but must be at all times in mediation guided towards a settlement which the two parties desire and not a settlement which he (the mediator) may feel is economically correct or in the national interest.

The agreements reached through the intervention of the mediator will perhaps seldom be perfect agreements as seen by those outside the dispute. If he helps the two parties to a settlement which they mutually agree upon, where they had been deadlocked previously, then the mediator has, nevertheless, achieved the 'perfect' agreement in that particular situation.

It must be understood that the mediator would be conciliating, not arbitrating, and his whole success would depend on preserving this distinction. Therefore, he must as a person, never act as an *arbitrator* in any dispute even outside his region.

At national level the mediation service should have a panel of special mediators available, again chosen in consultation with the TUC and the CBI. These 'special mediators' could be used on district or local disputes if required and the same principles of independence, conciliation not arbitration, and the use of discretion, apply to these national mediators as apply to those in the regions.

What I have outlined in these proposals for a NIMS is a variant on what operates in Sweden under the Mediation Act of 1906 (revised in 1920) and the Swedish unions who have constantly used this system have nothing but praise for the way it has operated. Some aspects of the Swedish system I have omitted, particularly the powers of the Warning Act of 1935, which means that seven days' notice must be given to the mediator in the district of any stoppage of work or lock-out. Another aspect of the Swedish mediation system which has not been included is the legislation of 1936. This makes it compulsory for the parties to attend when asked by the mediation officer.

These powers have grown into the system in Sweden because of the acceptable way in which the mediation has operated. It would be wise in any new mediation system in Britain to allow the same process to take place before compulsion to meet or notification of disputes is contemplated.

The Swedish mediation system is set out admirably in the book *Collective Bargaining in Sweden* by T. L. Johnston (Allen and Unwin, 1962), which describes not only the legislation but the operation of the mediation system in practice in the fixing of annual contracts in Swedish industry.

The National Industrial Mediation Service, although separate from Government and free from interference and pressure, would require to be attached to some government department for the purpose of primary administration. As the service must be seen to be independent, it is absolutely essential that it is not attached in any way to any of the government departments dealing with economic or industrial affairs.

In Sweden they have overcome this problem by attaching the 'Mediation Office' to the Department of Social Affairs, and some similar solution may be the answer in Britain.

The structure and guiding principles which have been outlined for a National Industrial Mediation Service meet the four requirements of independence, availability, conciliation and the likelihood of being used by both sides of industry, and would fill a gap which exists in practice, if not in machinery, at the present time in Britain. A service like this, properly developed, could be a valuable instrument in promoting better industrial relations in our country. It has the essential ingredients of voluntary operation and an absence of compulsion which should commend it to all those who negotiate at all levels in British industry.

Finally, in our industrial relations policy we have to recognise the need for investigation and information on industrial problems and other aspects which are important in collective bargaining at all levels.

During the 1964–70 Labour Government two important agencies were set up in these fields. The Prices and Incomes Board gave detailed information of pricing and wages problems which had in the past been a 'dark' information area in this country. It is a tragedy that this work should have been discontinued by the

Conservative Government. The information on monopoly prices was unflattering to those involved and did not do the private enterprise image any good. This no doubt was why the PIB got the boot.

Some similar agency with the kind of status enjoyed by the PIB should be reinstituted to deal with the vital service of supplying information and comment on the important factors in collective bargaining and in the cost of living.

The Commission on Industrial Relations (CIR) also fulfilled a valuable purpose in the investigating of trouble spots in industry. Many trade union leaders, including myself, have first-hand experience of working with the CIR in trying to find solutions in sections of industry where industrial strife has been endemic. The CIR have tackled not only the problems of bad relations between workpeople and management, but also the sometimes more difficult problems of differences between unions which were themselves a factor in the industrial discontent and upheaval in the firms concerned.

The CIR showed tact and experience in dealing with all the references they had handled up to their change of role in November 1971. One of the reasons for their success was again the absence of compulsion in the framework of their operations. Another reason was that they were usually able to look at a particular firm not in the heat or aftermath of a major industrial dispute (which is usually the lot of a Court of Inquiry) but in an atmosphere where industrial relations, although bad, were normal for that particular firm. This led to objective reports and their work on recognition issues, spheres of influence, domestic bargaining, dismissals procedures and their excellent report on facilities for shop stewards, have been important contributions to industrial relations over the last few years. One of the tragedies of the Industrial Relations Act was the diversion of the CIR into a framework of compulsion, and its changed role under an Act which is I think analytically opposite to the thinking evident in the CIR reports, which were based on the actual experience of field investigation by competent officials. The CIR should be reinstituted to carry out the role prescribed for it by the Labour Government.

Even with the best industrial relations policy there will still be disputes and these disputes will need the powers of inquiry. In these instances there is still need to retain the present power of the responsible Minister to set up Courts of Inquiry as necessary. The jurisdiction of these Courts should be as at present, with no power to impose a settlement on either side.

In concluding this chapter I bring together for easy reference the main measures which are necessary for a viable industrial relations policy. These are as follows:

1. Legislation. Guaranteeing basic industrial rights on
   (*a*) new contract of employment;
   (*b*) disclosure of information;
   (*c*) industrial democracy.
2. The provision of modern facilities for shop stewards.
3. Balanced procedure agreements.
4. The definition of negotiating areas in collective bargaining.
5. A mutual arbitration system (unions and employers only).
6. Reinstitution of the Industrial Disputes Tribunal.
7. Retention of the 'Industrial Court' in former role.
8. A new National Industrial Mediation Service.
9. Reinstitution of the Prices and Incomes Board.
10. Retention of the Commission on Industrial Relations in pre-IRA Role.
11. Retention of the Courts of Inquiry procedure with present powers and jurisdiction.

Each one of these eleven courses of action is capable of development and this is particularly true of the mutual arbitration and mediation service proposals. All of these proposals can be refined and improved upon and they are complementary to one another. Together they give us a much better chance of achieving our goal of better industrial relations, a more congenial working environment for workers in industry, and hence a happier and more united society.

Chapter 15

Prices, Incomes and Inflation

'If you are shrewd, strong and skilful, think a little and
work a little for the millions of your own class who are
ignorant, weak and friendless.'

Robert Blatchford, 1851–1943

PAST FAILURES AND A POLICY FOR THE FUTURE

The problem of inflation and the consequent measures to deal
with prices and incomes are acknowledged to be the most difficult
for economic management. This chapter analyses the reasons
why the Labour Government's attempt failed in the end and from
these draws conclusions, leading to proposals for a possible
future prices and incomes policy.

1964–70 – ANALYSING THE FAILURE

The failure of the Labour Government's policy on prices and
incomes must be qualified by the fact that it succeeded for a time
in holding prices. To that extent it succeeded for a time. But it did
operate unfairly and at the end broke down. To this extent it
failed. It certainly failed in trade union eyes.

The Labour Government's attempt to erect a prices and
incomes policy was the fourth such attempt since 1945. The 1949
freeze by Stafford Cripps, the price-plateau of the Tory's second
Government of 1955–9 and the Selwyn Lloyd 'Pay Pause' of 1961
were all finally ignored both by employers and workpeople, so the
Labour Government's attempt was fraught with bad omen from
the start.

The Labour Government's 1964–70 prices and incomes policy
was the most technical and precise attempt, on paper anyway, to

bring prices and incomes under some measure of control. They had very little experience from other countries to guide them.

The Swedish attitude to prices and incomes is, I believe, typical of the other European countries who have dabbled in these controls. After unsuccessful attempts to work out a mutual policy with the Swedish LO (equivalent to our TUC) the Swedes settled firstly for a period of centralised national bargaining co-ordinated through the LO (which had the advantage of preventing 'leap-frogging' since all the claims were settled in one round of negotiations), and secondly for what they called a 'moratorium' on wage and salary movements for a stipulated period whilst the economy passed through a difficult time. The moratorium is, of course, a finesse term for 'pay pause' or 'wage freeze', and it is usually only asked for in short periods of say three or six months and that infrequently. National centralised bargaining was only tried about three times between 1950 and 1960, and is now not popular.

Both these measures were very broad, designed to deal in general terms with a particular, critical situation and certainly not in the continuing and detailed way in which the Labour Government tackled the problem.

All the countries in Western Europe which have tried to regulate prices and incomes have started off with voluntary restraint. This later developed into more stringent control, and finally, under the strains and inequities these measures have produced, restraints have gradually been relaxed.

During the relaxation period the Government decrees on easing the squeeze have always lagged behind the actual thaw in negotiations in industry, so that the policy has really died long before the Government decides the date of the official burial. Governments in this position have then fallen back on fiscal and other more orthodox measures to control inflation.

Before looking at the reasons for the failure of Labour's 'prices and incomes policy', it is right to examine the arguments for and against such a policy.

THE NEED FOR A PRICES AND INCOMES POLICY

The Labour Government argued that ever since full employment became a permanent feature of the economic environment, prices had been rising. Since the war they had risen, on average, by about 4 per cent a year. The two worst effects of this are well known. Firstly, those on fixed incomes have suffered. In some cases (notably State benefits) it has been possible to some extent to compensate people for rising prices, but even this has not always been achieved. In other cases the injustice caused by rising prices has not always been eliminated.

Secondly, our prices have tended to rise faster than the prices of other industrial countries, with the result that we have had frequent balance of payments crises, as our exports have failed to make sufficient headway in other countries, whilst consumers in Britain have preferred to buy cheaper goods from abroad. This series of balance of payments crises has resulted in a periodic need to restrain demand and hence to reduce the rise in output. This in turn has had an adverse effect on investment and impaired the longer term prospects for growth. Since the only way to achieve a higher standard of living – the object of all economic policy – is to get a higher rate of growth, these effects of a failure to prevent prices from rising are obviously very undesirable.

For this reason a satisfactory prices and incomes policy was the cornerstone of the Labour Government's economic policy when it took office. At first, a purely voluntary policy was tried, but as time went on it became clear that this was not working fast enough to get out of the critical balance of payments situation inherited from the previous government. Indeed, during the year up to mid-1966 hourly earnings rose at the rate of nearly 10 per cent.

The Government eventually decided that the voluntary policy was not working fast enough, and therefore decided to introduce a standstill, which was followed by a period of severe restraint. It was eventually left to the TUC to operate a voluntary policy which included wage claim 'vetting' by the General Council and guidance to unions involved in claims.

AGAINST A PRICES AND INCOMES POLICY

There were two main arguments put forward during the 1960s against the need for an incomes policy. We are not dealing for the moment with the arguments against the prices and incomes policy of the Labour Government as such which arose out of the unfair operation of the policy. The two basic arguments which opposed the prices and incomes policy were more fundamental than operational difficulties.

Both viewpoints did recognise that inflation was the central

economic problem, but each had other methods of dealing with
this problem. One argument was that the old-fashioned regulator
of *unemployment* was the easy way to control inflation, while the
second view held that inflation could be controlled by *productivity*.
These views can be briefly summarised and evaluated as follows:

Regulation by Unemployment
Some economists say that a prices and incomes policy is too
complicated to operate and that the old remedy of unemployment
up to around 4 per cent is the only effective way to contain inflation at certain times in the economic cycle. This solution is a non-
runner in modern Britain, though I believe that the present
Conservative Government does believe it has a role to play in
damping down what it deems to be excessive wage increases.

Many economists have been hard at work trying to find out
just how much the level of unemployment bears down on wage
rate changes in present times. Some recent studies, notably C.
Gillon's *Wage Rates, Earnings and Wage Drift* (National Institute
of Economic and Social Research 1968), concluded that a 1 per
cent increase in unemployment meant a 3 per cent reduction in
wage rates. Professor Paish has argued independently that it is
impossible to operate an incomes policy (he does not mention
prices) with unemployment below 2½ per cent, whilst if unemployment is sufficiently above 2½ per cent (¼ per cent=60,000 jobs),
an incomes policy is superfluous!

There is, however, evidence to show that unemployment only
bears down on the level of wage increases in the short term. Once
unemployment has been at a certain level for long enough, a new
plateau is established and stabilised. At this point the familiar,
justified expectations of higher living standards reassert themselves and the incomes position is back to where it was before. So
even as an economic instrument, unemployment is not the long
term answer to inflation.

Regulating the economy by means of unemployment is out. It is
politically unpopular and it is regarded now rightly as being
wasteful and socially wrong.

Regulation by Productivity
The second argument is more up to date. It again begins by
stating the difficulties of operating an incomes policy, but con-
tinues to assert that the real problem is that incomes only appear

to be rising too fast because productivity and output are too low. Improve efficiency, increase investment, concentrate on productivity bargaining, and output will rise as quickly, and perhaps quicker than wages and salaries – or so the argument goes.

This argument may be true in the long term, but there are two serious drawbacks. Firstly, such a policy involving capital improvements in industry takes time because we would need to aim for an increase in output of something like 7 per cent per year. So in the *short term*, possibly for a few years, some transitory measures will be needed to keep inflation as low as possible.

Secondly, the highest price increases in the post-war period have come from the labour-intensive industries, and it is in these industries where the majority of productivity bargaining has been taking place. But there has been little apparent effect on the prices of the goods produced by these industries. This indicates that, unless there is a different kind of productivity bargain involving a pricing norm as an integral part of it, such deals are not going to produce lower prices automatically.

NO INCOMES POLICY WITHOUT SOCIALISM

There is, of course, one other argument against an incomes policy which is the blanket viewpoint that a fair incomes policy cannot be operated inside a capitalist economy. I agree with this view up to the point that there must be adequate control of the economy. Whether my idea of an adequately controlled economy would dovetail with those who argue that only in a socialist society can we have an incomes policy, is another matter.

To be more specific, I would think that given an economy with the kind of ownership and controls outlined in a previous chapter and also with the industrial relations proposals spelled out in the last chapter, an incomes policy would not fail because the Government lacked control of our economic direction, or because of lack of economic growth.

The problem of the transition from where we are now, economically, to where we want to be, has got to be faced. We cannot sit on our backsides and wait for a society which is sufficiently socialist to warrant a prices and incomes policy. If it is to be an integral part of our economic and social policy then socialists are not justified in rejecting it on their criteria as long as policies are being followed to change our society towards socialist ends. As long as we are reasonably sure that our Government is following socialist policies, then the right kind of prices and incomes policy should be supported.

What kind of policy this should be will be discussed later, as indeed will the question whether there is any need for it at all under certain conditions. One thing is agreed by everyone – that if there is an acceptable way to control inflation then it should be utilised. Inflation is a problem in our kind of society, and when it is accompanied by the modern phenomen of a high rate of unemployment, it bites deeply at even more families who are dependent on State benefits.

Agreeing with the need for 'something to be done about inflation' is one thing, but outlining even the broad path of such a control policy is far from easy.

WHY THE POLICY FAILED

Can we learn from the mistakes of the last Labour Government? Why did their policies fail? These were the reasons:

1. The prices and incomes policy was a major change in the role of the unions. For 150 years they had been concerned with trying to force increases from reluctant employers. Unions had bargained to obtain for their members 'what the market would stand'. If they did not push their claims to this limit during periods of full employment when conditions were favourable for bargaining, how were they to know that their restraint was not just adding to the profits of industry?
2. Employers did not like even the mild restraints which were placed on dividends and distributed profits.
3. The workers felt that the policy was operating more efficiently against wages than against prices.

   The phraseology of the incomes section of the policy was certainly more detailed and precise than for prices. Ceilings and norms were set for incomes, and the yardstick for obtaining increases above the 'norm' was extremely precisely fixed, being related to productivity, job evaluation and the revision of wages structures.

   Prices, on the other hand, were dealt with very loosely, and only two general conditions were laid down: prices increases could take place only when rising costs could not be covered by savings or by improved efficiency; and secondly, only when these rises in prices were necessary to finance new investment.

Both these criteria for price increases were so general that references to the Prices and Incomes Board were almost a formality. Increases were endorsed in almost all cases by the PIB and cynics said the Board was 'institutionalising inflation'. Referring price increases to the Board turned out also to be politically bad for the Government, because the PIB was synonymous with the Government in the public mind. Therefore, when the Board agreed to an increase, the people felt that the Government had in fact put the price up!

4. As the operation of the policy unfolded, it began to be seen that there was no effective way of enforcing the norms or of policing the criteria. Wage and salary settlements were made, and prices increased without reference to the PIB, or without notification to the DEP (Department of Employment and Productivity).

5. Productivity bargains were an accepted method of securing more than the norm, and these bargains were loosely interpreted by both unions and management. This favoured those workers who were in industries where such bargaining was applicable.

Statistics from the DEP in answer to parliamentary questions on the extent of productivity settlements, showed that in the first two years of Labour's office when the prices and incomes policy was voluntary, 3,000 notifications had been sent to the DEP on productivity deals covering over 6 million workers.

If all those deals had kept prices down in these industries, at least the productivity provisions would have been achieving something, but this was not so. Prices in these industries and firms which had concluded productivity bargains rose even faster than others.

The effect of this on other workers is only too apparent. Their wages were stuck on the 'norm' because their job did not lend itself to measurement, and also they still had the increased prices to pay from their stagnant pay packet. The productivity criterion bred immense discontent among workers because even in the labour-intensive manufacturing industries, which comprised most of the productivity bargaining, some industries were growing and could allow workers to benefit almost automatically while others were declining and had no room for increased output.

Workers therefore saw themselves falling behind through no fault of their own, but often by reason of geography and the supply and demand for labour.

6. Low-paid workers, who are often in jobs which do not easily permit piecework or payment by results, found that they were falling behind instead of being helped by the restrictions on increases. Conforming to 'the norm' for them meant, in fact, falling further behind the average. The Government in their 'low pay' provisions relied on traditional bargaining to improve the position of the lowest paid, but since the traditional methods of bargaining had widened the gap between the highest and lowest over the years, it was difficult to see how a reliance on 'the mixture as before' would improve the lot of the low-paid worker, even though exceptions were to be made in proved cases of settlements above the norm for these workers.

Some external action from the Government was necessary at this stage to ensure that this important part of the policy did work. The first steps towards a national minimum wage could have been taken, but they were not. As a result unions, including those who were genuinely trying to operate the policy, became disillusioned with the unfairness in operation of this aspect of the incomes policy. Those unions catering for occupations which are traditionally low paid grew increasingly bitter at a policy which they claimed was turning into a 'survival of the strongest and most prosperous'.

7. Unions were finding themselves unable to control wage increases, even if they had wanted to. Plant and local bargaining was on the increase, pepped up by the Government's emphasis on the need for more productivity bargaining and sophisticated methods of work measurement. Reports came from the PIB extolling the virtues of these devices, and workers and management at shop and plant level were putting into practice what the PIB preached.

This decentralisation of bargaining made it impossible to police the results. The 'latter norm' of $3\frac{1}{2}$ per cent which was supposed to apply to all annual increases, was absolutely inoperable and became successively outflanked, ignored and then derided.

These seven main reasons for the failure of the incomes policy could doubtless be supplemented by others, but by and large they do truly reflect the objections to the policy which ultimately brought its collapse. If the Government had been able to reach an acceptable social compact with the unions, and if the economy had been strong enough to allow higher increases than the norms visualised, then it might have endured under the strains.

The economy was groggy for the first five years of Labour's rule and the Government's fixation with the strength of sterling and the balance of payments confined its policies to extremely meagre limits in increased living standards. Had there been more liquidity immediately available, and a great deal more to look forward to, then the prices and incomes policy might have been more successful.

It is pointless to conjecture about what might have happened if the economic position had been better in 1964, but at least it is possible, now that the dust has settled on the issue, to draw some broad conclusions for the future.

NO FUTURE STATUTORY POLICY

The first conclusion to be drawn from the failure of Labour's prices and incomes policy is that there is no basis for a future statutory policy with built-in compulsory powers. It must be evident that if the wage and price increases *above* any fixed statutory norm cannot be challenged and prevented by sanctions of some kind, it is impossible to have these enshrined in statute.

It has always been known that a widespread evasion of the law makes the law impossible to operate. That is what happened at Betteshanger Colliery, and in the non-notification of wage increase and prices in the 1965–9 period. It also took place in the union-employer collusion to outflank the productivity criteria for increases above the norm during the statutory incomes policy. If the law cannot be enforced then the law should be changed or dropped altogether in the case of prices and incomes.

The change in the pattern of bargaining also makes national norms impossible to enforce. When most negotiations were at national level it was possible to broadly control and police national incomes norms. With the growth of plant bargaining, actively encouraged by the major unions in the country, it has become impossible to have a 'norm' or a 'guiding light' which can be enforced.

The proposals for a new industrial relations policy contained in the previous chapter also are based on the extension of plant and local bargaining. If, as seems sensible, national negotiations should deal only with minimum wages and conditions, then all other increases, including those to compensate for cost of living rises, will be negotiated at local or plant level. Such cost of living increases may well be included as part of a wages deal involving productivity or other bargaining matters, and it would be impossible to disentangle one from the other. The growth and daily extension of this kind of collective bargaining at plant level makes enforcement of a statutory incomes policy absolutely impossible.

The other argument against a statutory policy is that according to the experience in other countries as well as our own, an enforced policy only has a limited life. Under the strains mentioned earlier it breaks, and a cloudburst of increases follows in a short time which pushes up prices quickly. This flood of rising prices in turn engulfs those on pensions, State benefits and the low-paid workers.

Each country in Europe which has attempted a statutory policy has experienced the dam burst of wages and increases when the statutory lock-gates have been opened. Since, in Britain it appears to take about eight months to progress pension and benefit increases from the decision on the ministerial table to the Post Office counter, those unfortunate enough to be caught in the deluge suffer hardship.

For these reasons any future prices and incomes policy has got to be by consent, and the consent must be almost total as far as the unions are concerned. It is no use pushing a decision concerning a voluntary incomes policy through a conference, or at a trade union Executives' meeting in Croydon, with even one major union against. One union big enough to span a few industries, and operating against a voluntary incomes policy, means that the policy will disintegrate.

Operating a voluntary prices and incomes policy, even with total consent from the unions, does not mean that the Government has only to make brave speeches from time to time to call the tune. There are many measures which can be taken by the Government to make it work effectively and fairly. The main

N

fields for Government intervention would appear to be on prices, low pay, and what is called the 'social compact'.

KEEPING PRICES DOWN

There is a general consensus that the Labour Government's policy failed on prices. They had some success, but the policy certainly bore down harder on incomes than on prices. The British public, after the experiences of rising prices over the past ten years, are price conscious. A Government has all to gain politically from devising some broad measures for keeping prices down.

It is difficult to devise a workable policy to control prices, but it is not impossible. Great Britain has had price control in some form between 1939 and 1953 and an ostensible policy on prices under the Heath Government; Austria, Denmark, France, the Netherlands, Norway and Finland have also had policies to bring prices under public scrutiny. These price control policies can be summarised as follows:

PRICE CONTROL IN BRITAIN AND EUROPE

Price Control – Britain 1939–1953

The control of non-food prices was first attempted under the 1939 Prices of Goods Act. It was followed by the 1941 Goods and Services (Price Control) Act. The 1939 Act in its main provisions did no more than specify the principles on which the maximum prices to be permitted should be determined, without, however, facing the problems of enforcement and the necessity for prior definition of the goods whose prices were being limited. As a result its main provisions were for the most part unworkable.

The principle was that the profit earned per article should not be more than that which each firm earned on like goods in August 1939. It would clearly have been difficult in most cases to establish in a court of law what pre-war goods were to be taken as comparable, or what the price or cost or profit had then been. There was moreover, no inspectorate, so that action under the Act was initiated only on complaints from the public.

However, a subsidiary provision of the 1939 Act also allowed individual 'permitted prices' to be specified and this allowed a more detailed control to be built up. The Central Price Regulation Committee used this provision to work out a system of permitted prices for various branded goods, and later to sanction, often without any formal order, the prices of goods fixed by various trades or trade associations.

The 1941 Act gave wider powers to fix maximum prices or margins according to a variety of formulae. However, where the Act was chiefly more effective than its predecessor, was in that it was accompanied in some fields by production controls, which limited and defined the quality of the goods being produced. Even so, there were many difficulties in administering the price regulations, and many loopholes in the attempted definition of qualities. Outside this field, price control remained extremely loose.

Price controls extended over the greater part of food expenditure. Most of the major foodstuffs were rationed or subsidised or both, and in either case price control was both necessary and relatively easy. For many other foods, too, the Ministry of Food had control over supplies, and this too made price control possible.

At the end of the war price control covered about one half of total consumers' expenditure. Such a reckoning, however may perhaps understate the import of the price controls: because over much of the uncontrolled field, price control was for one reason or another either inappropriate or less necessary than in the controlled sector.

There was no appreciable relaxation of price control until 1949 and 1950. The rapidity of the price rise during this period also greatly increased the difficulties of control. In some cases the cost-plus controlled price (based on the historical cost of materials) came to less than the current value of the materials alone, so that if the price had been fixed on the usual principles it would have paid dealers to buy products to treat as scrap for their material content.

This revealed some inherent limitations in price control systems. It is obviously more effective where the product is more or less standard, but without standardisation and close control of specifications, it is difficult to ensure the maintenance of quality, and a form of price control evasion could clearly develop.

The system of price control was dismantled in 1952 and 1953. With the end of utility schemes, price controls over furniture and clothing were removed in 1952. The remaining Board of Trade controls expired in 1953, with the repeal of the 1939 and 1941 enabling Acts under which most price controls had been administered. (It is interesting to note that Britain abolished price control machinery at precisely the time that many of our European neighbours were busy constructing exactly these weapons.)

Price control in the UK remained fairly extensive though very loosely applied in many areas, for six or seven years after the war. The continued administration of price control for something like a decade would have been impossible had not traders, by a process of informal negotiation with government departments, been able to obtain increases in permitted prices when they could show that their costs had risen. Within these limits, price control during and after the Second World War was relatively successful. The trades concerned, however they may have disputed the details of its administration, hardly protested against its underlying principle.

Evasion, though not unknown on a minor scale, was limited. Prices over this period rose gradually and in line with costs, and widespread profit inflation does not seem to have been the rule.

In summary, the experience of price control in Britain in these years showed that price regulations could not be enforced in rigid detail against the opposition of the trade. But if, on the other hand, traders concurred in the purpose of the control, it probably sanctioned and strengthened existing tendencies. The climate of opinion for controls is therefore of the utmost importance.

Two further points should be made. First, the achievement of an effective system of price control necessarily requires a strong measure of control over the *standards* of goods involved. Second, the effectiveness of price control depends to a large extent on the strength or weakness of inflationary pressures on the economy. A comprehensive policy of price control must therefore seek to regulate these pressures if a broad consent to price stabilisation is to be achieved.

PRICE CONTROL IN EUROPE

These next summaries are designed to show some of the techniques used in six European countries to supervise and control prices. These summaries have been based on the following OECD Reports:

Policies for Price Stability (OECD, 1962); *Policies for Prices, Profits and Non-Wage Incomes* (OECD, 1964); *Non-Wages*

Incomes and Prices Policy (OECD, 1966); *OECD Conference Papers, 1971.*

Austria
Price policy in Austria consists of (*a*) statutory price control, and (*b*) price supervision by the Equipartite Price and Wage Commission. In addition, price policy is supported by action under the Cartel Law and the Anti-Profiteering Law.

Statutory Price Control. Under the Price Control Law of 1950 the Federal Ministries of the Interior and of Agriculture and Forestry have the power to fix maximum economically justified prices or charges, either on their own initiative or on application from other Ministries. Before doing so, they must consult the other Federal Ministries concerned and obtain the advice of the Price Commission, which is made up of representatives of the Chambers of Commerce, Labour and Agriculture.

Prices or charges are deemed to be economically justified if they correspond to the greatest possible extent both to the economic conditions prevailing in the production and distribution of the goods or services in question, and to the economic situation of the consumers of these goods or services. Maximum price orders may lay down other conditions, e.g. that if actual prime costs are lower than those used as a basis for fixing the official price, the difference must be paid over to the State (this generally only applied to imported goods). Manufacturers of new products falling within a general category covered by a maximum price order must apply for the prescription of an official price.

Although these powers were used extensively in the early post-war period, at present they apply only to a few basic foodstuffs, such as bread and flourmill products, milk, butter, certain sorts of cheese, and sugar; solid and liquid mineral fuels and their derivatives; electric power and gas supplies; and essential pharmaceutical products.

The responsibility for the following price developments lies with Administrative District Offices and the special Provincial Price Authorities. These have a fairly small staff, and exercise primarily a note-taking and educational function.

Price Supervision by the Equipartite Price and Wage Commission. The Equipartite Price and Wage Commission, consisting of representatives of labour and management, was set up in March 1957. Its authority was extended in March 1962. Following an agreement between the main industrial groups and the government, the employers' organisations agreed to invite their member firms to notify the Equipartite Commission of their intention to raise their prices, and to submit to it and/or its competent Price Sub-Committee the reasons for the intended price change, together with – to the extent possible – all the relevant data.

The Price Sub-Committee examines the submissions and the accompanying information submitted either by the employers' organisation on behalf of a whole branch, or by individual firms, in the light of cost increases and the general market and price situation. It may then recommend maximum prices for producers, wholesalers or retailers, which should not be exceeded. The same procedure has been applied also to important services.

If no agreement is reached by the Price Sub-Committee within five weeks after the submission of an application for an increase in prices, the Equipartite Commission must decide on the matter within a period of another six weeks. If no agreement has been reached at the end of this time, the applicant is free to charge the prices proposed. In the case of new or substantially modified products, manufacturers and distributors are not required to notify prices to the Equipartite Commission. This also applies to price increases for imported goods, provided such goods are not substantially modified and their value enhanced by being worked on or processed in Austria.

The Equipartite Commission has no legal authority and cannot, in principle, impose any sanctions. The Commission may, however, on the basis of a unanimous decision, request the authorities to fix the prices of certain commodities or services for a period of six months in accordance with the statutory regulations described above. In this way, the scope of the Price Control Law may be temporarily extended, for a period of six months, for the purpose of stabilising the development of prices. Such action is, however, only permissible if the price is made in a branch or by an enterprise or group of enterprises having a dominating position in the market. Moreover, under this procedure an official maximum price can be fixed only once on one and the same ground.

The Monopolies and Restrictive Practices Control Act. Under this Act the Monopolies Control Authority may intervene in price formation in any area where it believes a restrictive business practice exists or where an individual enterprise is exerting a dominating influence on the market. It can intervene in one of two ways: *by requiring advance approval for an increase in prices or profit margins, or by imposing maximum prices or margins.*

Exemptions from this general provision may be granted if warranted by the market conditions, the nature of the commodity, or its relative importance as to the total trade volume. An exemption may also be granted where the agreements or actions are of material importance for the advancement of efficiency, as, *inter alia*, in the case of structural rationalisation.

Enterprises producing or selling certain officially listed goods or services must submit their price lists or rate scales to the Authority, where they are open to public inspection.

The Price Supervision Act. This Act applies to areas where competition is not restricted within the meaning of the Monopolies Control Act but where the surmise *of the Authority is that price formation is unreasonable or that competition is not as keen as it should be.* The most important provision is that upon the request of a trade union, employers' federation, consumers' organisation, or on its own initiative, the Monopolies Control Authority may institute enquiries into prices charged for specific commodities if it considers that this would be in the public interest.

This temporary extension of official price control is primarily designed as a preventive measure and/or as a means of education, in order to restrain important economic branches or market-dominating enterprises – many of which are also subject to the provisions of the Austrian Cartel Law – from making arbitrary price increases detrimental to consumers, which cannot be justified from the standpoint of the economy as a whole.

If the governmental price authorities become aware that prices subject to an agreement reached in the Equipartite Commission are being exceeded, they may draw the Commission's attention to the matter and suggest that the price in question be officially fixed for a period of six months.

Denmark
Danish price control and regulation are governed by two Acts: The Monopolies and Restrictive Practices Control Act of 1955 (as amended); and the Price Supervision Act of 1963 (replacing

an earlier Act of 1956). The first of these is similar to legislation existing in many other countries in that it is primarily concerned with the effects on price formation of restrictive business practices. The more recent Act is, however, of considerably wider application.

Both Acts are administered by the Monopolies Control Authority consisting of a Board and a Directorate.

Appeal against the decisions of the Monopolies Control Authority can be made before a special tribunal, the Appeal Tribunal, the decisions of which can in turn be taken before the ordinary law courts.

In connection with the institution of inquiries, the Monopolies Control Authority *may impose a price freeze on certain goods or on the goods of a certain trade.* Such a price freeze is imposed for a period of three months at a time; the enterprises concerned must not without the consent of the Authority charge higher prices or apply higher margins than were in force at a given date. The presumption is that the period of such a price freeze may be extended beyond the originally stipulated three months if the inquiry instituted has not been concluded within that period.

One purpose of these inquiries is to encourage keener competition through publishing the results of the investigations into the prices and costs of specific goods. This also makes consumers more conscious of the relation between costs and prices in the selected field.

Where an inquiry made by the Monopolies Control Authority reveals the existence of unreasonable prices, the Authority is empowered to impose maximum prices and margins or indicative prices. Legal action can be brought against anyone violating provisions on maximum prices or margins, and the offender is liable to punishment of a fine or 'haefte' (a mitigated form of imprisonment). Indicative prices are not binding, but are intended to serve as guidance for traders and consumers as to the price that in general would be reasonable for the commodity in question.

While the Monopolies Control Act of 1955 provides individual price regulation as regards market-dominating enterprises and enterprises that are parties to agreements, the general price regulation provided in the Price Supervision Act of 1963 is applicable only to a whole trade.

France

The price control legislation in France dates from the beginning of the Second World War. Its main provisions were taken up again and codified by two ordinances of 30th June, 1945, amended and supplemented by later texts.

Since 1957 a number of important exceptions to the freezing regulations have been introduced. These have gradually reduced the area of control until today it is comparatively small.

The legislation in force does, however, enable the Government to return to a system of control at any time, and the responsible authorities have on several occasions used these powers to meet special situations or contain excessive pressures that were becoming evident in certain sectors.

Thus, to check the rise in food prices caused by the severity of the 1962–63 winter, maximum absolute prices or limited traders' margins were imposed in January 1963 for certain fresh vegetables, eggs and some cuts of pork. All these measures were withdrawn as soon as normal supply conditions had been restored. In March 1963 upper limits were set on trade margins for several products essential to farmers in an effort to go some way to meeting some of the claims of agricultural interests. Similarly, in April 1963, the rise in the prices of some widely-used industrial products led the authorities to re-introduce a variety of controls. In some cases limits were imposed both on factory prices and traders' margins. In others – particularly textiles – only traders' margins were controlled. In the case of textiles, the decision was postponed following an undertaking not to increase prices, and to reduce them where that proved possible.

Finally, in September 1963, to check inflationary pressures which were becoming evident in various sectors of the economy, the Government felt impelled to freeze producer prices for all industrial products at the level at which they stood on 31st August. For the same reasons it later fixed a ceiling for the prices of services mainly affecting industrial firms.

These recent examples of intervention are primarily regarded as expedients aimed at correcting or reducing the effects of temporary disturbances of the market; they do not imply general and concerted action on the volume and distribution of non-wage incomes. Corrections by price controls such as these, usually temporary in nature, are not intended to cause radical changes in structure.

Techniques. The basic position under existing legislation is that all prices are frozen at their level of 1st September, 1939, unless they have subsequently been freed, or frozen at a higher level, or subjected to some other form of supervision. The law puts no restrictions on the methods of control used, nor on the point in the economy at which it may be imposed. The following methods are distinguished in administrative practice:

1. Maximum prices are determined on the basis of cost data from representative firms which have to supply all the necessary accounting information.
2. Constructed prices are a variation of maximum prices where the producer calculates his own price according to rules laid down by the administration.
3. The method of prices control on a negotiated contract basis is similar to constructed prices but applies to products made to customers' specifications, mainly for some heavy mechanical and electrical engineering work, shipbuilding, aircraft constructions, etc.
4. Limitation of trade margins exists both in the form of limited absolute amounts and of limited percentages. Limitation of absolute margins applies at present to some foodstuffs, and to motor fuels, Limitation of margins in percentage terms applies to a number of food products and to a number of industrial products.
5. Under the system of freedom subject to official approval, manufacturers and suppliers of services, or their trade associations, may fix their own prices, but the administration retains the right to approve them before they come into force. New price schedules must be submitted to the authorities and only become effective if the authorities do not raise objections within fifteen days. These prices cannot be exceeded without a new submission by the interested parties and a new waiting period. This method applies to a few food products, and to a large number of industrial products.
6. The system of freedom subject to prior notification simply requires firms to notify the prices or price changes which they propose to apply. The administration has no right to object to them. The formality of notification does, however, enable it to follow the trend of prices and margins and to intervene

by reintroducing a stricter system if abuses should come to light.

7. As already noted, the freezing of prices is the basic provision of any French price legislation. Those products which are not submitted to any other regime or which have not been set totally free, are in principle frozen. In practice, most prices were freed after the general price freeze in 1957.

8. Complete freedom of prices is at present applicable only to those products which have by subsequent regulation been exempted from the general price freeze and have not been affected by any of the price stop measures taken in 1963. This is true for a number of food products, such as most meats and cheeses.

Netherlands

Although the legal powers of the government concerning price control are extensive, price policy in the Netherlands is primarily based on voluntary co-operation between Government and business. Price policy is the responsibility of the Ministry of Economic Affairs assisted by the Economic Control Office, a Government agency which keeps watch on the conduct of business with respect to prices.

Criteria. In order to achieve reasonable price stability the following rules have been adopted:

(i) wage increases are not to be passed on into prices;

(ii) a rise in external costs – and costs of raw and auxiliary materials – may warrant a corresponding increase in prices, whereas a fall in external costs should lead to a corresponding fall in the prices and final products;

(iii) in case of an increase in prices on account of an excessive rise in costs, the nominal trade margin – in money terms – is to be maintained; which is tantamount to saying that the percentage trade margin should be lowered.

Departure from these criteria may be permitted if necessitated by considerations related to the earning-power of the industry or enterprise concerned. Consultations are held every year with representatives of business to determine the exact interpretation of these rules.

Prior Notification. Price increases for all goods and services are subject to prior notification to the Minister of Economic Affairs together with a justification. With respect to proposed increases of the price of certain basic commodities the Ministry of Economic Affairs must be consulted in advance; since 1958 this has applied only to bread, milk, margarine and fuel.

Implementation. If in the view of the Minister of Economic Affairs a specific price increase is not justified, the industry or enterprise concerned is asked to rescind it. If this is not done, the Minister of Economic Affairs may use his legal powers, based on the Price Act. Most important is the power to fix maximum prices for goods sold in the home market. In the case of prices of goods and services subject to maximum regulations, the authorities are empowered to lay down rules for the form in which records should be kept in order to follow the development of costs. More generally, every person is obliged to supply such information as is deemed necessary to decide whether there is occasion to issue a price order.

Sanctions. When a price order has been issued, for a particular sector of industry or trade anyone who charges prices exceeding those laid down in the order can be summoned by the Economic Control Office. This has 200 controllers at its disposal, and can eventually prosecute.

Cartel Policy. Price policy is supported by cartel policy. The Economic Competition Act of 1956 authorises the Government to declare unenforceable agreements restricting competition which it considers are incompatible with the public interest. In the context of price policy, the decision reached in 1971 to declare collective forms of resale price maintenance non-binding is particularly significant.

Norway
Under the Price Act of 1953 the authorities possess extensive powers to intervene in price formation. Regulation of restrictive business practices is also covered by provisions of this Act.

The Price Directorate of the Ministry of Prices and Wages, with a staff of about a hundred people, implements the Government's price policy. *The Government Price Inspectorate, with nine local*

*offices and a staff of about eighty-five is responsible for verifying
the application of price regulations, and following the development
of prices which are not subject to regulation.* The Price Directorate
also takes part in this work. Furthermore, each municipality has
a Price Committee which plays an important role in the supervision of prices, particularly in keeping local industry and
commerce fully informed of the relevant price regulations.

Techniques. Regulations may apply to all levels, i.e. to the
producer level, the wholesale stage, the retail stage and to importers. A variety of techniques are used. They can be grouped in
three main categories:

(a) Maximum prices: apply to commodities such as milk and
    other dairy products, flour and flour products, fertilisers
    and feed concentrates, transport and hospital rates. In
    towns and built-up areas price regulation also covers rent
    and real estate prices.
(b) Price stop: at present provisional price stops are in force
    for prices and profits fixed by restrictive business associa-
    tions. This prohibition was introduced in December 1961
    to counteract a sharp inflationary price development, and
    has been maintained since.
(c) Regulation of profits: regulations concerning maximum
    profits apply to certain foodstuffs and their transformation.
    Retail profits on a number of basic general foods have been
    fixed by special agreements between representatives of the
    trade and the price authorities, e.g., cheese, sugar, a num-
    ber of soft drinks, canned foods, fats, soaps, etc.

It is not possible to calculate the proportion of the total production of goods and services which is subject to price regulation.
The figures below, however, show the weight in the consumer price
index of products subject to regulation in one form or another:

Maximum prices and special price stop arrangements	17%
Horizontal price and profit agreements (excluding goods which are also regulated in other ways)	14%
Maximum profits	15%
Total	46%

To the above must be added contributions from State owned industries and Government regulation in other ways than via the Price Act, amounting to 7 per cent. Altogether, therefore, products with a weight of about one half in the total index are subject to regulations of one form or another at the retail stage. At the producer or importer stage, products with a weight of about 40 per cent of the index are subject to price regulation.

The Price Act also authorises the fixing of minimum prices. This authority is, however, not at present utilised.

Criteria. Through regulation, prices shall in principle allow a reasonable profit on rational operations under normal capacity utilisation. In the administration of the price regulations consideration is given to the total profit situation for the enterprise concerned, in such a way that good profits on certain commodities or services, which are not subject to control, provide the basis for lower prices for the regulated items.

Prices of new products are in principle treated in the same way as corresponding products already on the market. This implies that, depending upon the circumstances, they may be subject to direct regulation, or to regulation or agreement concerning profit margins, or the price may be left unregulated.

If the Price Authorities consider it necessary, price formation of special products or group of products will be made the subject of a more intensive study. As the extent and importance of direct price regulation has been reduced, greater emphasis has been put on reducing hindrances to effective price competition and on supervision of prices and profit margins.

Control of Restrictive Business Practices. Price policy is supported by anti-monopoly policy. The Price Act provides for the reporting and registration of restrictive business practices and market-dominating positions. In 1957 producers' and importers' retail price maintenance agreements were prohibited. The individual supplier (but not associations of suppliers) may, however, quote advisory prices, provided that it is clearly understood the dealer is free to take lower prices. Furthermore, legislation introduced in 1960 prohibited horizontal restrictive arrangements on prices etc., and of restrictive practices in relation to tenders. General exceptions apply to exports, the sale of Norwegian farm and forest products and the products of the fisheries by producer organisations, bank and insurance services, and sales or deliveries from joint marketing organisations.

Finland
Stabilisation Policy 1968–70. The starting-point for the stabilisation of prices and wages was the devaluation of the Finnmark by 23·81 per cent in October 1967. It was obvious that unless special steps were taken, the situation would soon slide back to that which had made devaluation necessary in the first place. One reason for this state of affairs was the complex system by which all wages and prices were tied to indexes – a system designed to cushion everyone in Finland against the effects of inflation. At the start of 1969, for instance, wages would have risen automatically by 5–6 per cent merely by being tied to the index. To this would have been added the increase stipulated by the collective agreements. The interest rate was, because of the index linkages, as high as 11 per cent and would have risen continuously.

Simultaneously, unemployment was rising to a peak: 125,000 in January 1968. It was under these circumstances that the labour market organisations opened negotiations, presided by Mr Liinamaa, the State contact man, to stabilise prices and incomes. Quick results were achieved: In March 1968 a Stabilisation Agreement was reached between the labour market organisations, agricultural organisations, and the State. At the same time the commercial and industrial organisations signed a separate agreement to follow the stabilisation line in their own sectors.

The main points of the Stabilisation Agreement were as follows:

1. Wages and salaries were no longer to be tied to an index, neither were loans, interests, long-term purchase agreements, building contracts, etc. After the summer of 1968 the index would apply only to pensions.
2. It was decided to raise wages and salaries in 1969 roughly in ratio to the growth of productivity. This growth averaged 3·9 per cent per annum over the previous nine years, and it was agreed accordingly to raise all hourly wages by an absolute sum of 16 pennies, regardless of the type of work or current pay of the employee. Also agreed to were increases to certain social payments, which meant a further rise of 0·4 per cent in personnel costs. The first Stabilisation Agreement also applied to farmers, so agricultural prices were fixed simultaneously: they were raised by 2 per cent in

June 1968, and again in January 1969. The Stabilisation Agreement stipulated the enactment of a long-term Agricultural Incomes Act.

3. Prices were to be controlled as a guarantee to employees that their real wage increases would not be cancelled out by price increases. Wage controls were regarded as a necessary balance to price controls, but they were not to be enforced by the State; instead, wages were subject to collective agreements between the labour market organisations, as earlier.

4. The abolition of index-tying and enforcement of price and wage controls presupposed special powers for the State. Parliament passed an Economic Special Powers Act in April, to be in force in 1968–9. This kind of Act can be passed according to the constitution only by 5/6 majority.

5. The Agreement envisaged steps to cut down rampant unemployment. On this point the Bank of Finland was consulted, and special funds were granted to promote housing construction.

6. State expenditure was not to be increased, neither were tax bases to be altered.

7. Civil servants and public officials would have their own system of collective agreements, and a committee was set up for this purpose.

The first Stabilisation Agreement ended in December 1969. Well before this, steps were taken to continue Stabilisation. The agreement for 1970 was signed in September 1969. It provided for approximately the same policies as its predecessor: index-tying remained abolished and price controls were continued as in 1968–9. In fact, a list of commodities and services subject to price controls had been drawn up in summer 1969. The wage increase for 1970 was to be 18 pennies an hour, or 1 per cent, whichever was higher for the employee. An additional 1 per cent increase in total wages was to be applied as agreed between branch organisations.

Agricultural prices had been fixed under a three-year law passed in summer 1969. This Act stipulates negotiations between producers and the State, with the proviso that agricultural costs would be taken into account automatically, and that the productivity of agriculture and development of employees' wages in rural areas be taken into consideration at the negotiations.

As nation-wide unemployment had been substantially reduced between 1968 and the summer of 1969, the accent was now on alleviating regional and structural unemployment. Special measures were taken to promote training and to augment labour mobility.

In general the 1970 agreement did not alter the bases for State revenues. Certain prices went up at the start of 1970, such as postage and alcohol (a State monopoly in Finland). One factor in drawing up the terms of the 1970 agreement was the need for an anti-cyclic system. One of the terms, in fact, was that companies should make anti-cyclic deposits in the Bank of Finland.

The purpose of both Stabilisation Agreements has been to halt the advance of prices and keep wage and salary rises within the limits of growing productivity. Prices, however, are affected by factors other than wages – for instance, by the price of foreign raw materials. It is equally obvious that productivity does not rise at the same rate in every branch. So some increase of prices and some wage drift are inevitable. In fact, the two processes tend to balance each other out, resulting in an increase of real earnings, roughly in ratio to productivity.

The Third Agreement. A third Agreement on labour and economic policy was signed in December, 1970, but significantly it was not signed by the white-collar trade union Federation. It proved much more difficult to reach agreement on this occasion, and the President of the Republic intervened in order to urge the two parties to reach agreement. He presented a package of proposals to them and emphasised that his proposals were a complete package to be accepted or rejected as a whole. He proposed that price controls should be continued in their existing form while recognising that some of the proposed wage increases might, of necessity, lead to increased prices in some cases.

Results. Results show that Stabilisation has been a success. Prices rose steeply by 7 per cent up to March following devaluation, as was only natural, but since then they have proved to be astonishingly stable despite the sharp increases occurring in other countries. Between July, 1967 and July, 1968, the cost of living rose by 9·5 per cent; between July, 1968 and July, 1969 the increase was only 1·7 per cent, and from 1969 to 1970 it was respectively 2·7 per cent. In other words, between July, 1968 and July, 1970, the cost of living rose by a mere 4·4 per cent.

o

On the other hand the pay packets of industrial employees rose by as much as 11·8 per cent in 1968 and 8·7 per cent in 1969. Thus in 1968, during only part of which the Stabilisation Agreement was in force, their real earnings rose by 2·8 per cent and in 1969 by 6·3 per cent. This year, if prices rise by an average of 2·6–2·7 per cent, as seems likely, and wages by around 10 per cent, the real earnings of industrial wage earners will go up by about 7 per cent.

Unemployment was at its peak in 1968 but has since then declined rapidly. The average percentage in 1968 was 4 per cent; in 1970 it was down to 2 per cent – almost as low as the 1½ per cent prevailing at the beginning of the 1960s.

CONCLUSIONS

A number of points emerge from these international comparisons.

1. Legislation to Control Prices

Most of the countries examined have legislation which empowers specific government agencies to impose maximum prices and margins, or through some other standard to achieve price stabilisation through legal powers. In Austria, for example, under the Price Control Act of 1950 the Federal Ministries of the Interior and of Agriculture and Forestry have the power to fix maximum prices or charges. In France, legislation enables the Government to introduce a comprehensive system of price control at any time. In the Netherlands, the Price Act enables the Minister of Economic Affairs to fix maximum prices for goods sold in the home market.

The UK Prices and Incomes Act passed in August 1966 was therefore *not unique* in providing the Government with such comprehensive legal powers to stabilise prices. *European experience would suggest that there is a strong case for keeping reserve powers as envisaged in the 1966 Act to be used when necessary.*

2. Local Price Control

Few of the countries reviewed here have introduced any extensive measure of price control at the local level. In fact, the foregoing survey showed that only in Norway, Austria and the Netherlands has there been an attempt to decentralise the machinery for price control. In Austria, there are local Administrative District Offices and the special Provincial Price Authorities. But these have a fairly small staff and exercise primarily a note taking and educational function. The Netherlands Economic Control office – which is responsible for ensuring the observance of specific price orders – has 200 Controllers at its disposal who operate at the regional as well as the national level. Norway has gone farther than any other Western European country in this aspect. The Government Price Inspectorate with nine local offices and a staff of about eighty-five is responsible for verifying the application of price regulations. Moreover, each municipality has a Price Committee which plays an important role in the supervision of prices, particularly in keeping local industry and commerce fully informed of the relevant price regulations.

British experience so far suggests that some measure of 'decentralisation' as 'regionalisation' of the price control machinery is essential. At the very least, such units would make possible attempts to police a price control policy. Unfortunately, European comparisons cannot provide much help in this direction.

3. Price Criteria

A clear feature of European price control systems is *their flexibility*. In the UK the main effort of the PIB and the Monopolies Commission is towards stabilizing prices or charges themselves. In certain cases, however, it may be more effective to stabilise profit margins or trade margins at the wholesale level. There is considerable experience to be drawn from France in this respect, though other countries too adopt similar practices.

4. Absence of control over prices charged with Service Sector

It is clear from the foregoing survey that few countries have established machinery which achieves effective control over charges made by service industries. There are two particular problems here. The first is the absence of statistics of the numbers of units involved and their income distribution. The second is the fragmentation of the units involved.

As service industries and manufacturing labour-intensive industries are responsible for the highest rates of price increase in Britain, devising a system of price control and supervision for the major areas of the service industries will be an urgent task for a future Labour Government.

5. Pricing Norms

One further technique is worthy of mention. It is generally

assumed to be possible to fix future productivity rises in each industry. If this is feasible then this notional productivity rise could be fixed as the 'norm', and when prices are being reviewed in each industry, increases in costs *below the norm* should be expected to be absorbed and not passed on to the consumer. This would be a refined role for special offshoots of the little NEDCs, who could ensure an effective supervision of the pricing-productivity norm in their respective industries.

GENERAL MACHINERY FOR PRICE CONTROL

Some general Government machinery already exists which can be strengthened to bear more effectively on rising prices. Three aspects in particular: the Monopolies Commission, the Restrictive Practices Court and Consumer Protection, all have a direct bearing on the level of prices.

1. Monopolies Commission

The 1965 Monopolies Act strengthened the Commission and provided it with important compulsory powers over the prices and charges made by firms which it investigates. The Commission performs a very useful function. There are, however, two general problems arising from its operation at present. First, it works very slowly and can only examine a few cases each year. Second, the formation of the Industrial Reorganisation Corporation – concerned with structural reforms – requires the formulation of a more precise code on what are considered to be desirable mergers. There is some danger at present that the IRC and the Monopolies Commission will work in opposite directions.

2. The Restrictive Practices Court

Since its establishment the Court has built up a valuable series of case studies on existing kinds of restrictive practices which affect prices. In the present review being conducted by NEDC, the pricing aspects of its work must be reconciled with the code of pricing procedures now being formulated by the NBPI.

3. Consumer Legislation

The Consumers' Bill – presented in the last Parliament – was an important first step in consumer protection. Correct labelling is essential, but there is a much wider problem of ensuring that *adequate standards* are maintained. The Reith Commission's Report on Advertising concluded that the time had come to establish a National Consumer Board, and urges that 'A code of advertising practice based on the existing codes should be made statutory and . . . where voluntary supervision and negotiation fail to achieve adequate control the National Consumer Board should be able to intervene and proscribe. The new Board could also be provided with facilities for testing products to ensure value for money.'

In the industrial relations chapter we have already advocated the reinstitution of the Prices and Incomes Board. This body has also an important role to play in informing the public about price levels and product values. Some further powers are necessary to enable the NBPI to follow up its former prices and productivity investigations.

CONTROL IN THE PUBLIC SECTOR

The public sector is obviously an easier field for Government intervention on price control than the private sector. It is also an important 'price' sector because it contains a large proportion of the major service industries. Railways, Electricity, Gas, Air Transport are all services in which prices have increased in recent years above the average. Important changes are needed in whole areas of price administration in the public sector.

The basic principle underlying the 1961 White Paper, 'Financial and Economic Obligations of the Nationalised Industries', was that public corporations should, in most of the decisions which they make, behave as if they were normal competitive firms in a private enterprise economy. It was not denied that they all had 'wider obligations than commercial concerns in the private sector', but the authors of the White Paper believed that the twin aims of 'commercial practice' and 'social obligations' could be reconciled and harmonised once the public corporations were presented with a 'rate of return' which they should try to achieve.

The time is overdue for a new White Paper on pricing in the public sector. Its importance for the development of the public sector is clear. It would show clearly the Government's determination to stabilise prices in the public as well as the private sector.

It needs to be firmly stated by the Government that the old financial targets, although perhaps an advance at the time, have proved inflexible in practice. Targets should be set for a return on new investment, but the return on fixed present assets must be a

214/LABOUR: THE UNIONS AND THE PARTY

matter of pricing policy, and must include costs and returns which will not necessarily lead to the attainment of any particular financial target.

The size of the surplus (in terms of the 1961 White Paper the 'rate of return on assets') must be largely a matter of pricing policy. The danger in past thinking has been that prices will be determined by the need for some 'notional surplus'.

THE GENERAL LEVEL OF PRICES IN THE PUBLIC SECTOR

Public Corporations which find it easy to 'cover costs' – like electricity – can manipulate the surplus that they make to earn whatever rate of return they are permitted to squeeze from the consumer. The decision about the size of surplus to be earned is a decision about the degree of self-financing which is thought to be appropriate, and a decision about general economic policy, including the need for price stabilisation.

There is a strong presumption in favour of public corporations 'covering their costs' where costs are defined as the overall avoidable short- (and fairly long-) term outgoings. This is particularly true of and relevant for those industries where demand for their products is fairly responsive to price changes. Otherwise, consumers will be set the wrong 'signals' and will not be aware of the true alternative costs which they are imposing on the community.

In industries that operate under excess capacity and which could increase their output if there were greater demand, it would be preferable to cut prices rather than increase them, since if demand is responsive to price the surplus caused by the corporation might increase and, far more important, available resources may be used more profitably.

Decisions about the rate of surplus to be earned by different (and in particular competing public) corporations are crucially connected with long term planning considerations. So, for example, the surplus instructions which are given to British Rail and the Transport Holding Company are instructions that should reflect explicit decisions about transport policy.

THE RELATIVE PRICES OF DIFFERENT PRODUCTS

The structure of the prices charged by public corporations is largely a relic of the past, of the war and the pre-war habits of public utility price control. The 1961 White Paper made no positive recommendations in this field, and we should accept that prices should reflect relative costs of different products.

But the establishment of relative costs often involves an indefensible and arbitrary allocation of overheads. If all products were to be sold at prices that covered only their identifiable capable costs, overheads would not be charged for, and the 'surpluses' of public corporations which sell many joint products would be negative. Thus there must be an element of 'charging what the market will bear' in any pricing policy, although this should be subject to some political control.

Differential pricing for 'peak load' services is desirable, but often non-price interferences may produce the same or better results. Action, whether by pricing or by other means, should be pressed much farther and faster than in the past, in order to save socially valuable investment resources.

The general assumption that prices should cover costs should be heavily qualified and quantified rather than stated in vague and woolly terms. Sometimes the correct way to deal with these problems, despite many opinions to the contrary, may be to allow a certain amount of controlled cross-subsidisation to continue. It is at present recognised that transport services, for example, may, for commercial or political reasons, be offered at 'a loss' to encourage use of other more profitable services. BRS may find it necessary to undertake to deliver parcels to John O'Groats in order to be known as a national agency. Other 'loss-making' services may be planned parts of development of a general development plan of an industry.

Finally, it should be recognised that pricing policy in the private sector is often incorrect from the national point of view, and that therefore pricing policy in the public sector may have to be operated in different ways to take account of irrationalities in private pricing.

THE SOCIAL ASPECT OF PRICING POLICY IN THE PUBLIC SECTOR

We have earlier noted the urgent need to strengthen the measures providing consumer protection. In the public sector too, there is considerable scope for the strengthening of consumer protection. In particular, public sector pricing policies should be fashioned to take account not only of the financial factors mentioned above such as necessary rates of return on capital etc., but also must be concerned with the income levels and purchasing capacity of potential consumers.

We need to develop a pricing policy in which the consumer's as well as the producer's interest is fully considered. So far little attempt has been made by nationalised industries. Few national-ised concerns conduct adequate sales research. Even fewer translate their findings into their pricing policy to give it a 'social' and 'consumer' content. Public sector pricing policy could be a powerful instrument for improving the purchasing powers of the poorer sections of the community.

The recent legislation to set up a Minister for Consumer Affairs is certainly recognition by the Conservative Government that some action is necessary in this field, although their decision follows rather strangely upon their abolition of the Consumers' Association in 1971.

Appointing a Minister will do little by itself to focus the atten-tion and control which are necessary on prices, and here some serious consideration should be given to the setting up of a National Consumers' Authority which would be empowered to survey all consumer matters, and would not only give general advice to the public sector on pricing policy, but would also supply information to consumers and to all industries and services.

In line with sensible pricing policies, it would be imperative that the National Consumers' Authority had powers to test advertising claims made by manufacturers and operated under a statutory code of advertising practice.

This would at least ensure that the interests of the consumer were under constant surveillance by people who would have the necessary expertise to give judgements not only on cases submitted to them, but also in the formation of future pricing policy.

Such a body, charged with being the 'watchdog' for the con-sumer, would therefore combine the dual functions of monitoring advertising and advising and informing the general public on prices.

THE PUBLIC PURCHASING WEAPON

The public sector's demands for goods and services have consi-derable impact on the economy as a whole, and therefore on price levels, because they make up a large proportion of all purchases and capital investment in the country. In an average year, the public corporations alone account for about a fifth of all fixed investment in the country. The share of the public sector in investment in plant and machinery, almost entirely investment by the public corporations, has been rising in recent years and is now close to 40 per cent of the national total.

The importance of a proper policy for purchasing in the public sector, and the sad record of the absence of either policies or properly staffed purchasing offices in the past, suggests the following conclusions:

(a) The lead of the corporations such as the National Coal Board and the Central Electricity Generating Board should be followed in industry and in government. Where the volume of business justified it, strong separate purchasing departments should be established.

(b) The additional constraints on the bargaining powers of the nationalised undertakings, restricting their powers to manufacture either for their own use or for anyone else should be lifted. These restraints are economic nonsense in any case and should never be imposed on any future nationalised undertakings, for very good reasons quite unconnected with bargaining strength.

(c) If there is to be a national policy for 'buying British' or, say, for favouring a particular sector of industry, it should be a general rule, which is clearly recognised, and an opportunity should be given to debate it openly. It should not be a decision taken in a casual or unconsidered way and applied in a muddled manner.

(d) Benefits flowing from any such non-commercial purchasing principle should be fairly shared between the public buyer and the private supplier.

(e) Beyond these rather special, and, it should be hoped, rare, general directions, purchasing officers should be given freedom to drive a hard bargain with their suppliers, but rules of enlightened self-interest should apply. For example, the National Coal Board has found it worthwhile to plan purchases so that the two or three (or more) suppliers between them have some spare capacity at most times. This leaves scope for increased orders and keeps competition keen.

(f) The level of purchasing operations should be determined by experience, and not imposed by a dogmatic support of centralised buying *in all cases*, or for 'de-centralised' buying *in all cases*.

Some of these proposals are already being implemented, but there is enormous scope for further development, and in particular, a need to co-ordinate the purchasing policies of the public sector through a new National Purchasing Agency.

If it did no more than advise the public sector on purchasing methods, and on the level of operations advisable for particular articles or contracts, it would perform a valuable service. It could also foster the exchange of experience within the public sector.

It is to be hoped that it could be far more ambitious than this, and undertake purchasing on behalf of the public sector. It could marshal the whole market power of the public sector in this way, and if that power were intelligently used it would have beneficial effects on its private suppliers as well as producing savings for the public sector. The scope for such an agency to influence and stabilise prices would be considerable.

I have dealt at some length with the techniques of price control because I believe they have been sadly neglected by the newspapers and the mass media. For reasons only too well known, the Press and TV prefer to focus their attention on the wages element in costs to the exclusion of everything else. Retailers who always put a 'bit on for themselves' are not pilloried in the same way as workers or unions who are chasing wage increases. It is time that those who operate the prices mechanism in our country were brought into the arena of public scrutiny along with the unions when rising prices are being discussed.

The 'Prices Control' section in this chapter has been designed to show that some measure of price control is desirable and necessary, and that there are feasible techniques available to any Government that has the determination and will to use them. A large political prize awaits the next Labour Government if it tackles this central social and economic problem.

LOW PAY – GOVERNMENT ACTION

Apart from price control, the other most important area for Government intervention in a prices and incomes policy is in helping the low-paid workers. Government action here need not be restricted only to the concept of a National Minimum Wage, although this would be useful as a safety net. Low-paid workers are in need of assistance in other ways because the history of wage negotiations in this country, especially since the War, has shown that the present processes of collective bargaining are unlikely to improve the position of the low-paid worker in the short term.

Low-paid workers are to be found in areas where labour is plentiful and where industries are in decline, and in these cases collective bargaining is too weak a mechanism to improve their position. Even in industries or companies which are thriving, or in places where the demand for labour exceeds the supply, the low-paid worker usually exists because his job is seen to be less vital and important. Although he does better in comparison with similar workers in the less prosperous industries, he lags far behind the top workers in his firm. His job is often the most expendable, the first to go in a new investment programme, and though employers want to have such workers available in the factory, they do not want to pay high wages for this facility. Employers who do not quibble at putting pounds on the top rate dig in deeply when it comes to going above a few shillings on the lowest minimum rate.

If collective bargaining is not supplying the complete answer to improving the position of low paid workers, how can the Government assist? The Government could assist in three ways – by action on the statutory wage-fixing bodies, by encouraging money increases instead of percentages, and by a transitional levelling up *before* a prices and incomes policy was started.

ACTION ON WAGES COUNCILS

It is often ignored that over four million workers in this country have their minimum wages regulated by various kinds of Wages Councils and Boards. Nearly sixty of these fix minimum rates and they all fall within a narrow range of each other. It would there-fore mean no internal wages upheaval if all these wage regulating boards brought their lowest minimum rates to the same figure.

The Government at the present time supports these bodies not only with the law, but also by the expenditure involved in the mediation and arbitration of claims. In its role in a prices and incomes policy the Government could announce that Wage Councils etc. should all increase their lowest minimums to a certain figure by a certain time. This simple action would mean not only that industries covering 16 per cent of the total labour force would have a realistic minimum wage, but also that a very large proportion of low-paid workers would be affected because the industries covered by the Wages Councils and Boards operate largely in these areas of the labour market.

MONEY INCREASES – NOT PERCENTAGES

In the same industries covered by wage-fixing bodies and in the public sector where the Government can be expected to have some influence, they could also encourage the move towards money increases of fixed amounts instead of percentages. The percentage system means that those earning most get more from the increase than those earning least. Since the main ingredient in the claim is usually the rise in the cost of living, it follows that if there is a global amount which is to be allocated by the employer to settle the claim, then the percentage share out leaves those at the bottom with the smallest increase. This is an indefensible situation, because the cost of living rises by a monetary amount for all, *not* by a percentage of earnings. A global amount could be negotiated and a 'tapering formula' calculated whereby the lower worker would get a better deal, while differentials would not be upset too much. The TUC have advocated this same approach to the problem.

The Government could also help to restore much needed confidence in long-term agreements by encouraging the inclusion of cost of living clauses in all wage agreements in the Wages Council and public sector. At one time these were called 'escalator clauses', but the experience of the high level of inflation over the past few years has shown that they would have had a stabilising effect on wages bargaining and would have kept low-paid workers' wages in constant touch with prices.

Certainly, if long-term wage agreements are to be considered, then cost of living clauses, with 'thresholds' defined and the monetary increases fixed for each shift upwards in living costs, are an absolute necessity. This kind of agreement also puts a healthy, democratic pressure on both Government and industry to keep prices down.

TRANSITIONAL LEVELLING UP

One of the reasons for the failure of the prices and incomes policy which we examined was the fact that negotiations throughout Britain are taking place at different times. This means that no matter when a prices and incomes policy is started, some workers will feel that the new rules and criteria are affecting their increases because they have not settled their annual or biennial round of negotiations before the inaugural date. This is seen by them as starting off the new policy on unequal terms with other workers for purely chronological reasons, and certainly through no fault of their own.

This can be overcome by adopting a transitional policy of levelling up the annual increases. In practical terms it means calculating the average national increase over a period of about nine months prior to the inaugural date for the operation of the policy, followed by a Government 'fiat' that all workers who have had less than the average increase must be brought up to this figure by the date upon which the policy is due to start.

This does mean a hefty cost at the beginning of the policy, but without such a transitional levelling up, future norms are likely to be broken by those who were left behind and then the whole policy which depends on consent, collapses. This idea has been broached by Professor Hugh Clegg and is workable, because it is based on an American experiment called the 'Little Steel Formula' which operated successfully in the Second World War.

These measures mentioned involving action on Wage Councils, on influencing 'tapering' monetary increases as opposed to percentages, and in a transitional levelling up of annual increases prior to the inauguration of a prices and incomes policy, are all internal practical steps which can be taken by a Government to promote an anti-inflation policy. The final Government action which must be taken is in seeing that the prices and incomes policy operates within a socially just framework of society. This is known as the 'social compact'.

GOVERNMENT ACTION – THE SOCIAL COMPACT

The necessity for the right kind of social framework as a con-comitant of a prices and incomes policy has been raised by Harold Wilson. Speaking in New York on 4 May 1971 about Labour's difficulties on the operation of a prices and incomes policy during his period as Prime Minister, he said:

> For a statutory prices and incomes policy to be successful it must be based on consent: a wage freeze must be total; any statutory interference must be fair between groups, and individuals; any action of this kind must be made as far as possible tolerable by improved social services, and, being universal, it could not discriminate between the public and private sector.
>
> Above all, the lesson of our experience is that such a freeze can only be of short duration. In a national emergency, before anomalies make it totally unworkable and, as they do, discredit not only the policy, but even the system of society in which it operates.
>
> Restraint in wages and salaries would not last long if prices and especially key prices, were rising. By key prices I mean the principal elements in the expenditure of an average household, rent, bread, milk, school meals, commuter fares, shoes and clothing. In a general sense such a compact must be part of a national effort to raise living standards.

Mr Wilson was speaking here with hindsight, but he did pinpoint the need for action by the Government to go much farther in protecting the individual than his Government had done.

The compact which he spoke of, includes action on key prices, which we have already discussed, and also the necessity for fairness between groups of workers, which has also been examined. He also refers to the social compact, the framework of social justice, when he talks of the need for improved social services.

The social compact accompanying even a voluntary prices and incomes policy must contain not only improved social benefits, but also policies which will lead to and maintain full employment.

The social compact also means some significant shift in the redistribution of income and wealth in this country. This can be done by various taxation measures, such as increased Capital Gains and Corporation taxes, the introduction of a Wealth tax, which is already operating in some European countries, the closing of loopholes in the tax system which those with money enough to pay expensive accountants can profit from, and finally, with general budgetary measures to attack fiscal privileges of all kinds.

At the other end of the scale part of the increased income from the taxation measures mentioned should be used not to take sixpence off the income tax, but to take the low-income families out of the income tax bracket altogether. This last action would be a complementary measure to assist the low-paid worker, and this, allied with improvements in the social services used most by large families and the chronic sick, would create the kind of socially just conditions within which a prices and incomes policy could stand a chance of success.

The proposals outlined in this chapter on prices, low pay and the social compact, allied to the ownership and control, and industrial relations policies in the two previous chapters, would provide the kind of society in which *consent* to a prices and incomes policy could be forthcoming. The measures I have put forward would benefit every working man and woman and consequently all those in social need. What is good for these groups is good for Britain.

INSTITUTIONALISING INFLATION – AN ALTERNATIVE

Finally, to close this chapter we look at one other alternative to a prices and incomes policy. This is to accept that a certain amount of inflation is inevitable and build this into our economic plans.

This is 'institutionalising inflation' in the economists' jargon, but if there are too many strains in operating a prices and incomes policy in a free society like ours, then such planning for increased prices is worth consideration.

The argument here is that all economic factors can be planned for and in the long run, since society may prefer inflation itself to the remedies for its cure, we should try to assess the costs and disadvantages of inflation.

In an article on 'Industrial Relations', September 1970, David T. Lewellyn, Lecturer in Economics at Nottingham University, argues that institutionalising inflation need not lead to hyper-inflation nor need those on fixed incomes suffer if the Government planned ahead to mitigate the effects of inflation. Adjustments every quarter, under planned inflation, Lewellyn argues, would leave the pensioners better off than they are now where we already have inflation and where increases in pensions only come along every two years.

Lewellyn also holds the opinion that there would be less uncertainty about inflation if some plans were laid to deal with the effects of it on industry and individuals both in and out of work.

He finally illustrates the divergence of opinion between economists on inflation when he says that inflation need not be bad for industrial costs because it encourages growth. He bases this opinion on the fact that in a climate of rising prices, without periodic deflation to fight 'the bogey of inflation', there are higher expectations of rising profits and therefore higher investment, leading to greater efficiency.

Lewellyn's view of institutionalising inflation deserves a place in this study of prices and incomes in Britain because it could well be that his idea of planning for inflation (which is only one of several alternatives in his article) could operate with some loose form of prices and incomes policy. It could therefore be complementary to and not an alternative to a voluntary prices and incomes policy.

I am sure Lewellyn would agree that a combination of the two concepts would be the ideal solution to an economic problem which is likely to need tackling from both angles in the triple interests of increased living standards, economic growth and stability, and social justice.

A PART – NOT THE KEYSTONE OF POLICY

One mistake that must never be made by a future Labour Government is to lean too heavily on any kind of prices and incomes policy. Our experience and the experience of other countries teaches us that it is difficult to operate and is subject to strains.

If a Government feels it can measure up to its role in controlling the economy, in industrial relations and on prices, low pay and the social compact, then it is entitled to ask for the nation's co-operation to keep inflation under control. But this voluntary policy must be seen not as the keystone of its economic policy but only as a part.

If the Government feels that we cannot have a planned economy and a drive towards social equality without a planned prices and incomes policy, let them also remember that we cannot have a planned policy for incomes without a planned economy, and an economy is not planned unless it has social equality and social justice.

Chapter 16

Organising for Power

> 'He has not served who gathers gold,
> Nor has he served whose life is told
> In selfish battles he has won,
> Or deeds of skill that he has done;
> But he has served who now and then
> Has helped along his fellow men.'
>
> Anonymous

This final chapter examines the way in which policy is made in the Labour Party and the role which should be played by the trade unions in fashioning the policy of the party. Here we also have a look at some deficiencies in Labour Party organisation and make some suggestions for improvement.

All political shades of socialist opinion have a vested interest in an efficient and democratic Labour Party. We all want the party to be democratic so that our own particular point of view has a chance of becoming official party policy, and we all desire the maximum efficiency so that the party will be in a position to win power to put these policies into effect.

IMPROVING POLICY MAKING

Although the theoretical basis of the present method of making policy cannot be faulted on its democratic structure, there are still defects in the quality of the discussion which eventually leads to these decisions. I am not referring here to the block vote system of voting at conference, for I believe some kind of representative voting to be unavoidable and necessary if the policy

P

of the party is to reflect the wishes of all the interests of affiliated and individual members.

There has been a lot of rubbish talked over the years about the lack of democracy concerning the block vote, but as long as there is a structure of party membership which provides for both affiliated and individual members, then some kind of block vote is essential. The opposition to the block vote springs from a mistaken idea that only individual members are working at grass roots level for the party. What the anti-block vote brigade tend to forget is that the Labour Party is part of the broader Labour movement, which includes the Party, the unions, the Co-operative Party, and many other smaller affiliated socialist organisations.

Ordinary workers have only a certain amount of time available to work in the movement. If they choose, say, the trade unions as their sphere of socialist endeavour, they are still working within the Labour movement and to devalue their affiliated vote on policy decisions in the political forum of the movement is to be parochial in the extreme.

Financially it is true that the individual member pays £1·20 per year, against 10p for the affiliated member, from 1 January 1972. But only a small proportion of the individual members' subscriptions comes to the central organisation of the party, which is financed at present by 88 per cent from trade union affiliation fees and the remaining 12 per cent from the individual members and other organisations.

Trade unions, in addition to their annual affiliation fees, also contribute to local parties and are almost wholly responsible for financing the General Election campaigns. The creation of the National Agency Service has also meant that the central organisation is now responsible for more of the local party financing.

So from both points of view concerning financing and working for the movement, there are no grounds for devaluing the affiliated members' vote when decisions are being made in the Party.

Leaving the voting method at conference out of the argument, the problem still remains that the quality of decisions reached at conference leaves much to be desired.

The quality of policy making can be improved by both informal and formal means within the party. Formally, by improving political education within the party and aiming at policy making being a continuous process at all levels, rather than only at the Party conference, and giving constituency parties and regional conferences an opportunity to contribute to the making of policy.

Informally, there is still a cleavage in the movement between 'trade union leaders' and politicians, which can only be bridged by more discussion and consultation in depth on policy issues.

THE ROLE OF POLITICAL EDUCATION

If policy decisions are to be accepted by all, they must not only be decided by a conference discussion and voting system which is fair, but they must also be discussed through all the echelons of the movement. This means giving all members an opportunity to have a say in the debate leading up to the policy making decisions at conference.

A start has already been made on this by the participation programme which has now garnered constituency opinion on at least three policy subjects which require further study in the party. There is therefore a realisation by the NEC of the party that the principles of democratic participation must extend to party as well as to industry. This is a beginning. To extend its meaning fully, however, means equipping local parties with the necessary material and facilities upon which to base their opinions. This is one of the fields to which the party's political education scheme should be directed.

At the present time we are failing to give newcomers, or even existing members of the party, a clear idea of the socialist principles which lie at the heart of our movement. We also apparently find it unnecessary to teach members even the most elementary things about how Government operates, and the general principles of economics, international relations and social studies, without which it is impossible to reach informed decisions or appreciate what the party hierarchy are really talking about.

There is a grave danger here for the party, because the lack of political education with a direction means that participation in political controversy is confined only to a few, and this means that our claim that the Labour Party is a mass democratic movement becomes less true.

The quality of decision-making suffers not only because political education has been neglected in the past by lack of consultation, information and direction, but is also hampered by the lack of expertise at all levels in the party to carry out this important function.

As a party we rely heavily on voluntary effort, and we have sadly lacked a training programme to fit local officers of the party to carry out their duties both in educational and organisational work.

Teaching courses for the Political Education Officers in Constituency Labour Parties and suitable training courses to give Chairmen the necessary skills to make party meetings effective, are all part of improving the quality of the political discussion in the local parties.

This cannot just be left to chance or the good sense of whoever may be elected. Special information for each category of party worker should be available, outlining the rudiments of each party job and teaching the skills required. Trade unions have already been doing this for many years for their branch officers and shop stewards. The Labour Party must adopt a similar programme if it wishes to improve the quality of political discussion as well as its organisation and communications.

A workable approach to such a programme would be to analyse the skills required in each position in the party and develop the necessary information and teaching materials to give the training needed. This, coupled with a teaching course on the socialist background on economic and social principles for new members and the production of booklets as part of this introductory course, would provide a basis for the development of a practical political education programme for the party.

An outline for such a programme would be as follows:

(i) *Teaching Materials*

The success of educational activities within the party would depend firstly on the supply of teaching documents that provided the information to be conveyed to members, and set it out with regard to the varying levels of experience and the needs of different groups of members. Advice (perhaps in the form of check-lists) would be needed by tutors and discussion group leaders as to the steps in the examination of a subject, and guidance would be particularly necessary where it was proposed to get some feed-back from groups of students.

(ii) *The Party Meeting*

The party meeting must of necessity be the main instrument of political education. Perhaps, more to the point, the major purpose of members meeting together is to widen their understanding on all the affairs of the party so as to come to an individual or collective view, or a decision on some appropriate action. This means that it is largely concerned with education, however informal the approach. The quality of discussion within the party meeting will in part depend upon how effectively the party has serviced individual members with relevant information and encouraged more systematic examination of issues by groups reporting back to the local party meeting. These are discussed below. But many issues could be adequately presented at local party meetings with some visual aids, which would provide the framework for a disciplined discussion. They could be a series of professionally produced charts, which might in themselves be a self-contained story that did not need to be supplemented by a speaker. With the extensive interest in photography as a hobby, many party members would also have equipment for projecting slides, which could be used in a similar way for presenting aspects of the party's work. With the use of audio-visual aids, however, some background information would probably need to be presented by a speaker, for which some brief notes could be prepared.

(iii) *The Individual Member*

However keen a member might be to more adequately inform himself on party affairs, or to prepare himself for some new role in the party, or to represent the party on some public authority, it is not easy for him to seek out relevant information. The flow of information today in any large organisation is likely to be so great that any individual is likely to have considerable difficulty in retrieving particular information that he requires. This is the role of a library service. At local party level some collection of selected books, pamphlets and documents should be available to individual party members. The aim should be to have sets of documents for differing needs that are likely to be present at local level, e.g. party organisation; local government; education; as well as some introductory general reading on the party and socialist ideas. Transport House would need to provide a subscription service to local parties to enable them to keep their collections up to date.

(iv) *Study Groups*

In providing information that takes account of the needs within the party, good use could be made of study groups. Sometimes they will need to be based upon local parties or sections, or alternatively, the objectives that are aimed for might imply groups of members with more specific roles. Where the study project is based upon a fairly large unit in terms of members, such as a constituency party or regional organisation, it would probably be desirable for one or more study groups to prepare a report which could provide the basis of a disciplined discussion at the larger or more representative meeting. Where it is desired to use such study projects to feed back information and ideas to the National Executive, the major problem will be the planning of the timetable. The implications for the successful organisation of these educational activities is that they will require close co-operation between Transport House and regional and local parties.

(v) *The Tutors and Discussion Group Leaders*

It has been suggested that to be effective the provision of specific information often needs to be closely related to the initiation of developments in party policy. It follows that these educational facilities must be largely conducted by the party itself; and indeed, ideally they should be an integral part of the Party's system of government and methods of working. The main requirement in terms of teaching skills within the party will be for discussion by group leaders. However, it might prove useful in some of the more technical subjects for specialists within the party to supplement the basic information provided in the teaching documents with short introductory talks.

(vi) *Feeding Back Information*

The value of the results of the studies of local groups (where it has been intended to get some feed-back for the purpose of assisting the party in the development of policy of in applying policies) will in large measure depend on the care that was put into preparing the basic teaching documents for discussion group leaders. But such information will still need to be collated and analysed and the eventual decisions of the party fed back into the local parties and sections.

(vii) *Constituency Level Publications*

There is need to give information to members who do not attend party meetings. This can be met by the publication of constituency journals or bulletins. Local parties may need advice as to what ideas to publish and on how to express them.

CONCLUSIONS

The scope of educational services meeting some of the needs of the Party for more effective communications are unlimited. It would be necessary, therefore, for the party to have clearly stated priorities in the subjects in which information should be provided in these ways and objectives as to the different groups to be serviced. Initially only a very limited number of subjects might be handled in this way and for any one subject it might be necessary to restrict study groups to a particular region, or groups of local parties, or perhaps to women's sections or young socialists. However, it is desirable that as soon as practicable every local party and section should be engaged in such educational activities.

THE SOCIAL, ECONOMIC AND POLITICAL BACKGROUND TO SOCIALISM

We recognise here the need for the party to provide education for members in socialist principles and their application. We accept this as a commitment to be covered by a scheme of political education.

The needs for this work can be summarized as follows:

(a) Provision for new members;
(b) Young Socialists and students;
(c) the general needs of party members in this field;
(d) the need to do something for the party's full-time officials, such as arrangements for them to attend a linked or residential course;
(e) to ensure that there is a pre- and post- debate on the party conference agenda;
(f) new developments in party or government thought which invite debate.
(g) The importance of making members aware of the principles which underlie socialist thought.

There is need for a basic introductory course for new members. At the outset this would also be of general help for other party members, but in time as members want to move on to a more advanced course, it will become one primarily for new members.

The production should be undertaken, as a matter of urgency, of a series of booklets to meet the needs of persons seeking information about the background, development, structure and general policy of the Party. At present there is no publication of this kind available. Possible titles of the booklets could be:

  (i) Background of Socialist Ideas;
  (ii) Historical Growth of the Labour Party;
  (iii) The Labour Party and its Members (Structure and Constitution);
  (iv) The Labour Party and Social Conditions, Economic Affairs and Internationalism.

The writing of such booklets should not be undertaken by a committee but should be commissioned from individuals. The booklets should bear the imprimatur of Transport House. The style should be vivid and the aim should be to produce work comparable with the great formative influences on thinking of the Labour Movement like Paine's *Rights of Man* and Blatchford's *Merrie England*. These booklets should be prepared so that they may be used for planned reading by the individual himself, for postal study courses and study work. They should be available also to casual enquirers about the Party.

The party has also to accept responsibility for more sustained study. The development of education at this level could be powerfully supplemented by qualified tutors experienced in adult education, the provision of which may be beyond the resources of constituency parties. The party is not limited to its own resources and constituency parties could get into touch with the Workers' Educational Association for the arrangement of special courses which would be conducted by qualified tutors. In addition there are a number of local Fabian Societies which can provide tutors able to help in this work. Where the particular study is related to the party and the consumer, reference should be made to the help that can be given by the Co-operative movement.

The creation of a demand for, say, a course in the Development of Socialist Thought should be the subject of consultation between regional organisers and constituency parties. The fact that classes, if arranged through the WEA, might include people other than Labour Party members would not be disadvantageous to political education; rather the reverse as party members would benefit from the criticism of opponents.

Active support for this type of political education would be a new venture for many constituency parties. Pilot schemes with a good chance of success in a few areas are to be preferred to any attempt to impose a uniform countryside coverage.

A special effort should be made to establish such courses in university towns and in towns containing all types of colleges of further education, so that students who are members of Labour students' clubs may have an opportunity of widening their knowledge and understanding of the social, economic and political problems facing a Labour Government.

Young Socialists' branches and women's sections present excellent opportunities for developing of courses of this kind. Most of these organisations focus their activities on weekly meetings in which their members take part. There is thus opportunity for planned educational work to be sustained.

Members of Young Socialists' branches have a special motivation for the study of socialist principles for which the party must take responsibility. We have not been able to undertake a sufficiently close look at the work which may be required for Young Socialists and this needs more detailed consideration.

The successful promotion of political education at this level would depend to a considerable extent on the energies of the regional organising staff, already faced by extensive claims on their time. A special effort should be made to secure their goodwill and interest by arranging consultations and briefing sessions for them with party members employed in the administration and teaching of adult education.

If interest in this type of education is to be stimulated it will be necessary to provide opportunities for follow-on studies which might take the form of residential courses.

In addition to the booklets which I have proposed in a previous paragraph there should be published as a matter of urgency, suggested outlines and bibliographies for courses to be available as guides for those willing to assist in this work. Film strips as teaching aids should be commissioned and also made available to trade unions for use in the political aspects of their educational work.

As a general aid to political education at this level the party should discuss with the Fabian Society the possibility of making available bibliographies in the main fields selected for study, together with details of appropriate periodicals. Attention should be specifically directed to the publications of the Fabian Society. Information should be kept up to date by the issue of details of new publications in the selected fields, together with a limited coverage of reviews, to coincide with publishers' spring and autumn lists. The cost of this service should be covered by an annual charge to subscribers who should not be restricted to the Party membership. Properly developed, such a service would appeal to people beyond the usual range of political party propaganda, and could well be the means of attracting their interest to the Labour Party.

The Political Education Officer will need to have close liaison with the Fabian Society and the Workers' Educational Association in the development of this work.

TEACHING METHODS

There is also a need for training in using the new teaching methods for Labour's political education and on the conduct of discussion and the extension of 'learning by doing'. Education sessions should always include practical exercises, and these can be applied to political as well as organisation situations.

The development of new correspondence courses is also important because in some areas of the country it will not be possible to organise 'face to face' teaching and also the correspondence course encourages the use of written work which is an invaluable training to the political activists who will be involved in writing letters to the press, drafting resolutions and statements of the local party's attitude to political events.

REGIONAL LEVEL

At regional level the regional conference should be used more as a vehicle for contributing to party policy. This role has been curtailed in the past by the curtailment of discussion on certain topics. This has now been relaxed and advantage should be taken of this to have special conferences in selected regions to assist policy making on certain subjects.

Some regions have expert knowledge of certain areas of policy and have their own particular problems. They have an important contribution to make on these policies when national party attitudes are being formed. Organising special conferences in the regions is a task for the NEC in liaison with their specialist sub-committees and the regions concerned.

POLITICAL EDUCATION – NATIONAL LEVEL

Arising from one of the recommendations of the Simpson Committee on Party Organisation, a Political Education Section has now been established at Transport House. This section is headed by a Political Education Officer and should have the following tasks:

(a) analysing the party's needs in political education;
(b) determining the programme;
(c) preparing the courses;
(d) planning the teaching methods;
(e) training the tutors;
(f) planning the material;
(g) liaison with the organisation and research departments on training methods and materials;
(h) general administration of the education schemes throughout the party;
(i) external liaison with outside educational bodies.

If these tasks were carried out nationally with the programme already outlined at local level, there would be an increase in political awareness and efficiency which could transform the political activity of the rank and file of the Party, raise the quality of political discussion, and substantially lift the quality of decision making within the Party.

POLICY LIAISON WITH THE UNIONS

If political education is the tool to improve policy making within the party, how can we improve policy liaison between the party and the trade unions?

Some policy liaison is essential because it is becoming increasingly apparent that even with a trade union section on the National Executive Committee and a trade union group of MPs in the House of Commons, there is lack of understanding about policy objectives and the reasons for Party, or when in power, Labour Government, decisions. The need for some additional informal machinery was realised during the last two years of office of the last Government, and a small NEC liaison committee with trade union representatives was formed to meet a small cabinet committee each month. This arrangement proved valuable, but the policy liaison with the unions needs to be much stronger than that. The massive breakdown in communications which we experienced in 1964–70 between the unions and the party in Government must never be allowed to happen again.

If there were a coherent trade union political philosophy on all main issues contact on policy issues would be simple, but the trade unions are as riven by political divisions as the party itself, and therefore the trade union collective view at any given time on particular issues is not easy to obtain. True, there are discussions between the TUC and the NEC of the Labour Party, but these tend to be formal and concerned with particular issues, and cannot be said to add much to the pool of policy making for the party.

At top level in our movement there is a lack of political contact which must be bridged in some way. There is still a tendency in trade union circles to regard 'intellectuals' with suspicion. There is a saying, 'A nation that cannot trust its intellectuals cannot trust itself', but this is not accepted by some trade union leaders who use their suspicion to preserve the dichotomy between the unions and the Labour hierarchy.

This has led to political strife in the past and will do so again in the future if something is not done. As a party we have always been too soft in opposition on arguments that appeared to be dividing the industrial and political wings of the movement. This has meant that when a Labour Government takes power they have to argue within the Labour movement as well as with the general public on the policies which they intend to pursue.

The party has for many years now had this tendency of shelving awkward debates as though the 'halo of office' invested their argument with a piercing clarity which was absent when they were in opposition.

What is really required at the very highest level in the unions and Labour Party are several leisurely seminars to 'clear the ground' on major policy items, and these should be taking place now when the party is in opposition. I know that all people at the top are busy, but it really is inexcusable that no meeting of minds, free from pressure of immediate conference decision, is taking place in our movement.

Time must be found for some discussion of the problems concerning the transition from the kind of society which we have at present to the socialist society we all want to see. It will not be achieved by everyone at the top sitting pat on their own particular theories or approaches to problems. We can all learn from each other, politicians from trade unionists and vice versa.

If the will is there, it should be possible to arrange several 'two-day meetings' a year with a carefully prepared agenda, at which some of the policy issues already mentioned in this book could be discussed. At least the industrial and political wing would be able to define the common ground and could then concentrate on discussion in depth on the controversial issues which remained.

Agreement on major policies at top level would not be the end of policy disagreements in the party, but such agreement would provide a beginning for deeper discussion in the movement than has been the case in the past.

There is no formal way of making such meetings part of the structure. They must develop because those involved recognise the need for them if the movement is to avoid the mistakes of the past. Someone, somewhere is waiting for a lead on this. The movement's future success may well depend on the willingness of a few people to recognise the necessity of this kind of regular, pressure-free, political 'get-together'.

A policy concordat between the unions and the Parliamentary Party would then leave the movement free to tackle the main problems of organisation which confront the Labour Party at the present time.

The Party Organisation Committee, which I chaired in 1968 and 1969, produced recommendations which have already been put into operation, and these include:

1. The new National Agency Service.
2. A new role and status for the General Secretary.
3. The appointment of a Deputy General Secretary.
4. A Political Education Section with a full-time officer.
5. A new Regional Council for Greater London.
6. Replacement of Women's Sections by Women's Councils.
7. Restructuring of Home Counties organising areas.
8. Yearly submission of amendments to annual conference.

9. Increased Women's and Young Socialists' representation to
to annual conference.
10. Wider discussion at the Women's and Young Socialists'
conferences.
11. The training of Assistant Regional Organisers in public
relations.

These and many other minor changes are now operating, but
there are still some major problems remaining. It would not be
appropriate to deal with all of them in this chapter, but two are
outstanding and demand attention – the decline in the number of
full-time agents, and the financing of the party.

THE AGENCY SERVICE

There are approximately 620 Constituency Labour Parties and in
1971 there were only 128 full-time agents servicing constituencies.
Thirty-nine of these agents are employed in the National Agency
Service.

This is a grave situation because the 128 full-time agents are not
in the strategic constituencies, those considered to be marginal.

A first organisation priority is to place a full-time agent in
each marginal constituency and progress must be made on this
before the next election takes place.

This probably means a further extension of the National Agency
Service which is now centrally financing (with some minor help
from constituencies concerned) almost one-third of the full-time
agencies. A substantial increase in the number of full-time agents
paid for by the party means that we are back once again to the
problem of financing the party.

FINANCING THE PARTY

Although fund-raising schemes have a role to play in increasing
the party's coffers, and other ventures such as a Labour Party
Motor Insurance Scheme and Labour Holiday Agency are also
likely revenue earners, the real money to finance the party's
activities is going to come from affiliation fees.

The party's financial position in 1971 is well known to all concerned. The estimated deficit for 1971 was around £160,000, and

with the same level of finance this yearly deficit would grow to around £400,000 per year by 1975.

So the need for speedy action was essential, and the proposals at the 1971 conference were badly needed. These proposals, which were approved by Conference, meant that a 2½p increase in affiliation fees for unions etc., would take place in January 1972, 1973 and 1974. This meant that by 1974 the affiliation fees would be 15p per member per year, or double the 1971 level.

The 'staged increase' approach to affiliation fees and also to individual membership dues is long overdue. Unions only change their rules and consequently their political levies every three or five years, and some long term projection of Labour Party expenditure and income required was necessary.

What is now required is for this projection of expenditure and income to be extended to 1980, and the new affiliation fees should be linked to a programme of improved organisation, including an extension of the National Agency Service, and a purposeful political education programme. Given the projects for which the extra cash is to be used, I am confident that the affiliated and individual membership will respond.

At the present time nearly 80 per cent of the party's income is spent on salaries. This leaves too small a margin for the political activities which are calling out for attention.

The proposal made in an earlier chapter to permit unions to finance the party from their general funds would liberate much needed finance for political purposes, but as demands increase and affiliation fees rise, it is only natural that the membership will want to see value for money.

BUILDING A BETTER PARTY

The proposals outlined in this chapter for improving the quality of political discussion, the provision for adequate participation by the party in forming policy, the closer liaison and political 'concordat' with the unions, will all lead to a climate which will encourage members to pay more with a good heart.

As in the proposals on industrial relations, this chapter has tackled the problem of organising for power from the grass roots up, and this surely is the natural way for democracy to grow in the political wing of our movement.

As we depend on the pennies of workers, not the pounds of the employers, we will never have all we would like in an efficient socialist party, but we can have a much better party than we have at present. More democracy, more political education, better communications are a good start upon which a better party can be built.

Chapter 17

Conclusion

'Diversity of opinions on theoretical grounds is never
dangerous to the party. There are, for us, no bounds to
criticism. However great our respect may be for the
founders and pioneers of our party, we recognise no
infallibility. . . .
Science, whose sphere is ever widening, continually
disproves what it previously held as truth; it destroys the
old decayed foundations and creates new ones. Science
does not stand still for an instant, but moves remorselessly
over every dogmatic belief, in perpetual advance'.

> Wilhelm Liebknecht, close friend of Karl Marx, and the
> father of German Social Democracy: *No Compromise, no
> Political Trading*, 1918

In the Preface to this book I stated that I had firmly anchored the
historical section of the book in the events that had influenced
trade union political thought. For that reason the historical
narrative might not give due importance to other relevant events
which were milestones in the development of the trade unions.
I am conscious of such omissions, but if the book were not
to do a 'historical stagger' over the whole scene, some selection
of events had to be made.

Historically the book was concerned with the forces, in terms of
ideas, events and people, which made the early clubs in the 1800s
burgeon into political flower and create and sustain our Labour
Party. This look back will probably be of most interest to younger
members of the movement who will find under one cover, some
chronology of the political history of the unions combined later
with analysis and contemporary policy proposals.

ON TAKING NOTHING FOR GRANTED!

The study of these events has taken nothing for granted. Many may think that the questioning of the reasons for trade unions being in politics is elementary and needs no answer. But those who feel like this do so because they have made up *their* minds on this long ago! In pubs and clubs today some working men still say that the unions should not be in politics. Leave that to elections and to the politicians, they say. But this question does need an answer, and as illustrated, trade union political activity can be justified on almost pure industrial grounds.

Equally, the step from political activity to being aligned politically with one party, may seem to many to be an inevitable step, but again the trade union experiences of the 1964–70 Labour Government did lead many trade unionists to think deeply about the trade union links with the Labour Party.

True, there is nothing like a dose of Tory medicine to push ideas of political neutrality aside, but if these ideas are latent they could be incubated by some future events. So the case for alignment with the Labour Party, which after all is the chosen political instrument of the unions, had to be stated in modern terms. That alignment is required more today than at any time since the end of the Second World War. In affairs at home and abroad we have need of a political party which will reflect the views of those who labour for a living.

PAST EVENTS AND PRESENT OPINIONS

Our walk with history in the early chapters has thrown up all manner of analogies with later events. The arguments at the formation conference in 1900 are still with us. The well defined groups of opinion present on that day, seventy-two years ago, may have splintered, but the main groups are with us now and still argue about the same things.

The direct action philosophy of 1910–13 and the revolutionary ferment between 1921 and 1926 are still here today, in small political groups.

As in all cases with small minority opinions, a lot of dedication goes a long way, and although these opinions are politically 'way out', many young people are struck with the same piercing clarity that affected Nye Bevan when he first listened to Noah Ablett on the 'virtues' of direct action.

Without a knowledge of the history of the Syndicalists how can we evaluate the strength of opinions held today by these socialist evangelists, and let us not forget that the frustration of many people with politics, which in this country is synonymous with frustration with and contempt for the democratic process and Parliament, has drawn more under the 'direct action' banner now than at any time in the last forty years.

THE NEED FOR A 'SOCIALIST DEBATE'!

The examination and analysis of the competing philosophies for the heart of the Labour Party in the chapter 'Which Political Way for Labour?' could not have been tethered in present reality without an historical hitching post on which to tie our arguments.

This kind of analysis is badly needed in our movement at the present time. We can languish in our present political philosophical doldrums and be swept back to political power because of the ineptitude, lack of compassion and mistakes of the Tories, but the endemic economic and social problems will still be there in three years time, perhaps even aggravated by the Tory mismanagement of five years. If the problems are still there, and we have not settled our political direction, then we are going to be back in the old mid-sixties routine of disunity, disagreement and disillusion.

What we therefore need at present in the Labour movement is a fresh statement of the problems in our society today. Economic, social and moral problems should be presented in this statement, not with the view of providing a background for conclusions already made by the leadership, but presented in a manner to initiate a party debate at all levels.

In Fabian and other socialist publications some Labour Party members have already seen that the end of the last Labour Government marked the end of an era of thinking within the party, and are already posing future problems which will have to be solved by the next Labour Government.

The NEC of the party, in statements at the 1969 and 1970 Annual Conferences in the publication of study group reports and in the development of the 'participation' programme, have also recognised that some old problems have to be approached by different policies, and new problems need 'in depth' policy discussion.

It should be the task of the Political Education Section of the party to set this debate in motion.

In advocating party discussions I realise that it will not be possible to confine this on a pragmatic level. Many in the Labour Party will find it impossible to think out these policies without first charting their political direction. They may first want to discuss the general 'means' by which we intend to achieve socialism in Britain – and why not?

Neither Marxists nor Democratic Socialists should avoid the kind of re-examination which I have attempted in the chapter 'Which Political Way for Labour?'. Leibknecht's advice at the beginning of this chapter is sensible and timeless.

For too long now we have not argued our socialist beliefs in depth, and this is 'bad medicine' for a socialist party. The fundamental disagreements which arose during the last Labour Government surely demand that we argue these out to find how far we agree and what divides us. Even holding each other at 'thought's' length is eminently better than the ideological abyss that divided us in the troubled days of 1968 and 1969.

The expansion and better planning of political education within the party has a major role in ensuring that the debate on socialist beliefs does not generate into political mayhem.

In arguing out whether the old Marxist or the new Crosland-Galbraith thesis (or some amalgam of the two) is right for Labour in the 1970s, we must avoid the charges of 'socialist insincerity' which were flung at the revisionists in the 1959–60 Clause 4 controversy. If these two schools of thought do represent the majority opinion within the party, it is essential to realise that basically they both want the same kind of society. No side is entitled to claim that they are the purer or more sincere socialists simply because their ideas are the most ancient or the more modern!

The party lately has become a lot more tolerant of minority groups. Whether we have 'come of age' politically will depend on whether we can conduct a fundamental discussion on socialist principles without rancour and disintegration.

I place great importance on the need for an examination of which political way we intend to travel in the 1970s and 80s, because without our compass set in an agreed direction it is impossible to plot our policies, and then stick to them with determination when we are in power.

The three policy issues which have been examined in this book are the major areas where the unions and a future Labour Government are likely to be at loggerheads. What kind of owner-ship and control policy we have for the economy, should follow logically on from our debate on the means we intend to use to secure our ends. The success of our policies on industrial relations and prices, incomes and inflation, will depend almost wholly on how effective is our control of the economy.

THE INDIVIDUAL – A POLICY FOR CONSENT

In both sets of proposals outlined on industrial relations and inflation, one central theme stands out. The individual has got to be convinced that he counts for something and that he has a say in his or her industrial and economic destiny.

In industrial relations the proposals seek this by integrating industrial democracy into our industrial relations system, by building up from the individual worker and by a framework of industrial mediation that is seen to be fair.

The prices and incomes proposals are also individualised, for they are based on consent and not statutory compulsion. The techniques in respect of price control, low pay and the social compact, are again designed to build a fair framework within which free collective bargaining can operate and raise living standards for the individual.

This brings us to the heart of the Labour movement itself and the need for a *continuing process* of policy making instead of the quick, sharp stab at policy which we take at conference each year.

The previous chapter seeks to give to the member the same opportunity to influence the policy direction of the party as he would have in respect of his firm or industry under the industrial relations proposals. As a democratic party we can do no less than this. If we can revitalise the party by giving the members the facilities to take part in policy making and achieve a closer liaison with the curious, then our party will not wither as living standards improve.

The road to decline, which D. W. Rawson says is the way of all Labour Parties who improve living standards, will not apply to a party which keeps contact with the aspirations of its adherents, and whose members feel that they matter.

OUR PARTY – HEALTHY, UNITED AND LASTING

I have promised myself that I will not end with a long peroration. I have tried in the historical section to adduce the necessary lessons, and in the analysis and policy proposals to be specific, because this is not a time for misty pronouncements.

These in my opinion put down important political anchors on what I believe to be common political ground. In our present circumstances this is the first step towards forging a healthy, united and lasting party, whose policies can in the future give intellectual, social and moral satisfaction to its members and raise the quality of life for all the people of this country.

This is a difficult but rewarding task in which we 'all must labour' for the common good.

Bibliography

Political Studies, September, 1969, D. W. Rawson
History of British Unionism, Henry Pelling
Labouring Men, Professor E. J. Hobsbawn
Constitution and Aims of the Philanthropic Society
Labour Defended, Thomas Hodgskin
Thomas Hodgskin, Elie Halevy
History of British Socialism, Max Beer (National Labour Press)
Critique of Political Economy, Karl Marx
Das Kapital, Karl Marx
Report to the County of Lanark, Robert Owen
Invitation to First T.U.C., – 1868, T.U.C.
Evidence – Royal Commission on Trade Unions, – 1867.
Trade Union Illegality – Hornby v. Close, 1867
The Beehive, George Potter
The Labour Leader, Keir Hardie
The Miner – 1887, Keir Hardie
Political "Formation" Resolution – T.U.C. 1899.
Labour's Early Days, George Shepherd, N.C.L.C. Pamphlet
1904 Labour Representation Conference, Arthur Henderson
Unemployment Resolution – 1905 Labour Representation Conference.
L.R.C. Executive Committee Report – 1906.
Britain for the British, Robert Blatchford, 1902
Trade Union Act – 1876
Trade Union Act – 1913
The Miners' Next Step, Arthur Cook – Noah Ablett
Reflections on Violence, George Sorel
British Syndicalist – March, 1911, Tom Mann
In Place of Fear, Aneurin Bevan, William Heinemann Ltd.
Pocket History of the British Working Class, Raymond Postgate, N.C.L.C. Publishing Society

Report – Second Congress of the Comintern, 1920, V. I. Lenin

Left Wing Communism, 1920, V. I. Lenin

10th Congress of Communist Party Report – 1929, J. R. Campbell

History of British Socialism, Max Beer, National Labour Press

The Workers' Weekly – 1924, J. R. Campbell (Communist Party) – Editor

The British Labour Party, H. Tracey, Editor., Caxton Publishing Ltd.

The World of Labour – 1913, G. D. H. Cole

A Verbatim Report – 1934, H. G. Wells and J. V. Stalin, New Statesman.

Collected Poems – 1955, Stephen Spender

A Social History of the Thirties and Forties in Britain, 1963, Harry Hopkins

Future of Socialism – 1956, Anthony Crosland, Jonathan Cape.

Necessity for Communism – 1936, John Strachey

Contemporary Capitalism – 1958, John Strachey

Coming Struggle for Power, John Strachey

The Stagnant Society – 1961, Michael Shanks, Pelican – Penguin Books

Necessity of Communism – 1932, John Middleton-Murry.

Studies in Class Structure – 1955, G. D. H. Cole, Routledge and Kegan Paul

The Managerial Revolution, James Burnham

The End of Laissez-Faire (Essays in Persuasion), J. M. Keynes

The New Industrial State, J. K. Galbraith

American Capitalism, J. K. Galbraith

State and Revolution, Vol. XXI, V. I. Lenin

Prerequisites of Socialism, Eduard Bernstein

Marx and Trade Unions, A. Lozovsky, Martin Lawrence Ltd.

The Challenge of Marxism – 1963, J. R. Campbell

Aneurin Bevan, Vol. I, Michael Foot, MacGibbon & Kee

A Short History of the British Working Classes, G. D. H. Cole

May Day Manifesto – 1927, T.U.C.

Royal Commission on Trade Unions and Employers' Association – 1965–68, H. M. Government

A Fair Deal at Work, Central Office, Conservative Party
Report, Cmnd. 4668 – 1971, C.I.R.
Collective Bargaining in Sweden, T. L. Johnston, Allen and Unwin
Wage Rates, Earnings and Wages Drift – 1968, C. Gillon, N.I.E.
   and S.R.
Policies for Price Stability, O.E.C.D. 1962
Policies for Prices, Profits and Non-Wage Incomes, O.E.C.D. 1964
Non-Wage Incomes and Prices Policy, O.E.C.D. 1966
Conference Papers, O.E.C.D. 1971
Speech – New York, 4th May, 1971, Harold Wilson
Industrial Relations – September Issue, 1970, T. Llewellyn
No Compromise – No Political Trading – 1918, Wilhelm Lieb-
   knecht

Index